45511

P
90
.S4413

Servan-Schreiber,
Jean Louis.

The power to inform

DATE			

THE POWER
TO INFORM

THE POWER TO INFORM

MEDIA: THE INFORMATION BUSINESS

Jean-Louis Servan-Schreiber

Translated from the French with the cooperation of
Paris Research Associates

McGraw-Hill Book Company
New York   St. Louis
San Francisco   Toronto

P
90
.S4413

123456789BPBP7987654

Library of Congress Cataloging in Publication Data

Servan-Schreiber, Jean Louis.
The power to inform.

Translation of Le pouvoir d'informer.
1. Mass media. 2. Communication. I. Title.
P90.S4413   301.16'1   73-15822
ISBN 0-07-056317-9

Grateful acknowledgment is made to the following for permission to quote passages from copyrighted material: Thomas Y. Crowell Co., Inc., for *Pressures on the Press* by Hillier Krieghbaum, copyright © 1972 by Hillier Krieghbaum and Ballantine Books, Inc., a Division of Random House, Inc. for *Divorce Corporate Style* by Don Gussow, copyright © 1972 by Don Gussow.

To Denise Servan-Schreiber,
mother of journalists

Acknowledgments

To Russell F. Anderson, who was the first to encourage me to write this book.

To Hubert Beuve-Méry, Jean Boissonnat, Jean-François Revel and John Peter, who kindly agreed, with pencil in hand, to read this book in manuscript, and whose advice and detailed comments have considerably improved it.

To Sabine Nicole, my assistant since 1965, who has helped me at all stages of my work and who virtually knows this book by heart.

To Claude, my partner in life, who has given me what an author needs most: lots of love during the writing of this book and lots of critical remarks while rereading it.

Preface

The one subject that the media rarely illuminate for the public is the subject of the media itself. Like most other industries, the press—whether in print or on the air—dislikes having its behind-the-scenes stories openly revealed. Only when crises develop that directly affect or involve the media (newspapers, magazines, radio, television) do they become a topic of analysis or commentary by the media themselves. Even then, the picture that emerges is somewhat hazy.

The public, uneasy at newspaper mergers that eliminate some dailies and confronted with the demise of such major publications as the *Saturday Evening Post, Look,* and *Life,* may all too readily believe that the printed press is in its death throes. Strikes by various labor unions within the media, including those that take journalists out of the city room and off the air, may lead the public to believe that the commitment to a free and continuous flow of news is less important to the profession than negotiating favorable union contract terms. Scandals about payola or the suspicion that many news items are actually a form of concealed advertising may increase public discomfort about the accuracy of information conveyed on the air or in print. And charges that the press is biased and that it molds public opinion without being answerable to anyone have been a particular bone of contention in the United States, one of the few countries that has constitutional and traditional guarantees of freedom of the press in all media. Americans might think better of their own news coverage if they contrasted it to the controls imposed on radio and television in many European countries, where the broadcasting media are state monopolies or strictly regulated by the government.

Any media "insider" will quickly recognize how much of the information about the media that reaches the public either falls short of the mark or is too often weighted to serve certain interest groups rather than to serve truth. For this reason I have attempted in this book to present the immediate and anticipated problems of the information industry: not only the story of the death of certain journals but of the growth of others that reflect new trends; the difficulties and advantages of technological progress; the ways the conditions within the media and the media themselves affect the lives of media professionals as well as those of readers, observers, and citizens.

If I, a French journalist, focus primarily on the American press and television, it is to some extent because they represent a quarter of the dailies and a third of the television networks in the world and to an even greater extent because—despite their limitations and room for improvement—the American information industry is the one to which the rest of us can turn for the most up-to-date, thorough, and systematic sources. But American readers may also find comparisons with, for instance, Canada, Europe, and Japan illuminating, insofar as they show how well the Americans have done in some areas and how much room there is for improvement in other areas.

Today the power of government seems to be conditioned by the complexity of the social system it represents; the power of political parties is checked by the countervailing power of the voters and public opinion; the power of labor leaders is frequently overwhelmed by the dissident views of its rank-and-file; and the power of university trustees and administrators has hardly totally recovered from the shock waves of student protest and agitation in the 1960s. The only power that has continued to assert its strength and to grow is the power to inform: growth based in part on spiraling technology but primarily because information has proved over and over again to be the line of communication necessary to the functioning of all other power blocs.

The power to inform—and to do so freely, conscientiously, and responsibly—is not only essential to the media but to citizens. It is central to sorting out the conflicts and issues in our postindustrial societies.

Contents

Part 1

Is the Press Still a Money-Maker?

Chapter 1

The Fall
of the Dinosaurs

Man, small creature that he is, never ceases to be fascinated by the fall of a giant, be it a sinking battleship whirling its propellers, a massive bridge collapsing into the gorge, a slain whale lying with its belly in the air or a mighty oak crashing earthward. . . .

Newspapers and magazines, with their millions of readers, are among life's more familiar giants. When one of them perishes, it has a profound effect on the public, which is at a loss to understand the event. The death of publications is not necessarily preceded by a noticeable period of decline, change in editorial content, or even a decrease in circulation. Thus the shock as America's general interest magazines, the largest in the world, began to disappear. *Collier's,* with a circulation of 4 million, folded in 1956; the *Saturday Evening Post,* with 6 million, in 1969; *Look,* with 6.5 million, in 1971, and *Life,* which had deliberately reduced its circulation from 8.5 million to 5.5 million, expired at the end of 1972.

The gradual dying out of the colossus of a species inevitably brings to mind the dinosaur—that fifty-ton triumph of the animal kingdom which, over the span of its eighty-million-year existence, evolved from the size of a chicken to that of a house. Every last one of the dinosaurs disappeared, leaving seemingly weaker but more adaptable animals in their place. Their history, which has intrigued schoolchildren for generations, poses a disquieting question for adults: do great size and power portend decline?

The shock occasioned by the fall of the magazine "dinosaurs" always engenders a barrage of dire predictions, such as the imminent end of the written press. But as little is known about the real reasons for a magazine's disappearance as about the extinction of the reptilian titans.

Did the dinosaurs' overwhelming size make them so phleg-matic that they fell prey to more agile enemies? Did their bird-sized brains, separated from their massive bodies by inor-dinately long necks, react too slowly to crisis? Did their abnor-mal size make them too susceptible to disease? Or was it merely the appearance of creatures better adapted to the changed envi-ronment which signed the dinosaurs' death warrant? Similar questions, put in terms that apply to the problems of the press, can also be posed for giant publications.

THE MISFORTUNES OF THE PRESS

Since the end of World War II, the written press has faced a series of crises—the fall of large-circulation magazines being only one of the more obvious symptoms.

Until the 1920s print was generally the sole means of dispers-ing the news. The advent of the radio broke the printed press' monopoly, and then—for the past twenty-odd years—television became the prime vehicle for disseminating the news, providing entertainment, and reaching the public with advertising mes-sages. In the United States, where television developed earliest and the most rapidly, it was not long before the written press began to run into difficulties: in 1947 alone twenty-four dailies disappeared. Today there are scarcely forty cities where two or more dailies still go to press, and in the majority of these cities the morning and evening newspapers are owned by the same publisher or share the same printer.

As for magazines, the first real warning of things to come occurred shortly before Christmas of 1956, when *Collier's* (a weekly founded in 1888) and its sister publication, *Women's Home Companion* (a monthly founded in 1873), were simul-taneously discontinued. In a single day 2,800 people lost their jobs. Someone with a rather biting sense of humor went so far as to tack a black-bordered card reading "We regret to inform you that there is no Santa Claus" on publisher Crowell-Collier's bulletin board. And yet on the eve of their disappearance these two magazines together were selling more than 8 million copies per issue. This significant and cruel disaster was greeted with the same kind of reaction in the publishing circles as was the sinking of the *Titanic* in nautical circles. From that moment on, the publishing industry began to realize that other serious developments might be pending.

Five years later, in 1961, another mass-circulation magazine, *Coronet,* went down in spite of the fact that it had over 3 million readers. However, it was not until the final demise of the *Saturday Evening Post,* in February 1969, that the general public was really aware of the seriousness of the situation. The *Post* had been considered as integral a part of the American way of life as Coca-Cola. Founded in Philadelphia in 1820, it had become a weekly pastime in millions of homes. As a result of its well-known covers—each depicting a scene of small-town or rural family life—and its editional content, the magazine had become a mirror of day-to-day living in America.

By 1913 the *Post* was selling 2 million copies, and by 1960, despite television's phenomenal growth, the circulation figure reached a high point of 6.5 million copies. Commercially, the *Post* set records no other publication has yet broken: in 1930 it alone accounted for 30 percent of all American magazines' advertising revenues.

The death throes of this colossus were particularly illuminating. From 1961 on, it suffered a loss of advertising revenue that its management tried to stem with a succession of desperate measures. They continually changed editorial direction, leaving their readers extremely bewildered. Four successive presidents of the Curtis Publishing Company (publishers of the *Post*) proved to be incapable of reversing the financial situation. Finally, the last of these, Martin Ackerman, a thirty-six-year-old lawyer with no previous publishing experience, decided that an unprecedented amputation would be the appropriate remedy. The *Post*'s circulation was halved to 3 million with the aid of a computer, which eliminated the less-educated and less-wealthy subscribers—i.e., those readers of least interest to advertisers. It was hoped that the new, lower advertising rates that ensued and a "higher quality" readership would work together to make the *Post* attractive to advertisers again.

Madison Avenue greeted the move with some amusement (particularly when they learned that the computer had eliminated, among others, Ackerman himself), but it was far from convinced that the *Post,* which went from weekly to bi-weekly publication at the same time, could become an advertising money-maker overnight. Ackerman was finally forced to fold the magazine, which by then was no more than a ghost of its former self anyway, and return to his law practice.

Look's demise in October 1971 was more rapid but certainly no less poignant. The magazine had only begun to lose money (officially, anyway) the previous year. However, the amount of money lost in 1970—$5 million—was no meager sum and, based on the continuing decline of advertising income, the loss would have doubled in 1971. Unlike the *Post,* neither its publication schedule (bi-monthly since its debut in 1937), nor its format, nor its editorial direction were altered. The magazine's circulation was cut from 7.5 million to 6.5 million one year before its disappearance, but the resultant cut in publication costs was insufficient to adjust the publication's profit curve.

When sixty-eight-year-old Gardner Cowles, who had founded *Look* thirty-four years earlier, held a press conference announcing his decision to discontinue publication, he in effect liquidated the major achievement of his professional career and put a thousand people out of work. *Look* had learned its lesson from the disaster of the *Saturday Evening Post.* Recognizing defeat, it made a prompt decision that avoided prolonged agony for employees and saved money for the parent firm, Cowles Communications.

Of America's four general interest large-format magazines without a specific editorial "line," *Life,* the largest of them, survived *Look* by only a year. Introduced in November 1936, only a few months before *Look*'s appearance in 1937, *Life* had the largest advertising revenues of any magazine in the country, reaching $170 million worth of ads in 1966, its most prosperous year, before falling to $110 million in 1971. In 1970, *Life*'s circulation reached 8.5 million copies actually sold each week. Nevertheless, the annual losses totaled as much as $10 million, and Time, Inc., had to absorb the deficit. Less than two months after *Look* was dissolved, *Life* announced a self-inflicted circulation cutback which brought its number of subscribers down to 5.5 million (3 million less than it had been eighteen months earlier) in the first few months of 1972. To advertisers, on whose evaluation of where to spend their advertising dollars the survival of the last of the dinosaurs depended, it seemed— despite repeated denials by *Life's* managers—like a replay of an all too familiar scenario.

Such publishing difficulties are by no means restricted to the United States. Similar afflictions were shortly to cripple the daily newspapers and large illustrated magazines of other industrialized countries.

In France, the number of daily newspapers fell from 414 in

1900 to less than ninety in 1971. Their combined circulation stagnated at 12 million while the French population increased by 25 percent between 1941 and 1971. In Paris only thirty-two of the papers launched in 1945, during the enthusiasm of the liberation of France, are still around a brief twenty-five years or so later. Despite mergers, regroupings of papers serving large areas under a single newspaper, and the advantages of combined advertising rates, the number of dailies in the red continues to grow.

Since 1970, *Paris-Match,* the French equivalent of *Life,* lost advertising and decreased its circulation. Although it is France's only weekly picture magazine, it sold less than 800,000 copies in 1971, or not quite one French family in fifteen. The four giants of American publishing (*Collier's,* the *Saturday Evening Post, Look,* and *Life*) together found their way into one home out of three when competition was keenest.

In Great Britain, *Picture Post,* the country's sole illustrated large-circulation magazine, disappeared as early as 1957, and for the past twenty years Fleet Street has been rocked by a continual national newspaper crisis.

In Germany, where there are more than a thousand dailies (each small town seems to have its own), mergers and take-overs are constantly diminishing their number. The only country that is an exception to the rule of the disappearing daily (as well as to many other rules) is Japan, where a powerful and vigorous daily press manages to maintain peaceful co-existence with a television network that is developing at a lightning-like pace.

POOR STRATEGIC DECISIONS

Two major factors are generally credited with responsibility for the death of america's large magazines: the advent of television, which made news photography outmoded and took away advertising, and the ruinous circulation race which caused magazines to spend more money to attract new readers than could be offset by income from new subscriptions. These economic factors certainly played a decisive role, but there were other causes as well. Otherwise, how would *Look* have been able to continue showing profits for thirteen years after *Collier's* folded? How else could one explain the fact that *Reader's Digest,* which is dependent on the same mass market, still prospers today? Obviously, basic errors in management must have been made somewhere along the line.

Between the two world wars, the Curtis Publishing Company was the incontestable giant of American magazine publishing. In addition to putting out the century-old *Saturday Evening Post* and the *Ladies' Home Journal,* the leading women's magazine, the Philadelphia firm consolidated its success with a number of specialized publications (interior decorating, hobby, and children's magazines). But in 1937, H. Fuller, then president of the company, made a decision which at the time seemed to follow a certain "industrial" logic: Curtis would concentrate its growth on the printing side of the business rather than on the magazines themselves. Curtis thereupon acquired a sizable amount of forest land, paper pulp factories, and giant printing plants—all of which were money-losers. The magazines' profits, which had been remarkable over a long period of time, were hardly sufficient to make up for the losses in the industrial sector. In addition, Curtis' directors and administrators (businessmen rather than journalists) were too slow to adapt the magazines' editorial policies to the changing American society. When the problems of having neglected the editorial realm became evident, it was too late. Facing catastrophe, Curtis president Martin Ackerman made one more bad move by deciding to concentrate all his efforts on the *Post* (which he was ultimately unable to salvage) and to unload the *Ladies' Home Journal* (which was sold to Downes Publishing and has since become a very sound profit-making venture). Was it really the "crisis of the press" which led to the downfall of the Curtis empire or simply the fact that its management consistently made unsound decisions?

By the same token, the unfortunate strategic mistakes made by Gardner Cowles, founder of the publishing group which bore his name, Cowles Communications, can also be attributed to human error. Until the very end he did everything he could to save the one magazine that truly interested him: *Look.* In an effort to keep the badly bleeding publication on its feet, he gave up his two money-making properties: the *San Juan Star* and *Family Circle.* The latter, sold to the New York Times Company in 1970, made the most astounding progress of any magazine in America the year following the sale, with advertising receipts taking a 40 percent giant step forward.

Cowles had made other unprofitable investments. In the 1950's *Flair*, a women's monthly directed by his wife, was totally bankrupt when it closed down; the *Suffolk Sun*, a daily newspaper begun by his son in 1966, folded three years and $12 million later; *Venture*, a travel magazine introduced in 1964, was never once in the black during its six-year existence. As was true with the Curtis Publishing Company and the *Saturday Evening Post*, Cowles' real money-eater, *Look*, was the last to go, but only after it had devoured the empire its earlier prosperity had helped to create.

In the case of other magazine empires, while decisions made in the heat of competition for short-term advantages did not always provoke a "twilight of the gods," as in the case of Cowles and Curtis, they often later had devastating repercussions.

From the turn of the century on, the two principal American women's magazines, the *Ladies' Home Journal* and *McCall's*, had been waging a commercial war. In 1962, Herb Mayes, the inventive and editorially oriented new president of McCall's Corporation, decided to strike hard and overtake the *Ladies' Home Journal* once and for all. He made three decisions without precedent in the world of publishing:

1. *McCall's* circulation would immediately be increased by 1 million subscribers, for a total of 8 million—a record circulation for any women's magazine.

2. Every page of the publication, recto and verso, would be printed in four-colors, making *McCall's* the magazine richest in the use of color in the world.

3. Color advertising pages would be sold at the same rate as the black and white pages.

Ad agencies and competitive magazines, which had never witnessed such tactics, were convinced that *McCall's* now had an unbeatable edge. Only later did it become evident that the magazine had taken on heavy expenditures without any guarantee that advertising revenues would follow. And, because the inflow of advertising revenues was less that anticipated, *McCall's* was on the verge of closing. Eight years later the magazine had changed beyond recognition. Its size had been reduced by a third, color was used sparingly, advertising pages were minimal, and circulation had fallen back to under 7 million. The mighty assault had turned into a long fizzle. Herb Mayes resigned and the more prudent *Ladies' Home Journal* again outdistanced its perennial rival.

This same obsession with high circulation figures rather than high profits caused the executives at *Life* to commit a major error. *Look* and *Life,* both introduced within a short time of one another, considered themselves archrivals from the beginning. *Look* appeared every other week, so that *Life,* published weekly, seemed in effect twice as powerful. But *Look*'s circulation was always 10 to 20 percent above that of *Life* (probably because the former only put out twenty-six issues a year rather than fifty-two and thus had a lower annual subscription rate). As a result the publishers of *Life* could never feel completely happy: the world's leading weekly should also have held the lead in circulation.

An opportunity to outdistance *Look* presented itself in 1969 when the *Saturday Evening Post* folded. The death of the *Post* left millions of subscribers orphaned. *Life* offered to take over 1 million of them, pushing its circulation up to 8.5 million in one fell swoop, more than half a million above that of *Look*. But *Life,* already deeply in the red, had in reality taken on a heavy financial burden with its increased circulation. Traditionally, readers who are switched from one magazine to another in the middle of a subscription renew only in very disappointing proportions. Nevertheless, *Life* felt it had achieved another small triumph when, in October 1970, *Look* decided to decrease its circulation from 7.7 to 6.5 million as a result of its own economic difficulties. Still blind to the realities, the publisher of *Life* noted in a memo to his employees that by abruptly cutting off half a million subscribers *Look* had shown itself to be a bit thoughtless in its obligations to readers.

Yet three months later *Life,* waist-deep in deficits, was forced to take the very same steps of reducing its circulation—in this case from 8.5 to 7 million. The anticipated profits of "buying" a million of the *Post*'s subscribers less than a year before had to be written off as a loss. And, immediately after *Look* closed down in October of 1971, *Life,* finally free of the pressures of direct competition, again decided to cut back its circulation by 1.5 million, bringing it down to a mere 5.5 million. What marvelous subject matter for the "moral" of a La Fontaine fable!

TWO WORLDWIDE ILLNESSES: UNIONS AND POSTAL SERVICES

Placing the blame for publishing's woes on television, as many publishers are wont to do, is a vast oversimplification. Conversely, it is just as unfair to brand publishers as their own gravediggers. Even the best of executives make a substantial number of poor decisions over the course of their careers. When mistakes are made in a healthy corporation, they can slip by virtually unnoticed and are more than compensated for, both psychologically and financially, by the successes. Within the press, however, badly weakened by overwhelming competition from the "tube," the tolerable margin of error is lowered—like a sick patient's resistance to germs.

As is true for all other industries, the press is subject to special difficulties that are directly linked to its own inner workings: newspapers must deal with disproportionately high printers' salaries; magazines are troubled by worldwide hikes in postal rates.

Printers' unions are a constant source of nightmares for every publisher in the world. Arthur Ochs ("Punch") Sulzberger, publisher of *The New York Times,* told me at the beginning of the 1970s that union negotiations would play a greater role in the future of his newspaper than sophisticated electronic equipment. Union troubles are nothing new. In the nineteenth century, workers in European printing plants, particularly the typesetters, were among the first to organize powerful unions. (Since the very nature of their work meant that they had to know how to read and write, they were the elite of the working class.) In addition, daily newspaper employees are in an excellent bargaining position because (in contrast to the situation of the manufacturer of automobiles that can be stockpiled) the losses incurred by management during a newspaper strike can never be recouped. Even yogurt is less perishable than unsold newspapers. Therefore it is not surprising to find that printers have always been able to command astonishingly high salaries. Today in the French provincial town of Clermont-Ferrand they earn 65,000 francs a year ($14,000) or 20 percent more than the average French executive.

Like other groups that see their privileges as vested rights, the printers' unions have increasingly concentrated their efforts on protecting their jobs, thus reinforcing a guildlike spirit opposed in principle to technical innovation. Unions systematically resist the installation of new equipment which could improve performance levels.

If a newspaper replaced a press capable of putting out 25,000 copies an hour with one that produced 70,000 an hour, printers refused to make it work at more than 40 percent of capacity. If the new press requires half as many men to run it, the unions have agreed to allow it to be put into use only if the same number of workers are retained.

The limit was reached when *The Wall Street Journal*'s composition room adopted automatic linotype machines that replaced keyboard operators with punched tapes. Only after the management agreed to keep all the former comp room employees did the union permit the new machinery to become operative. The management had no choice but to pay linotypers to sit around and look at the new machines. What executive in his right mind would continue investing in costly modern equipment and at the same time retain in its entirety one of the most expensive manpower forces in the world? *The New York Times*' 1970 Annual Report summed up the dilemma: the newspaper had to agree to a 42 percent increase in printers' wages over a three-year period, but were unable to obtain increased use of new equipment in exchange.

As New York's daily newspapers began to disappear one after the other, union leaders must have known that they could stop the trend by being a little more flexible in their demands. Yet time after time they chose to see their members lose their jobs rather than compromise. There are some signs of grudging willingness to bend a bit as the unions begin to realize that the possibility of further shutdowns is real, but the future effects of union negotiations are by no means certain.

There are few reasons why typographers should be paid more than other workers today. Their skills are as commonplace nowadays as they were rare one hundred years ago. In the interim the strength of their unions has made up for the uniqueness of their qualifications. Their inflexibility has spelled death for a great many newspapers, and other deaths will follow. In the competition for leadership in profitability being waged by the two most powerful newspapers in the United States, *The New York Times* and *The Los Angeles Times,* the latter has a definite advantage for the moment: by means of a questionable but effective sixty-year-old company policy, *The Los Angeles Times* has always been able to keep its printers from unionizing. But how long will it continue to fight off pressure to unionize?

Whereas the corrosion-like disease of daily newspapers lies in its Malthusian union negotiations, magazines are subject to the increasingly prohibitive cost of sending their publications through the mails.

In Western Europe and Japan, the major means of distributing periodicals is still newsstand sales and home delivery, but in the United States the prosperity of magazines was built on mail subscriptions. The advantages of this method are considerable: no unsold subscriber copies; the signing of a long-term contract with a reader who, unlike the newsstand buyer, cannot forget or simply decide not to buy the magazine in a given week; payment in advance (what other industry in the world regularly receives payment for its merchandise a year in advance?). Finally, and most important, because information cannot really be considered a normal commercial product since it unquestionably has a social function and because all governments attempt to conciliate the press, government post offices charge very reasonable rates for delivering magazines. In 1971, it cost 7 cents to mail a periodical in the United States, 6.5 in Great Britain, 4.5 in Germany, 1.30 in France and 1 cent in Italy. Compared to the 30 cents to $1 paid by the subscriber, shipping costs have, on the average, remained inexpensive—often being nothing more than a token payment.

Unfortunately for publishers, post offices (like any other manpower-based service that cannot be automated easily) in the developed nations have begun to realize that they are losing money on the delivery of all these millions of copies of newspapers and magazines. To avoid heated arguments with the publications, a few governments have continued to let the taxpayer make up for the deficit. In the United States, where there is a certain consideration for the reality of costs, it was decided that even if the post office should not go public, at least it might be turned into an independent, profit-making endeavor free of government aid.

At the beginning of 1971 in the United States the post office's new board of directors announced a five-year plan for increasing postal rates that jolted all of the magazines' yearly income statements. For example, *Newsweek,* which only made $1.5 million in profits in 1970, was faced with $2 million in supplementary costs. Of course, the more subscribers a publication has, the harder it will be hit by the postal hikes. For certain of the dinosaurs of magazine publishing, it has already meant extinction. When Gardner Cowles realized that *Look*'s postal expenses would jump from $4 to $10 million in five years, he knew that the end was in sight.

Today, magazines that are primarily sold over-the-counter have gained the advantage in the United States, but there are only a few publications of this sort (notably *Woman's Day* and *Family Circle,* which are both sold exclusively in supermarkets to 7 million readers, and *Playboy,* which relies on subscriptions for only 24 percent of its circulation). Others are trying to put together private distribution systems, which will cost them less than the planned increased postal rates but more than they are now paying. The solutions adopted by American magazines will be of great interest to their European counterparts, which have already begun to experience similar postal-rate increases in their own countries.

CONFUSING YESTERDAY AFTERNOON WITH TOMORROW MORNING

"You can see at a glance that our industry is a bit unusual." Every consultant hears these words or some variation on them during the course of his first hour of talks with a company president, whatever the business may be. His professional experience has taught the consultant that there are more similarities than differences between any two given organizations, and he knows that that is precisely why he has been called into the president's office. But the business executive, totally immersed in his own particular difficulties, has a real need to believe that his is a special case.

Among those industries that consider themselves unique, the press undoubtedly feels that it presents the most special case of all. I confess that for a great many years in the profession I too was convinced that this was true. Even when my blind adherence to this belief had been tempered by the knowledge that the problems of the press were relative, I still found myself resorting to the handy refrain both as a device for recruiting executives and as a catch-all explanation for poor profits. And people believe you. The public—and even consultants—more readily acknowledge the singularities of putting out a publication than they do of an assembly line for battery-operated fans.

However, there is one area in which publishing, apart from its particular problems, clearly shows its similarity to other industries. Its management suffers from the same myopia that impairs the vision of all decision-makers: they mistake yesterday afternoon's problems for those of tomorrow morning.

For instance, newspaper staffs are hired, trained, and paid to *continue* in the footsteps of their predecessors. Innovators are rare. No one is there to stop or eliminate outmoded practices. Nevertheless, when matters come to a head, the hangman's role is invariably given to someone who is unprepared for the job both professionally and psychologically. Therefore, the person responsible for instituting changes naturally puts off doing so until the last possible moment—which is usually a moment too late.

Another situation common to all industries is the life cycle of its products: ordinarily, rapid growth is followed by a long leveling-off period, and then a more or less rapid decline. To avoid this, marketing experts are hired to predict the moment of decline so that the product may be taken off the market before it starts losing money and another product can be introduced to replace it.

Too few magazine publishers use this tactic. Despite all evidence to the contrary, they act as though the interest of readers and advertisers can only grow. Yet entire sectors of the press have gone out of style right before their very eyes.

After the Second World War, Europe's romance magazines had a meteoric take-off. The photo-novels published in *Confidences, Bonheur, Nous Deux,* and *Rêve* sold as fast as presses could print them. The quality of the printing was as distressing as the plot level of the stories, yet the mass public gobbled them up. However, an increase in personal income and, even more important, education finally checked the attraction for this semiliterate literature. For over ten years, their circulation has been tapering off in France, gradually at first, then very quickly. The same drop in popularity was obvious in Italy a few years later. The fact that this form of magazine publishing remains very prosperous in Spain, a country which has only begun to develop, seems to indicate a high correlation between the success of these journals and low economic prosperity. They probably have ten more good years ahead in Spain and fifteen in Portugal, but after that they may prosper only in Turkey and on the African continent.

Cultural change has also a profound effect on American publishing. At the beginning of the century the features readers preferred were serials in daily newspapers, and novels and short stories in magazines—in brief, fiction. A hunger for facts favored the creation of such magazines as *Time* and *Reader's Digest* in the 1920s, which, in turn, modified the nation's reading habits. By the time the *Saturday Evening Post,* which relied on fiction for the bulk of its editorial content, woke up to the fact that reader interests had changed, it was too late—the magazine's audience had grown as old as its formula.

Fiction as the essential element for the success of a magazine (which held true for almost a century) enjoyed a longer life cycle than photo-journalism. Photo-news magazines became a major event at the end of the 1930s with the introduction of *Life* and were quickly imitated abroad, but began to decline early in the 1960s—an obsolescence accelerated by television.

The essential lesson to be learned from the downfall of the giants of magazine publishing is that they were mired in yesterday's problems, not anticipating the enemies waiting in the wings.

The first problem among the four large-circulation magazines *(Collier's, Post, Look,* and *Life)* was competition among themselves. All four were pursuing a similar group of readers and identical advertisers, and there were too many of them for all of them to continue to succeed (as is true today of the large women's monthlies, whose readers are similar enough to be considered almost identical).

The reason was that during the 1950s the enemy had changed: while magazines had been vying with one another, television had steam-rollered advertisers. The magazines then threw themselves into a hopeless circulation drive to increase their subscriber lists in proportions that would enable them to offer advertisers a reading audience comparable in size (taking into account the fact that each copy of a magazine is read by several people) to that of the more popular television programs. They sunk fortunes into an absurd and futile numbers race. Even if the total increase could match the number of television viewers, magazines obviously could not provide sound and motion. Yet, strangely enough, they almost won the ruinous struggle. At the end of the 1960s, studies (such as that conducted by General Foods) showed that the two media had a comparable advertising impact, in any event, were complementary. At that time, too, television's phenomenal growth had reached a plateau. Would the large magazines be restored to health?

Not for long. Once again the enemy had changed. The numbers fad had passed: advertising agencies began to refine their targets, aiming at a specialized audience for their products. The magazine dinosaurs, gorged with circulations in the millions, would not offer advertisers "useful" readers at the same rates as small, specialized publications. It was the specialized magazines and not television which took away the last of their advertisers.

When at the end of 1971 *Life* finally found itself alone on the market, there was practically no market left. *Look*'s disappearance had not meant increased advertising for *Life*, but had simply given it an opportunity to reduce costs by sharply cutting its huge circulation. For the first time, *Life* no longer had to try to surpass the circulation figures of a direct competitor. But advertising in the last quarter of 1972 and projections for 1973 showed a downward trend that spelled the finish for the magazine.

Thus, by focusing on the past, smart men were constantly losing the battle of tomorrow at the very moment that they thought they had won that of the day before—thus precipitating the downfall of the firms they directed.

THREE SIMPLE CONCLUSIONS

Witnessing the demise of the giant magazines with their millions of subscribers, the average person could grasp the fact that a periodical's prosperity was not necessarily proportional to its sales curve. This is a complicated matter, the nature and consequences of which even the professionals have trouble measuring.

But, outside of in-depth analysis, the publishing disasters brought to light three historical facts which the press would do well to bear in mind.

The importance of the printed press in modern society is on the downgrade. Its monopoly on mass communication was broken by radio and television. As the late Pierre Lazareff, editor of *France-Soir,* told his employees some ten years ago, "At one time when something happened people rushed out on the street to buy a newspaper; today they go home and look at television."

Whatever the inherent drama of certain events, it cannot be denied that television coverage increased their immediacy and also, in turn, had an impact on their development. The role played by magazines and newspapers will be transformed, minimizing their "hot news" function and forcing them to more "in-depth" analysis.

Convenient ways of proving the contrary have been devised by those who have a direct interest in keeping advertisers from deserting the printed page. On the other hand, a total decline of the influence of the printed press will take longer to come about than has been predicted by those involved in television and other audio-visual equipment.

Newspaper and magazine publishing involves tremendous sums of money that are within the reach of only rich men and business organizations. There is no longer such a thing as an independent press. However deplorable this truth may be, it has already become self-evident. In the United States, the effort at greater concentrations undertaken by several newspaper chains (the largest, Gannett, has bought fifty-three dailies) is being accelerated. By now, a few newspaper chains own over half of the country's papers.

In Germany, a single man, Axel Springer, owns the bulk of the daily newspapers of that country, and most of the magazines belong to one firm: Grüner Jahr. In Great Britain, two giant firms—International Publishing Corporation and the Thomson organization—were able to gain control of the majority of the country's daily newspapers and periodicals within the span of a few years; ownership of the remaining publications is divided among a few smaller groups.

In France, ten or so enterprises have, by mergers or acquisition, taken control of the regional press. In Paris, with the sole exception of *Le Monde,* all of the daily newspapers are linked with industrial organizations or press conglomerates which often (as in the case of *La Croix, Combat, L'Aurore, Le Parisien Libéré* and the late *Paris-Jour*) finance their deficit. Most of the influential magazines are owned by either Hachette, Prouvost, or the Groupe Express.

In the world's industrialized countries there is probably not one sane investor who would even dream of starting a newspaper. All the gaps have been filled (except in the case of small local publications in the United States). In fifteen years, five attempts at introducing new Parisian dailies have failed after going deeply into debt. For magazines the situation is somewhat more fluid, but, as it turns out, only because there seems to be room for specialized publications with restricted circulations— the only ones that have been successfully introduced in recent years. The era of conquests of millions of readers has come to an end.

Advertising has become practically the press's sole source of income, which is dangerous for both its financial independence and its morale. Extreme as it may seem, this statement is far from an exaggeration. Advertising has worked like a habit-forming drug to make the press dependent upon it. Two examples: during the first thirty-three years of its existence, the *Reader's Digest* did not accept advertising but nevertheless had comfortable profits. In 1950 it opened the door to this new source of income, which was intended only to be complementary. Fifteen years later, in 1971, the pages of the *Reader's Digest* included $62 million worth of advertising in its American edition alone but, despite this sum, which is huge for a monthly, the publication, because of rising production costs, had a great deal of trouble balancing its monthly statements. The firm's profits are now mainly dependent upon products other than the magazine.

In France, *Le Monde*, which is owned by its employees and which is particularly proud of its independence, had a long-standing policy against letting advertising account for more than half of its income. Today advertising accounts for more than 70 percent of its revenues, even though *Le Monde* charges more per copy than any other French daily newspaper.

For many newspapers and for most magazines, advertising brings in more than 80 percent of their revenue; for this reason, their existence is quite fragile. At the least sign of recession industrialists the world over begin an economy drive that includes a cutback of their advertising budgets. Through various economic cycles over a period of years, advertising agencies have tried to convince their accounts that in fact it is exactly when the need to generate sales is greatest that advertising budgets should be increased. Perhaps someday these persistent efforts will succeed in reversing the trend, but for the time being top corporate executives will continue to economize on advertising expenses before cutting back their own salaries.

Thus, recessions bring with them advertising budget economies that may outlast the recession itself and the cutbacks will inevitably doom marginally profitable publications, even those that may be at the height of their popularity. If one takes into account the effects of economic fluctuations and the formidable competition from television, as well as the various and often irrational reasons that agencies decide to place ads in such-and-such a publication rather than another, one begins to understand why newspaper publishers have become obsessed with the problem of gaining ads and have been led to make editorial concessions for the sake of it.

Television's inroads into modern life have haunted the printed press for over twenty years. It is easy to see why, but—as happens with many new problems—inappropriate historical comparisons have obscured reasoning. For instance, the prophets of doom believed that the press would meet the same fate as the horse-and-buggy when the automobile had appeared a half-century before. Publishers today realize that, despite serious crises, the press is far from being a historical relic. Focusing on more comparable precedents would have avoided many sleepless nights.

If Wall Street financiers had known at the beginning of the century that the telephone, invented thirty years earlier, would one day be at the base of the largest enterprises in the United States (A.T.&T.— 1 million employees), they might very well have rushed to sell off their stock in Remington and Underwood, the two big typewriter manufacturers, but they would have been wrong to do so. The telephone has not replaced letter writing; much to the contrary, people have never written more letters than they do today. The telephone may be vital to modern life, but a parallel need for the written word has triggered the founding of entire industries—such as the copying machine.

Only now has the press begun to wake up to the fact that the birth of a second child in a family does not mean the end of the world for the first-born. It is never pleasant to realize that one is no longer the one and only, but even a two-year-old can adjust to the new situation in time. To the extent that the printed press indulges itself by attributing most of its miseries to the diabolical tube, its condition will continue to deteriorate. But then, after all, it is always easier to put the blame on someone else than to work at self-improvement.

Chapter 2

Buy Me Five Hundred Thousand Readers

Throughout the world daily newspapers and magazines lament the fact that each copy has to be sold below cost. And, since it has become a standard practice to proclaim unprofitable undertakings as public services, newspapers everywhere are asking their governments for one form or another of financial aid so that they can carry out their "mission" as disseminators of news. This was not always so. Before the blossoming of advertising, relations between readers and their newspapers were based on a sane and simple economic principle: the purchaser paid for each issue at a price equal to its cost plus the publisher's profit. In this sense, the economics of journals was basically analogous to the profit system of book publishing, but with less risk, since sales of daily or weekly publications can be predicted with far more accuracy than for a single work.

Newspapers of the mid-nineteenth century depended for their existence on high newsstand prices. Today, as we discard the morning newspaper after having read the headlines and four or five articles, we forget that the newspaper was for a long time looked upon as a luxury item. Consequently, newspapers were read at the club or café, where they could be found waiting for the reader, carefully rolled on a wooden holder (a customer-attracting device comparable to the advent, in the 1950s, of barroom television sets which night after night kept bars full until the wee hours of the morning). A friend of my grandfather's, after having purchased and read the morning edition of his favorite newspaper, crossed half the city of Paris on foot to bring it to one of his uncles. Every issue bought found its way into the hands of a large number of readers. But the total number of sales per publication was only in the thousands or tens of thousands.

The financial equilibrium of the press was not only maintained by a cover price above the means of the majority of the public; expenditures were limited. It took two months for news of a battle with Indians in America to reach Europe, but improving the rapidity of news gathering was not considered worth the high investments entailed. Nor was there any question of covering all of the news—from sports and politics to fashion and foreign affairs—on a daily basis. A handful of journalists, severely underpaid, put to press a maximum of six to eight pages a day. Then a small team of delivery men toted the copies to the city's news sellers (there was, of course, little question of national distribution). However, no one newspaper was abundant enough in news to satisfy all readers. Several dozen newspapers were available in a single city, each one reflecting its own particular political leanings or simply the opinion of its combination owner–publisher–editor-in-chief and, frequently, also that of the printer.

The only familiar form of advertising at the time was the classified ad. These small inserts of unillustrated print served as well for announcing the creation of a new cough syrup as for finding a cook or selling a house. For the publisher, it was an additional source of revenue, but inconsequential—certainly not enough to dispense with a circulation-based revenue structure.

It was not until the end of the nineteenth century that the various necessary elements converged for the emergence of a truly popular press, capable of being widely distributed. This meant a railroad system that could travel through an entire European-size country in a single day; presses that could produce tens of thousands of copies in a matter of hours; a telephone and telegraph network that made news as perishable a commodity as fresh fish; and, above all, a compulsory school system which created a reading audience. At this juncture, businessmen who wanted to sell consumer goods needed advertising to make their products known to the public.

Publishers quickly realized that they had before them an opportunity that could totally restructure their economic setup, bringing them far greater profits and at the same time increasing their power. But in order to attract advertisers, newspapers would have to be purchased by as large a number of readers as possible, not the select buyers that had previously sustained them. The obvious means of achieving mass circulation was to sell newspapers at a reasonable price—that is, to sell below costs while deriving profits from advertising. This gave rise to what became known as the "penny press" in the United States.

Circulation revenues, which had once accounted for 100 percent of a publication's total income, fell to 80 percent, then to 50 percent. Today it hardly accounts for 30 percent of the income of prosperous dailies. The bet paid off far above anyone's wildest expectations. Newspapers print in the hundreds of thousands per edition in a given city, reaching as many as several million copies in countries like Great Britain and Japan, where they are distributed nationally.

With the changed economic base of the publishing industry, the primary goal was no longer to sell news to readers but rather to sell readers to businessmen for advertising. While technology and business innovations were affecting publishing concepts, the press was also modifying the world in which it was evolving. At the same time that it continued to fight for its freedom from government controls, it hardly noticed that little by little it was falling prey to advertisers.

An immediate result of the struggle for mass circulation was unruly competition for the loyal readership of the largest possible number of buyers, the key to large advertising budgets. Daily newspapers, magazines, and, in turn, television, all found themselves in a race for the largest audience.

NEWSPAPERS GOBBLE ONE ANOTHER UP

The numbers race was run in two phases. During the first, at the turn of the century, the new cheap price put newspapers within the range of large numbers of potential readers and all of the papers were able to increase their circulation. However, just when newspapers had fully exploited the reader market, radio came onto the scene. This signaled the end of a great era of expansion of the daily press but not the end of competition for readers. Previously, newspapers had all been able to tap a seemingly inexhaustible public reservoir; now they would have to steal readers from one another.

Throughout this first phase, as in any pioneering period, newspaper publishers had a good time. Not all went so far as William Randolph Hearst, who fanned the flames of the Spanish-American War to increase circulation, but all made use of sensational headlines. If the news of the day was not spectacular enough to meet their needs, they created news by disclosing some scandal, real or invented. It was during this era that the press, overstimulated by the race for high circulation figures, developed some of its least commendable characteristics. Getting a scoop and thrilling headlines counted far more than accuracy in news reporting. The essential method of newspaper distribution was newsstand sales. To keep the public buying, newspapers had to reactivate reader interest daily; in so doing, they brought on the first wave of distrust and uneasiness from the public, which sensed that the press was trying to stimulate its curiosity artificially.

Fortunately for the medium of print, at the same time that attention-catching headlines and the written word began to be threatened by competition from radio between the two world wars, news photography made its debut, giving the popular press a whole new face and revitalizing its hold on readers. As early as the 1930s, daily newspapers began to look the way they do today.

Despite the dismal predictions, the massive onslaughts first of radio and then television did not kill newspapers, but they did manage to slow down and, to a certain extent, to bring to a standstill an over-all increase in readership.

During the second phase, it was necessary to continue the mad race for high circulation figures in order to present a dynamic image to advertisers (and because the natural reflex of the head of any enterprise is to nibble ceaselessly like a rabbit at the largest possible share of his market). Hence, like any lucrative industry that can no longer expand, publishing soon found itself in an era of concentration. What made this necessary was financially devastating battles to obtain readers. The first objective was not to bring up circulation figures immediately but, rather, to wipe out a weaker competitor. Publishers rarely competed over editorial quality, because they did not feel that readers would be sufficiently responsive to make the effort worthwhile. Instead, they waged promotion campaigns. In France, for example, audiences are vied for with games. Contests and prizes—which take readers away from competitors but have nothing to do with a journal's news function—have become a major weapon.

At this stage of the race two major victory strategies are employed by the press: a fight to the finish in which one entrant, bled white by ever-mounting costs (salaries, printing expenses, promotion campaigns), finally falls by the wayside, leaving its readers to the victor, or the perhaps more humane method whereby the stronger contender buys the weaker. However, even then, most of the staff of the acquired organization eventually lose their jobs, but the publishers recoup most of their financial outlay and sometimes a great deal more.

A modification of the outright acquisition process consists of the signing of an "agreement." Certain aspects of costly competition are bypassed: the two publications, printed on the same presses, retain their separate names, a single advertising rate is established, and the profits are shared. Individuality is seemingly maintained while duplication of costs is eliminated.

To sum up what has happened in reality during this second phase: more power concentrated in the hands of fewer newspapers. In the last fifteen years, four London dailies have folded (this may not seem like a significant number except for the fact that London newspapers each have a national circulation in the millions). In Germany, sixty-three dailies have been eliminated either by suspension of publication or by mergers. In France, the ninety journals which still go to press are in reality controlled by twenty or so groups which have established among themselves a series of noncompetitive agreements.

And the tendency will continue. In New York, since the shutdown of the *"World Journal Tribune,"* itself the result of a merger of three newspapers, only the *Times,* the *Daily News,* and the *Post* remain. In Paris, the death of *Paris-Jour* in January 1972 (which was, strangely enough, the only Paris daily whose circulation had risen regularly over the years) left only ten papers, all of which, with the exception of *Le Monde,* lost money in 1971. Nevertheless there are still too many publications competing for the same market, and their number will continue to drop. In London, a troubled Fleet Street speculates over the name of the next victim. Nevertheless, the press as a whole is not under threat; those publications that are able to survive will do very well.

This, in fact, is why the final stage of concentration, that which is now developing in the United States, no longer has as its objective the elimination of competitors (which has already been largely accomplished anyway) or increasing circulation (which is considered to be impossible). A dozen groups are simply engaged in a financial concentration by methodically acquiring independent newspapers considered to be good profit-makers. The publications are bought at a high price and generally allowed to keep their editorial and political independence (which, in any case, they exercise very discreetly). As a result of this movement, which began less than fifteen years ago, more than 50 percent of America's newspapers now belong to national "chains." At the moment there is no end in sight to this trend, except, perhaps, through reactions of a public which is becoming increasingly concerned about the placing of such a huge concentration of power in the hands of so few.

MAGAZINES BUY THEIR READERS

While dailies got off the ground as early as the nineteenth century, magazines represent a more recent form of journalism. Their origin dates back to the mail-order catalogues and dress-pattern books of the turn of the century, which gradually began to include practical hints and fiction serials. Only a relatively advanced society could support this less-vital form of publishing, since it did not perform the service of carrying the news of the day, local birth and death announcements, or classified advertising.

Magazines could evolve thanks to two "holes" in the advertising market which newspapers were unable to fill: because magazines did not have to carry up-to-the-minute news they could service rural areas too remote and too spread out for rapid distribution; and, more important, they could offer "national advertising coverage." In other words, if a business wanted to introduce its product to the entire country at once (e.g., to achieve mass distribution), a fortune would have to be spent running the same ad in all the different local publications, particularly if it was necessary to repeat the ad. Hence the attractiveness of magazines, one issue of which can reach millions of rural and urban homes. The longer time span between issues than for dailies makes it possible for magazines to use quality press work, thus offering advertisers an advantage which, even today, newspapers simply cannot approach: the use of color. Dailies frequently do try to supply color, but the quality remains generally subaverage.

The key to magazines' success, however, still remains their millions of readers. With one exception (the New York *Daily News*), no American newspaper surpassed until very recently the million-copy mark, while more than a dozen magazines put out over 5 million copies per edition. And since each issue of such magazines as *Time* is estimated to be read by more than four people, the actual audience they reach is composed of tens of millions of consumers. Before television, magazines constituted the only real mass medium.

American magazines have perfected a more systematic and precise means of running the numbers race than their European counterparts. The great advantage of the large American magazines is distribution through subscription, which accounts for up to 90 percent of their circulation.

For the publisher, subscription sales are virtually an ideal system. It means he reaches the reader directly, which saves him the 50 percent commission of distributors. Subscription mailings avoid an untold number of unsold copies, which can be anywhere from 15 to over 50 percent of the print run. Payment in advance by subscribers helps build a cash balance which is on the whole not available to other industries. In addition, the publisher has a subscription list on file which he can profitably sell other businesses for mail solicitation (including other magazines).

However, the greatest of all advantages of subscription circulation is its built-in ability to measure the possibility of increasing circulation at a given time. It is quite simple, after making a few tests, to predict how many new subscribers can be anticipated by spending a specific sum on promotion.

If the publisher wants to pick up some half a million new readers over a six-month period, the best way to gauge the possibilities for growth is to ask the circulation manager: "How much will it cost us to get 500,000 new readers in six months?"

As I said earlier, newspapers discovered that it was no longer a question of selling news to readers but, rather, selling readers to advertisers. Magazines, going one step further, realized that, thanks to subscription sales, they could "buy" readers at a cost calculated in advance and sell the use of them to advertisers.

The succumbing by the United States to subscription sales took place in two stages, each employing radically different business techniques.

The first era: pre-World War II. The weapon: door-to-door sales. The era's champion: the Curtis group (*Saturday Evening Post, Ladies' Home Journal,* etc.).The steam-roller technique of the traveling salesman was in full swing. Teams of twelve men, using four cars, would infiltrate an untapped city, setting up headquarters in a centrally located hotel. They left only after having combed every apartment and home in the area that figured in their plan of attack.

It was the lady of the house who received them. In her eyes they were probably more prestigious than vacuum cleaner salesmen since they represented a more exalted product: magazines. In fact, they often represented several periodicals, and once they got into a home, would try to take advantage of the situation by peddling a weekly magazine for the head of the family, a monthly for the wife, a publication for each of the youngsters, varying according to their sex and age group, and, as a bonus, a large, book-size color album or two. Because their travel schedules made it impossible for them to return on a regular basis, the salesmen would try to convince the subdued housewives that it would be a far better deal to take each subscription for three years (for the price of two) or even five years (for the price of three). Before leaving, the salesmen might easily have chalked up subscriptions worth $50 to $100, magnanimously allowing the new subscriber to pay over an eighteen-month period (amounting, nevertheless, to payment in advance for subscriptions of two or more years in length).

This is what is known in the trade as high-pressure sales. Renewal rates, after the initial subscription ran out, were often extremely low, but the technique still turned a satisfactory profit. It wasn't until half a century had passed that the American public caught on to the system, decided it had had enough and, *en masse,* learned to close its doors. In 1969, Congressman Fred Rooney strongly attacked this sales method. Cowles and later Time, Inc., then decided to close down their affiliates which were still using the method.

Other more subtle methods complemented door-to-door sales. One consisted of exploiting a persuasive group of amateur salesmen: children. Under this system, a school would receive a letter asking it to organize a contest among its pupils. The students would be divided up into competing teams, the winning team being the one that in the span of four days sold the largest number of subscriptions to relatives, friends, neighbors, passers by, shopkeepers and so forth. As a reward for the school's co-operation, a minimal percentage of the price of each subscription would be donated to the institution to buy new uniforms for the football team. Often an entire city would be saturated in less than a week.

CAUGHT IN THEIR OWN TRAP

As a society becomes more sophisticated, thanks to education and material prosperity, forcing one's foot in the open doors of people's homes becomes less effective and less acceptable. After the war, therefore, a "soft pressure" approach was adopted— subscriptions solicited by mail. This was magazines' second era in the numbers race, and the undoubted champions were the Time-Life group *(Time, Life, Fortune)* and the monumental *Reader's Digest.*

Because a letter can be tossed into the wastebasket with relative ease, the responses are, of course, lower than when using door-to-door salesmen. For every hundred subscription solicitations mailed, on the average only two orders are received. This obviously represents a heavy investment, particularly as it is frequently necessary to send the subscriber several bills, spaced three to four weeks apart, since only a minority pays up after receiving the first notice. And because half-price trial subscriptions are generally short term (less than six months) the subscriber has scarcely paid his bill before he begins to receive letters asking him to renew his subscription. If he doesn't succumb immediately, he will probably be inundated with ten or more renewal offers, for, as long as the cost of obtaining a new subscriber does not exceed the value of the renewal, it is in the publisher's interest to continue his efforts.

Computers calculate the profitability of each letter, stop or modify the length of subscriptions, watch over billing, and yield valuable statistical data. In the last few years computers have even been typing promotional letters (as well as renewal offers and bills), slipping into the text two or three references to the addressee's name or the city where he lives. This is, of course, more expensive than running off a regular form letter, but the proportional increase in returns makes the extra cost worth while.

Direct mail selling is the sole form of advertising the effectiveness of which can be tested in advance, and the impact of which can be continually improved by refining one aspect or another. Virtually everything has an influence on the returns: the season during which the mailing is made; the appeal of the envelope; the length of the letter; a price of $1.97 as opposed to $1.85 (and it is not always the cheaper rate for which the returns are best); whether a choice of two different subscription lengths is being offerred (a choice often reduces orders because it forces the recipient of the letter to think, that is, to come to a decision). Mail-order selling is a precision marketing technique which makes use of applied psychology at a profit.

Publishers send out tens of thousands of letters for each of their magazines yearly, and regularly pull in the subscriptions, bill payments and renewals predicted by their computers. It is in this context that the concept of "buying" a subscriber can perhaps be best understood. For each $2 subscription that comes in, fifty to 100 letters costing from $4 to $6 had to have been mailed out to potential subscribers. The first renewals (rarely do more than half of the trial subscribers renew) do not compensate for the initial investment, which can be amortized only after several years.

After 1945 the majority of magazines used all of the subscription sales methods simultaneously: door-to-door, direct mail, and even telephone solicitations. They had to kindle the flames with all available wood if they wished to keep the fires burning for quick expansion, faster growth than their competitors, and an enjoyment of advertising riches which continued to mount at a rate which was then twice that of the American Gross National Product.

Between 1946 and 1971 *Time* tripled its circulation, reaching 4.5 million; *Newsweek* multiplied its 1946 circulation by 3.5, and *Business Week* by 4.5. *McCall's,* which had 3.5 million readers in 1946, added 5 million more in twenty years; *Reader's Digest* has increased its circulation by 500,000 every single year for the past fifteen years.

By 1956 the magazines all became aware that television had

edged its way into three-fourths of American homes, and a last-gasp scramble for circulation ensued. Quite a few publications, believing it was still possible to expand, wore themselves out trying to acquire an ever-increasing number of subscriptions. However, after so many years of being intensively badgered, the American public (which by then was spending three hours a day in front of the television) was becoming unresponsive. Returns began to flag, making each new subscription more and more expensive to obtain. Renewal rates for general interest magazines fell, on the average, to below 50 percent, a situation which forced *Look's* circulation manager, for example, to turn up 4 million new subscribers in 1970 simply to maintain the same circulation.

The rigorous circulation-campaign method of "buying" new readers began to backfire on its creators. Magazine circulations continued to increase, but in a way that was more and more unreal and overwhelmingly expensive. One can say with certainty that, if publishers had not sunk enormous sums into promotion, under the impact of television the circulation of the large magazines would inevitably have declined. That is precisely what happened in France to *Paris-Match,* which depends almost exclusively on newsstand sales. In ten years its circulation fell from 1.4 million to 800,000.

The mounting spiral has been reversed. Between 1967 and 1972 the rate of advertising growth has been slower than that of the American economy on the whole. At the same time, inflation has caused magazine production costs to skyrocket. In addition, the most careful advance planning has been affected by imminent postal rate increases which strike at the heart of a magazine's ability to survive. Considering the effect on the costs of soliciting readers by mail, sending bills and renewal reminders, and shipping the magazine itself, the straining for new subscribers has begun to resemble the painful spring-back of an overstretched rubberband.

A COUNTRY SATURATED BY TELEVISION

When television is not subsidized (and therefore controlled) by the state, advertising is its only means of support. From this comes all of the medium's specific problems in the United States. As soon as television came onto the scene about a quarter of a century ago, its overwhelming success was a bonanza for television-set manufacturers; an entire country had to be supplied. The infatuation with the new magic box was such that the fascinated public indiscriminately absorbed anything it was offered. Therefore the networks (CBS, NBC, ABC), which created the programs, took the path of least resistance in terms of quality—a laxity they would never completely overcome.

The unleashing of America's purchasing power on this marvelous gadget meant that the country was saturated with television sets in record time. In 1950 fewer than 4 million sets had found their way into a mere 9 percent of all U.S. households. Four years later, half of America's families had installed a television set in their living rooms, and by 1962 50 million sets were being tuned in for more than five hours of television watching a day in 90 percent of American homes.

With its twin tradition of private enterprise and freedom of the press, it was natural that in the United States television broadcasting should be in commercial hands. But no one who came in on the ground floor foresaw what the long-term cultural consequences of such a choice would be.

In most other countries of the world, the state runs the television stations in whole or in part. Even in England, cradle of the freedom of expression, the BBC, a public enterprise, with two channels, shares part of its audience with ITV, the commercial channel, which is free to rent (under the terms of a renewable contract) the frequencies it uses. The advantage of television under government auspices (there are also many drawbacks) is that monetary considerations are not its biggest problem. Many countries finance television programming by making set owners pay an annual tax, which is generally lower than the price of a daily newspaper subscription. If the tax yield is insufficient to cover costs, the state budget makes up the difference. When in France and Italy the state finally decided that it could enjoy additional income from television advertising, commercials were inserted between programs, rather than in mid-program, to avoid upsetting viewers' habits.

In the United States, television began without government subsidies and the networks had to operate within the restrictions of profitable yearly income statements, thus more often than not forcing the networks to adopt programming concepts that would yield quick profits but would provide no long-term vision of serving the public. During its early years, many financiers considered the new-born medium an excellent way to gain tax advantages by losing money. Publishing corporations as weighty and as prosperous as Time, Inc., and the New York Times Company were in a position to buy one of the national networks for what would today seem like a mere token sum. In the end, they decided against it (a decision from which they have not yet recovered). The only way for the television networks to assure a rapid inflow of cash was to get advertisers to package entire programs; this would take responsibility for an hour or two of programming out of their hands and would cut down on the exorbitant costs to the networks of putting a program together. Of course, soap and toothpaste manufacturers had little interest in becoming patrons of the arts. They chose the more popular types of programs (games, variety shows, situation comedy and adventure series) and crammed them with commercials, which, to assure capturing viewers' attention, were systematically interjected into the shows at peak moments of interest.

Later on, the networks, which had become highly profitable, were in a position to face up to the sponsors and push commercials to the end or beginning of each program. But internetwork competition and the need to show increased profits at the end of each season cut off this possibility. American television, which had become the world's most powerful and influential source of news and mass culture, had put itself exclusively into the hands of producers of consumer products.

The power of American television and the competition between CBS, NBC, and ABC should have played a role in improving programming. Paradoxically, they have had the exact opposite effect.

Because television is able to attract millions of viewers daily, the rates for commercials have been pushed so high that only the largest advertisers can afford them. Predictably, manufacturers that sell products that are bought by just about everyone (food, household supplies, personal-hygiene products, automobiles) are most attracted to television. Programs therefore have to appeal to mass taste and offend no one, thus assuring the lowest of cultural levels.

Competition only serves to accentuate this tendency, since each channel understandably wants to get the lion's share of the "prime-time" audience (from 8 to 10 P.M., when the greatest number of viewers are tuned in), and to be more popular than its two competitors—one more guarantee of low-quality programming.

Having battled back to back like this for so many years, the three networks have practically fought to a standstill. Each has managed to hold on to about a third of the nation's viewers, leaving local stations and the educational or public service channel (financially desperate as a result of its no-advertising policy and almost total lack of government aid) with only the crumbs. It seems unlikely that the networks, stuck like three pachyderms in a narrow river basin, will make much effort to improve the quality of programming and risk losing viewers.

American homes are saturated with television sets (there is often more than one to a household), Americans' days are saturated with hours of television viewing (or, perhaps, hypnosis), and broadcasting schedules are saturated with insipid serials, which, in turn, are saturated with commercials. Intellectually speaking, American television has lost a great opportunity. An American cartoonist, Conrad, summed up the problem with a drawing showing a family (with the face of each member drawn to resemble a SMILE button); sitting glued before a television set in the shape of a garbage can.

WHO LOST THE RACE?

For several generations now, newspapers, magazines, and television have wasted all their energies on the numbers race, forced by their advertising-based financial set-up to attract great masses of people. Many publications disappeared as a result, but American society as a whole was the real loser. Instead of encouraging innovation, bold ideas, cultural diversity, and continued public education, advertising—because it is directed to the masses—has imposed conformity. Daily newspapers all tend to look alike and their biggest fear is scaring off readers. All the women's magazines hand out the same advice, recipes, and illustrations. Except for special events, every evening spent before the television screen is as barren as the next. In the matter of children's programs, chopped up with ads for chocolate-flavored dry cereals, this descent to the bottom of the intellectual barrel has reached critical proportions.

33

To be sure, similar problems exist in all capitalistic countries (though one can easily argue that, in countries that reject the economy of the marketplace, advertising is replaced by political propaganda, which is worse). But nowhere else is advertising as highly developed as in the United States, where it represents 2 percent of the Gross National Product.

Fortunately, in the past few years advertising itself has begun to be more innovative, recognizing the need to break up viewer monotony and to get more audience response for less money—thus opening up the possibility that programming too can at least partially break the mold of sameness.

Chapter 3

Unspecialized Publications Step Aside

If in 1967 anyone was taught a bitter lesson by the difficulties of publishing it was thirty-eight-year-old John Veronis, then president of Curtis Publishing's magazine division. After the anguished demise of the *Saturday Evening Post,* his crown jewel, one might have thought he would switch to a more stable line of business. On the contrary, he not only decided to remain in publishing, but did so with the daring of the captain of an ocean liner who banks his future on an experimental pedalboat: he went into partnership with Nicholas H. Charney, a twenty-five-year-old psychologist fresh out of college, and launched with him a psychology monthly based in San Diego, five hours by plane from New York and its concentration of media and ad agencies. The two immediate major questions were: was there enough of an academic audience for a specialized publication of this sort, and could the publishers assemble a readership that would attract advertisers?

Three years later, Veronis and Charney had not only succeeded in launching *Psychology Today,* but they had also made a fortune selling the infant publication (and its large book publishing and book club operation) to a major conglomerate, Boise Cascade, for the eyebrow-raising sum of $21.3 million. The same man who had had a hand in one of the biggest failures in the history of contemporary publishing had, in record time, totted up an equally unprecedented capital gain (which he and his partner lost later in the equally daring, but this time unsuccessful, venture of revamping the *Saturday Review*).

Certainly the *Psychology Today* episode indicated Veronis and Charney's considerable talents as innovators, entrepreneurs, and businessmen; more importantly, it demonstrated the potential vitality of an industry that many were already referring to in the past tense. However, the only thing that

Veronis' *Saturday Evening Post* and *Psychology Today* ventures had in common was the fact that they both involved publishing magazines. The marketing approach between the two had undergone a radical change. General magazines were dead, long live specialized publications!

A FRAGMENTING SOCIETY

On the evening that *Look's* folding was announced, in September 1971, one of the most noteworthy commentaries on the end of the "general interest publications" came from television commentator Eric Sevareid. Predicting that the changes evolving in the communications field would bring about even greater fragmentation in a society that had already become too diversified, Sevareid claimed that the real hazard was not a monopoly of information, but, rather, a Tower of Babel.

In so saying, he first of all made a plea for the cause of television, which had been accused by Agnew and others of having too strong an influence on public opinion. But Sevareid was also underscoring the swift acceptance of heterogeneity in place of social coherence and conformity. Americans today find that, as a result of an era of progress from which their country benefited before any of the other industrialized nations, their immense, reputedly homogeneous society of 200 million individuals is fragmenting. What are the basic causes of the profound evolution that has forced the media to diversify?

Job Specialization: The more complex a society is, the more necessary it becomes for everyone in that society to play a role in a restricted area he knows thoroughly, so that things are kept functioning smoothly. The preference for teams of competent specialists over the intuition of an exceptional generalist is at the foundation of American management. Today this specialization has created subgroups which barely speak a common language when one of them has to communicate with another. Within the same business firm, engineers and researchers, moneymen and management live in different worlds. At the same university, history professors are out of touch with biologists, professors of literature are unlikely to meet with mathematicians. To meet the needs of these subgroups, publications strictly tailored to their fields of interest are required.

The Assertion of New Freedoms and Tastes: As American

36

society became more "permissive," magazines developed to cater to the interests of different groups that were asserting their potential for new markets in magazines. Sexual, class, age, regional, and spare-time differentiation in tastes made themselves felt. A new type of women's magazine emerged in *Ms.;* the special services and delights of a major city were catalogued in *New York;* mildly sex-oriented magazines like *Playboy* began to receive serious competition from the more forthright *Penthouse* and started a similar magazine, *Oui; Rolling Stone* serviced the youth culture beyond paying particular attention to rock music; the *National Lampoon's* extraordinary success rested in the appeal of *Mad* magazine's type of humor for college graduates. The list is long and will continue to change as additional segments of American society demand a magazine to fit their needs. Magazines specifically aimed at a Black audience, for example, continue to spring up—ranging from journals with a definite political or social orientation, to slicks.

Liberal Education: For one thing, a greater interest in culture and increased knowledge of the world have played a strong role in the diversification of Americans' tastes. And for another, since World War II, the education system has tried to cope with the problems of a greater influx into the schools for a longer period of time. In other words, Americans have had to cope with all the problems of mass education. This has led to the diffusion of learning norms and values, and the concomitant multiplication of varied curricula and standards at schools and universities. Perhaps few Americans under forty years of age today have received an identical education.

The Consumer Paradise: In a market as vast and prosperous as that of the United States, any well-presented idea can create a limited but highly lucrative submarket for itself. The era of standardization corresponded to a time when all families were concurrently equipping themselves in durable goods. Today they can afford to be more fussy. The era of the 15 million Model-T Fords belongs to the past. Chevrolet, one General Motors line of cars, may display as many as forty different models on a single page of advertising. One of the main attractions of the eternal Volkswagen beetle could be the fact that, for the purchaser of this anti-Detroit car, it is a way of showing independence from the traditional American overemphasis on large size as a symbol of prestige.

Increased Leisure: Confined to jobs which bring them little satisfaction other than earnings, the great majority of Americans—affluent by world standards—seek to express themselves in their leisure activities. Thanks to the thirty-five- to forty-hour work week, weekends off (and, in the near future, more four-day work weeks), Americans have embraced a wide variety of sports, from bowling to scuba diving, from surfboards to pleasure boats, all of which have created new markets. Also, the ability to take vacation and business trips abroad—on a scale undreamed of by previous generations—has helped to diversify American interests in food, wine, art, and architecture, making the United States one of the most sophisticated markets in the world for a great variety of products.

People with the means and desire to do so have found new ways to express their interests by identifying and joining together with others of similar interests, which gives them the feeling that they are leading more meaningful lives.

Advertising caught on to the new consumer trend and adapted itself accordingly. While it had already been acknowledged that it was inadequate to run the same January tire ad in Chicago, which is covered with snow at that time of year, and in Miami, where crowds tan on the beach, now it was recognized, for instance, that for certain items it is more productive to use different sales pitches and media to reach black and white women. Surfers would be too expensive to reach if it were necessary to run an advertisement intended exclusively for them in a general interest publication like *Reader's Digest.* Also, the same individual will not react to a liquor ad found in *Life* as he would to one in *Gourmet.* By refining their techniques, marketing and advertising have forced the media to do the same.

THE PUBLIC AS A SALAMI

Facing competition from smaller, more specialized means of communication, in response to advertisers' demands, the mass media realized that it was no longer possible to sell their audience as a whole and devised techniques for cutting it into slices.

Daily newspapers, finding that concentrations had led to the coverage of increasingly large territories, began to offer multiple regional editions. Two to six pages within the regular news edition of a French newspaper consist exclusively of local news.

Ouest-France, which covers ten *départements* in Brittany, actually publishes thirty-five different editions. Every day 250 different pages are composed for the paper, to make up different regional editions averaging about twenty-eight pages each.

The national newspapers in Japan and Britain obviously cannot satisfy the interests of readers and the needs of local advertisers with a single edition that gives news slanted toward the interests of the capital city. Therefore, not only do the national papers have local inserts, but they do their printing at different sites throughout the country as well. Actually, this amounts to producing different newspapers in several locations but retaining a single name for all of them.

Even certain American dailies whose circulation is limited to local areas (usually consisting of a single city and its immediate vicinity) are spread too wide to serve all of their readers. *The Los Angeles Times,* which has reached the million mark, now publishes varied pages for certain suburban areas, as does the high-circulation *New York Times.*

But daily newspaper customers are not sliced the same way in the United States as they are in France, where regional publications most often have a monopoly. With no competitors (except, occasionally, small, meager weeklies), the large regional French dailies are forced to meet specific local needs for information (such as publishing a list of pharmacies open on Sundays and holidays in every small city).

In the United States, despite the fact that the daily newspaper reader is standardly depicted scanning the news over his morning cup of coffee, there are four times as many evening papers as there are morning ones (1,400 versus 340). However, most of the largest newspapers—those servicing the major cities—are published in the morning. The evening dailies are generally local organs that provide news and advertising listings for the day-to-day needs of a given region. *The Los Angeles Times* covers a huge urban area of 10 million inhabitants, but nearly a dozen evening papers, all "neighborhood" publications, continue to prosper under the *Times'* shadow.

Regional specialization is in itself not the total answer for the dailies. As a result of the proliferation of advertising some newspapers have become so thick that few people have time in a single day to read through a whole issue. Therefore they are often divided into separate sections, sometimes into separate inserts. One section covers national and international news; another, sports; a third, the financial pages; classified advertisements are grouped together; and there may be a separate women's page with practical advice and "handy hints." At the family table, the father may be reading the financial pages, the son the sports section, the mother those parts of the paper that particularly interest her, and the classified ads may lie around unread unless some member of the family is particularly involved at the moment with wanting to buy or sell a small item or is looking for an apartment or job.

The arrangement of a paper into sections is a convenience not only for the reader but for the advertiser, who can decide in advance what section will produce the best results for his advertising dollar. An individual ad is actually read by only a third or fourth of the newspaper buyers, but at least the ad is likely to be seen by those readers who are directly "useful" to the advertiser.

Many of my friends who read *Time* or *Newsweek* in Paris have come to the erroneous conclusion that "There really isn't much advertising in American magazines." The slim, sixty-page publication which they buy in Paris actually contains no more than ten pages of advertising. Unfamiliar with the sophisticated methods used to slice up the readership like a salami, they are unaware that the same week the New York edition carried perhaps sixty pages of advertising and the San Francisco edition forty-five, and that the Italian edition of *Time* may have four fewer pages of advertising than the French one.

At the end of 1950s magazines discovered that many advertisers could no longer afford advertising rates which, as millions of subscribers continued to be recruited, had become astronomical.

By publishing editions for different parts of the country, magazines were able to offer business firms the choice of advertising only in editions destined for specific geographical areas covering several states, a single large city, or, in the case of the weekly newsmagazines (which are the only ones with sufficient worldwide circulation), Africa, all of Europe, or simply Ireland. The largest publications put out up to fifty regional editions. Not all of these were profit-making, since regional advertising pages brought in, at best, only 10 to 20 percent of a publication's revenues. National advertising continued to be by far the main source of revenue for magazines.

True, up to now magazines have not on the whole tried to offer regionally adapted editorial content along with regionally adapted advertising. In the future, though, if they wish to compete with television's increasing trend toward regional area programming, some magazines may have to think about revising this policy of standardized editorial content, which was originally dictated by cost factors. A newsmagazine such as *Newsweek* could increase reader following in California appreciably if, in addition to its national pages, it provided Californians with four to six pages of more local news that concerned them more directly. After all, with a population equal to half that of France, California certainly merits a few pages of weekly news.

Publishing separate editions with regional advertising makes sense only in those countries where different parts of the nation are comparable in wealth. Up to now, no French magazine has dared to take this step. Paris holds such a dominant place in the country's economy that publishers fear—and, for the moment, rightly so—that special advertising editions would be so heavily concentrated on the Paris market that regional editions would be deadly thin.

In recent years, the computer's infinite flexibility has made it possible for American magazines to acquire more precise statistical breakdowns of their readership. With the aid of zip codes, the country's wealthiest neighborhoods and suburbs (according to census figures) can be grouped in such a way as to provide advertisers with an audience that enjoys better-than-average purchasing power.

Demographic information enables a magazine such as *Time* to direct itself to the several hundred thousand students, doctors, or businessmen who are among its 4.25 million readers. In this case, specialization creates internal competition problems: with its "businessmen's" edition alone, *Time* can offer advertisers more readers than *Fortune,* published by the same corporation. *Business Week,* whose advertising rates had grown at a faster pace than many of its advertiser's budgets, introduced in 1972 an industrial edition (thus excluding bankers, insurance men, and professionals in other service fields), which ran additional pages in the editorial section. Nevertheless, by slicing up the readership in this way, the publisher runs a risk: if, in the future, the majority of advertisers find that their needs are satisfied by only one of these slices, the new editions, instead of bringing in additional advertising, could show a net loss for the magazine.

Facing the same problem of cutting up the public in a way that is most useful to advertisers, American television has managed to find a possible solution. When stations are on the air virtually the whole day (few other countries in the world start broadcasting in the morning), the television audience is hardly of the same quantity and quality several hours in a row. Therefore, television can be more flexible in meeting advertisers needs than the printed press and thus presents formidable competition.

In the morning and afternoon, a television audience consisting largely of housewives is the same audience that is attractive to advertisers in large women's monthlies. At mealtimes, particularly during the dinner hour, television displaces general magazines directed to the entire family. From 10 or 11 P.M. on, the stay-up-late audience is made up primarily of young adults. These are the hours when lower advertising rates enable local advertisers to break into the late movie or talk shows with advertising monies that might otherwise be spent in daily newspapers. The unfortunate viewers are bombarded with advertising messages that are produced locally and that may be fairly amateurish. This is a perfect example of how the public can be sliced up by age group (the under-forty generation, with its great purchasing power), sometimes by sex (if it's a horror film, the commercials will be directed to male consumers), as well as by region.

On Saturday and Sunday morning only children are presumed to be awake, and they are treated to an interminable parade of outdated cartoons interspersed with commercials urging them to eat more sweets. Only since the beginning of the 1970s have producers tried to create better programs for children.

With its versatility, it is not surprising that television is considered the perfect commercial medium.

UNLIMITED SPECIALIZATION

The advantages of slicing up the public by region has its limits, especially if little more is known about readers than their zip codes. For instance, the impact of an advertisement for certain products or services may be diffused in a general interest magazine. The editorial "environment" can play a critical role in the directness and intensity of the reader's response to a specific ad. It is not necessary to have studied marketing for three years and to have a computer at one's disposal to be aware that an ad for a new book is more effective in a literary review, that an ad for car seat-covers does best in an automobile monthly, that one for an anti-flea product belongs in a pet magazine, that one for a fishing reel gets the most action if run in a sports fishing journal, and that an ad for machine tools should be placed in an engineering publication.

Engineers, doctors, and sports enthusiasts make careful distinctions between editorial content and advertising when looking through a newspaper or general- interest magazine, but tend to be more receptive when they have a periodical that covers their specialty or hobby.

The specialized press, which focuses its articles and illustrations on a small number of subjects, has a considerable psychological advantage over generalized magazines: it talks to readers about themselves, about things that really matter to them, about professional success stories, the problems and issues that are unique to their particular area of interest. In these ways, the specialized press mirrors very important facets of the reader's personality and thus holds his attention. Discovering that there is a magazine which deals with one's specific tastes, profession, social group, or city gives certain importance to one's own existence.

Each new trend, fad, serious social movement or issue, if it can be related to some consumer product, rapidly creates a press geared to identifying, describing, promoting and serving it. Even if someone has only a temporary need for information in a particular area of interest, it is possible to find a publication that suits that need or that has been especially created for it. Each transatlantic air traveler, for instance, will find in the pouch on the back of the seat facing him a magazine prepared by the airline with practical advice and, of course, enticing ideas for other trips. When he arrives at his destination, the traveler often finds that his hotel has left on his night table a journal which names previous clients of the hotel and contains advertisements for restaurants and stores in the city. Departing the next morning, he will leave this publication behind, for once out the door he no longer belongs to the transient social group constituted by virtue of being occupants of the hotel.

43

The categories of interest that are capable of supporting a specialized press are almost unlimited. The most obvious of these can be broken down as follows: *Locality*—within New York City the different boroughs and even the different neighborhoods within the boroughs sustain one or more prosperous newspapers. *Professional*—there are not only magazines for electronical engineers, but publications for marketing men in the electronics field and even for management personnel in the electronics industry (the professional or trade press is by far the oldest, most varied, and most lucrative of the specialized presses). As Don Gussow explained in his recent book *Divorce Corporate Style:*

> I could not imagine enjoying a more rewarding and satisfying career than as a business magazine editor and publisher.
>
> While the average person knows little or nothing about trade papers (or business magazines, as they are known today), just about every one identified with business, industry and the professions at any sort of executive level has some kind of involvement with this unique but very practical and valuable medium. Many executives in a long list of industries would be lost without their favorite business magazines.
>
> Trade journals or business magazines provide news and information about a particular business, industry, profession or function. While the medical field is the largest, with over 350 different periodicals and with an annual advertising volume in excess of $100,000,000, just about every trade, industry or profession has at least one or two of its very own specialized magazines. And some have many more. For example, the computer field has twenty different publications, the electronics industry has more than a dozen and the chemical, food, metal and other basic industries have numerous magazines. But there are trade journals for plumbers, funeral directors, bakers, candy manufacturers, soft drink bottlers, machine tool people, pet shop operators, accountants, lawyers, teachers and insurance men. About 2,500 business and professional magazines are published in the United States, and thousands more throughout the world. It is a big, unusual, highly specialized business with an annual advertising revenue approaching one billion dollars in the United States alone.

Hobbies—There are monthlies for archers, numismatists, butterfly chasers, and modern jazz enthusiasts. *Age*—There are magazines for children of different age groups, as well as those that meet the needs of teenagers, college students, and young working people who identify with the youth culture. And certain magazines are aimed in large part at the interests of the more affluent retired people. *Sex*—One of the major categories under this heading is women's magazines. *Seventeen* is one of the most prosperous women's magazines in the United States despite the fact that its readership, by virtue of its name, is limited to a small sector of the public. From the feminist magazine *Ms.* to *Cosmopolitan* (which preaches sexual liberation for women without social emancipation), there exists a feminine press which is far more specialized than that of the traditional large women's magazines. Certain of these specialized women's magazines, such as *Marriage,* must obviously constantly renew their supply of readers. Many magazines are thought of as male oriented because of subject matter that has traditionally been considered as falling within the masculine domain—sports, technology, business, etc. In this way, a general magazine like *Argosy* is fully cognizant of the "masculine mystique." Magazines like *Oui, Penthouse, Playboy* and *Genesis* all say on their covers that they are directed toward men, and only in this sense may they be considered specialized. There are magazines for both sexes *(Man and Woman, Sexology)* and for those who are single or divorced *(Single* and *Singles,* for example). *Ethnics*—As the great waves of immigrants came to America, there were publications for people of Irish, Swedish and German descent as well as journals published in Spanish, Chinese, Hebrew, Yiddish, and Portugese, or English-language publications addressed to specific ethnic audiences—all destined for Americans of diverse origins. The Black press has gone through several periods of strong development. And, of course, the audience for specialized publications is further broken down into smaller categories: *California Pilot, Black Sport,* and *Business West* are only a few examples.

There are 9,000 different periodicals published in the United States and more than 2,000 in France. These figures remain fairly constant, but they do not always stand for the same 9,000 or 2,000 publications. Every year a certain number fold as a result of the decline of various specializations and a great number of journals are introduced to attract new subgroups.

ONLY THE ONES WE NEED

For publishers of specialized magazines, the most important consideration is not obtaining maximum circulation but servicing a homogeneous audience in order to maintain advertiser interest. If *Golf* magazine found that a high proportion of its readers took winter vacations and decided to add a winter sports column, it would run the risk of attracting skiers who may not play golf, thus diluting the total readership's interest in editorial content and ads directed toward golfers. Therefore, it would be wiser to create another magazine directed to skiers alone, if there are enough of them to constitute an audience for such a magazine.

The way to preserve the value of a magazine's readership is to refuse subscriptions to readers who are not within the magazine's target area. McGraw-Hill's *Business Week,* which is directed exclusively toward executives with responsible positions, asks subscription "candidates" to fill out a questionnaire concerning their work status. If the prospective subscribers are doctors, retired persons, students, or accountants, they receive a carefully worded letter explaining that *Business Week* is reserved for business executives. Obviously it would be a bit awkward to have to tell them that the real reason they have been turned down is that they would not be valuable advertising "prospects." Indeed, there are few doctors who can place orders for cranes or computers.

This policy has its drawbacks. Naturally, promotion returns are lower if "conditions" are imposed. When, using the same system, I introduced the monthly magazine *Le Management* in France, we made control tests which offered subscriptions without screening questionnaires. The results were 40 percent higher. However, since reader quality was of essential importance, I decided to stick with the questionnaire method, knowing that it would limit the circulation to 20,000 copies.

Another drawback of the selective subscription list is that it all too easily stirs discontent among those who are refused. Take, for example, a man who, because his name appears on a list of American Express card holders, receives a subscription solicitation from *Business Week,* which relies heavily on such lists of people with high purchasing power. The man decides he is interested in subscribing and sends back the order card.

Fifteen days later the postman brings him an embarrassed letter from the magazine, which has turned down his subscription request because he is a dentist. Even if the man no longer has any illusions about the bizarre workings of postindustrial society, he still probably would not calmly accept the turndown ("First they beg me to subscribe and now they don't want me"). The management of *Business Week* does admit that if an individual insists, they would let him subscribe.

Selected subscribers bring more advantages to magazines than the creation of a specific market for their advertising salesmen. By the use of detailed questionnaires, specialized publications can gather (and record on computers) precise information about their subscribers and can, for example, produce lists of their readers who work in the aeronautic industry or are under thirty-five years old. This is exactly what *Business Week* did when it began renting, at a substantial price, tailored subscriber lists to mail-order companies whose products were of interest only to narrow groups of clients.

Magazines whose specialization is geographical come up against still another problem involved in reader specialization. The most prosperous among the specialized regional magazines is *Sunset,* a monthly unread outside the Western part of the United States for the simple reason that *Sunset* does not want circulation except in that part of the country. Dealing solely with "life style" (gardening, travel, decoration, cooking), *Sunset* is a mass-circulation magazine; with sales of over 1 million, it surpassed *Life's* circulation figures for that section of the country. The members of the Lane family, owners and operators of *Sunset* for two generations, have warded off any attempt to enlarge· the magazine's distribution by refusing to sell it throughout the country or to seek subscribers beyond the boundaries they set up. In spite of this restrictive policy—or, more likely, because of it—*Sunset* ranks twenty-fifth in the nation for advertising revenue.

A new arrival on the publishing scene, *New York* magazine, made a similar decision when it was introduced in 1967. Observing that the venerable *New Yorker* had long overstepped the boundaries of the city whose name it bears, *New York* decided to concentrate its sales solely in the New York metropolitan area which, with over 10 million inhabitants, constitutes one of the wealthiest advertising markets in the world. As a result, no newsstand sales were made and no subscriber solicitations were conducted outside metropolitan limits. *New York* even went so far as to charge a significantly higher subscription rate to anyone living outside the designated area who nevertheless wanted to receive the magazine. In contrast to *Sunset,* articles in *New York* are written by some of America's best by-lines, which gives the magazine increased general interest and importance. Finally, however, a tearful letter from an exiled New York woman who complained about the financial discrimination of her high subscription price moved George Hirsh, then the magazine's publisher, to do away with the costlier "out-of-area" rate. This was of little consequence, though, because the very fact that the magazine conducts no national promotional campaigns keeps its circulation restricted to the New York area, just as its originators had intended.

All of the publishers of specialized magazines did not have the foresight to limit their circulation targets. A good example of the risks involved in indiscriminate growth is *Scientific American.* This excellent monthly was transformed by Gerard Piel with the aim—admittedly quite difficult to meet—of presenting the scientific discoveries and issues of our time in language that would be understandable to laymen while avoiding cheap popularization. The task was immense, making it necessary for journalists to spend days on end with the scientist-authors, men who were far more at ease with a test tube than an inkwell, rewriting their words in readable form without distorting their thoughts. The goal was met, and today *Scientific American* is considered the best scientific magazine in the world.

However, the magazine's editorial success seriously jeopardized it financially. As long as *Scientific American*'s circulation remained modest, advertisers of scientific equipment (microscopes, scientific calculators, etc.) flocked to the magazine, lured by the quality of its audience and its reasonable advertising rates. But *Scientific American* readership grew steadily, and, once it had reached the point where it was putting out several hundred thousand copies per issue, advertising rates had to be raised, making it out of reach for manufacturers of small equipment to continue advertising in the magazine. In addition, businessmen, students, commercial engineers—all of little interest to scientific equipment firms—now made up a large proportion of its readers.

Alarmed by the sudden loss of advertisers, *Scientific American* tried to give itself a new look, launching promotional campaigns which purported that its readers were, on the whole, decision-makers. This was an attempt to get in on the lucrative business advertising market. There, however, *Business Week, Fortune,* and others offered advertisers more concentrated groups of middle- and top-management readers, and the results were disappointing. By aiming at a fairly general readership, *Scientific American* compromised its very existence. In an ideal world this would not happen to a publication whose educational value is unquestionable. But, alas, the rules of the economic game prevail.

Ultimately, the logic of specialization and the desire for an undiluted market led some publishers to make a stab at free distribution. Today ever-increasing lists of the members of any given profession are available. Anyone who wants to can secure the names and addresses of all the physicians in a nation. Why, then, spend a fortune trying to sell subscriptions to doctors when, at the most, only 20 to 50 percent of them will respond? It is far more profitable simply to send them copies of the magazine free. Even the system of free distribution will still result in a modest print-order (there are 40,000 doctors in France; 200,000 in the United States). This makes it possible for the publishers to guarantee pharmaceutical manufacturers that the group they wish to reach is 100 percent covered. The situation would also hold true for electronic engineers or urban planners. The major problem, of course, is that other publishers may have the same idea and thus there is a strong possibility that the unwitting engineer whose name appears on an alumni list will receive three or four free magazines in his field. Editorial quality then becomes crucial. The publisher must be able to prove—through reader surveys—that the magazine is not only received but read as well. Magazines that do not meet this conclusive test will have trouble finding advertisers. The paradox is that the editorial quality of free periodicals may be higher than in those that charge a cover price. Advertising agencies, however, wonder just how seriously interested readers are in something they have not paid for, and it is this factor which is the major rein on the proliferation of free professional magazines.

When the groundwork has been carefully prepared, this method of controlled circulation (a euphemism for "free") makes highly precise marketing possible. Take the example of Gilbert Kaplan who, in 1967 at the age of twenty-five, launched *Institutional Investor,* a magazine of top editorial quality designed exclusively for those engaged in the newly developed business of managing huge stock investment funds. Firms of this type are few in number, but handle considerable sums on Wall Street. Kaplan put together a list of only 20,000 names, sent them the magazine, and pulled in financial advertising from corporations, banks, and stockbrokers. A year later, he repeated his success by creating *Corporate Financing,* a publication which also dealt with money management but which was designed only for financial directors of major firms. In 1972, he refined his target area further by introducing *Pension,* a periodical available only to managers of powerful retirement funds. Obviously, none of these magazines is known to the general public, but the professionals who happily receive them constitute an exceptional advertising market.

The advantages of specialization in a magazine are not limited to advertiser appeal. If a publication can create a bond between itself and its devotees it will benefit from reader enthusiasm when it lends its name to other enterprises.

This trend marks a new departure in publishing, which began by selling news, information, and dreams to readers. Later publishers began to sell readers to advertisers. Now they have started to sell products and services to their readers. Two main business functions of a journal have become establishing a publication's market and image, then capitalizing on that to cement relations with readers. This favorable condition can be used to advantage in creating spin-offs such as other, more specialized publications, which benefit from public trust in the parent magazine or firm.

Another facet of publishing widely practiced today is selling to subscribers the product which most complements a magazine: books. The greatest successes in this area have been achieved by *Reader's Digest,* which publishes condensed books (the literary critics find them loathsome, but the public adores them), and Time, Inc., whose science, nature, geography, and cookbook series are put together with editorial techniques drawn from the magazines. Enormous success and huge profits are available to those publications that inspire great reader confidence in products bearing their name.

As was at first true of advertising, ten years or so ago the selling of related products was considered to be an adjunct of a magazine's principle activity and an opportunity for supplementary profit. But as the decline in advertising revenue and mounting production costs made journals less profitable, supplementary income from the sale of related products has become essential for some journals. In several countries of the world, local editions of *Reader's Digest* would lose money if book profits did not exist.

Today's generation of publishers on the whole deal in marketing-oriented conceptions and count on selling books, posters, games, records, audio-visual cassettes, seminars, conferences, packaged tours, and, of course, other publications to their readers. And why not? If *Time,* the pet of genial, austere Henry Luce, can go into the pots and pans business, the practice can't be all that bad.

Chapter 4

Advertising: Detestable and Indispensable

Clay T. Whitehead, the young (in his thirties) director of the White House Office of Telecommunications Policy, announced on February 17, 1972, in Denver, Colorado, that "the government does not feel that advertising is in itself essentially evil." The subject of the talk was his opposition to a proposal made by the Federal Trade Commission to present "counter-advertisements" which would have the right to attack fraudulent or simply doubtful claims made by manufacturers.

What makes Whitehead's statement so astonishing is not the fact that a Republican administration, therefore closely linked to business circles, is giving its support to the advertising industry in the face of opposition from a regulatory agency of its own government, but that it is doing so in such a defensive manner. It is certainly a far cry from the "What's good for General Motors is good for the nation" philosophy of the Eisenhower years. President Nixon himself felt compelled to affirm in an October 15, 1971, nationwide television broadcast that he felt profits were a necessity. The statement was about as earth-shattering as the Pope confirming the existence of God in his Christmas message. Nevertheless, the mere fact that the President felt compelled to make the statement indicates that yesterday's dogmas are in the process of being challenged in the United States.

It is fortunate that "advertising is not essentially evil," since every time the giant American business machine produces $100, $2 are allocated for advertising. This is, by far, the highest proportion in the world: in Japan advertising accounts for 1.14 percent; in Germany 1.56 percent; and in France only 0.90 percent. The $20 billion that Madison Avenue distributes each year surpasses the value of the total Egyptian and Pakistani G.N.P. combined (on which more than 100 million people live).

In view of the tremendous sums at stake, it would be a bit difficult to deny that advertising contains the seeds of corruption of journalistic independence. It is, in effect, part and parcel of modern capitalism. It subsidizes and, as we saw earlier, conditions the information systems of most of the world's countries. In addition, advertising is by its very nature a form of information—whatever its ulterior aim. But today, despite its power, it is subject to a more serious and fundamental re-evaluation than ever before.

THE MEDIA'S HABIT-FORMING DRUG

Publications began by accepting small amounts of advertising, which was, early on, considered a welcome source of extra revenues. Then they started counting on advertising to finance their development and pay their executives' expense accounts. One fine day, they realized that they were no longer able to do without it and found themselves within a hair's-breadth of bankruptcy if any year's ad billions decreased rather than increased. Certain publications which had previously been beyond reproach in their commitment to editorial and artistic independence seemed to be willing to compromise their standards (sell their cover, for example) to pull in more advertising. In the same way that the human body becomes addicted to amphetamines, the information industry had, in half a century, become totally dependent on advertising.

In the United States, 66 percent of all magazines' revenues are from advertising, and in France the proportion is sometimes even higher. More than 50 percent of a daily newspaper's financial resources are based on ads (90 percent for *Figaro,* 75 percent for *The New York Times*). Advertising also accounts for television's total revenues in the United States and for a rapidly increasing proportion in France (none in 1967, $110 million in 1972). Whatever overall policy or administrative system is in force, when such a tremendous proportion of the media's very ability to exist comes from a single source, it is equivalent to advertisers' having stockholders' rights—despite the press' proclamations to the contrary.

Each medium needs advertising far more than advertising needs it. The proliferation of newspapers, television networks, and new media, the market development of which is only beginning, have given the ad industry a wide choice. When, at the request of H.E.W., cigarette commercials were excluded from American television at the beginning of 1971, a large portion of the advertising dollar which would have gone to television went instead to the printed press; ironically, cigarette sales, far from declining, went up—although at a slower rate of increase than in the past.

Every type of advertising has its preferred media adapted to its needs and the public to which it is directed. Looking at the top twenty-five advertisers for each medium, one finds that there is an overwhelming preponderance of commercials for household products (food, cleaning supplies) on television; that advertisements for transportation (cars, tires, airlines) appear prominently in the pages of daily newspapers, and that cigarette, liquor, and automobile advertisements are stressed in magazines. The national advertising budgets for television and magazines (daily newspapers are less likely to be affected by national budgets since they depend primarily on local advertisers) are drawn for the most part from 500 large corporations which work with 200 principle ad agencies.

Despite the potential for control of the content of the media, agencies and advertisers do not, on a day-to-day basis, take full advantage of their power. To be sure, certain companies are still convinced that, by inserting a page of advertising in a publication, they earn the right to have an article published about themselves. Some old-fashioned industrialists may even go so far as to naïvely announce to advertising salesmen, "No, for the moment I don't need any advertising, but how much will it cost me to have a one-page article printed?" To the extent that such ploys succeed, the fault lies largely with publications themselves, particularly those small specialized trade journals which over a long period of time have allowed themselves to be bought in this manner.

However, as business practices have become less crude, industrialists have learned that a policy of "if - you - write - about - my - company's - strike - I'll - give - my - advertising - budget - to - someone - else" risks antagonizing publishers. And, although journals cannot live without advertising, it is rare that they cannot keep their consciences clean by sacrificing one advertiser at a time. It is simply a matter of how far they can go. The independence of the press, as it is now defined in France, gives the media the right to criticize a new car (this is a recent change in the rules of the game), but it is still taboo to release a study of the automobile industry's disregard for passenger safety.

The major reason that advertisers' direct or pre-emptory interference with the media is rare (though it still exists) is that their power is such that it would be unseemly to make it felt too often. Just as intelligent parents refrain from constantly flaunting their raw power over their children but instead use gentle persuasion, the more power the members of the business community have over the media, the more likely they are to handle them with kid gloves.

Editors of newspapers and magazines are always ready to tell the story of the article in the public interest that cost them an important advertising budget to show how editorially independent their publications are. But the same men are far less eloquent (perhaps because they are less conscious of it) when it comes to discussing the self-censure which has become second nature to many journalists and the VIP treatment given to press releases from the PR departments of most large firms.

THE DISTORTED MIRROR

Advertising does not shape a periodical through financial pressure alone. Its very presence in a publication creates a typographical obstacle course for the reader. In those daily newspapers that carry the largest amounts of advertising, the reader may have to leaf through entire sections where no more than a meager column per page is devoted to news or features. In magazines, articles are frequently continued at the back of the publication, where narrow strips of copy are lined up against column after column of advertising.

The mere presence of advertising pollutes the editorial environment of the printed press as greatly as it does that of television, and in Europe often to an even greater degree. The ideal solution would be to group all of the ads together in one section of each publication. But advertisers are not very likely to accept this idea and the press cannot risk alienating them. It is the reader who has to accommodate his reading habits to layouts that bunch reading matter and ads together. Some magazines and newspapers do not have overflows of advertising pages and make for eye-pleasing reading. But because pages devoid of advertising are generally one of the surest signs that a publication is facing financial deficits, such pleasures are usually short-lived.

Many readers are aware of this and unconsciously try to get the feel of a publication's weight before reading it, just as one might try to size someone up by the expression on his face. If they find the journal a little on the thin side, they may be concerned about its future. For example, subscribers to *The New Yorker* may feel alarmed about the continuation of the weekly at the beginning of each year. But the skinny January issues are as seasonal an occurrence as winter migrations. Advertisers, like migrating birds, all go into action at the same time of year. In the weeks immediately preceding Christmas, advertising content is usually at its zenith. And then suddenly, at the end of December, the number of advertising pages drops by 80 percent. Publishers have learned to bow to this reality.

Another way in which advertising has conditioned publishing is that it is virtually impossible to think of creating a newspaper or magazine without it. Many publications that fulfill a need or interest for a large reading public might be launched every year, but advertisers would not find them attractive—or at least not attractive enough. Thus only publications certain of attracting an advertising market are created, even if there is no obvious social justification for them. This explains the present decline of opinion magazines which, as a result of their diversity, vigor, and even their extremism, should remain at the center of a democratic press. Lack of advertising has helped kill them.

According to a formula devised by French media critic Professor Henri Mercillon, "There is no patron of the arts more ruthless than advertising." In other words, advertising finances only those endeavors that serve its purposes and withdraws its support once their usefulness has been exhausted.

As a patron, advertising is not only ruthless but sometimes underhanded. Certain ads are designed to look like news features in an attempt to get the message across to unwary readers or viewers. Advertising pages can be camouflaged by presenting them in article form, using the same type face and layout as the publication in which it appears. Even France's most scrupulous newspaper, *Le Monde,* accepts these ads, which are accompanied only by a discreet disclaimer that the "page was produced by Agency X" at the end of the article.

In fact, it is on television that news and advertising run the greatest future risk of being confused with one another. The "tube" needs an awesome quantity of programs, and many local networks, particularly in the United States, simply do not have the means to fill up their air time with quality broadcasts. Advertisers have taken advantage of this weak point by becoming producers themselves. Large advertisers can put together seemingly noncommercial one-hour programs replete with their products (which are all carefully presented to their best advantage, of course) and then offer the shows to television stations across the country. Some stations turn down such programs, but many need them to "fill in the gaps." Thus for a production cost of only $183,000, Lockheed Aircraft obtained air time that under normal advertising rates would have cost them $500,000. Small television stations are so hungry for films that, as some satirists have said, if blank film were sent out to a hundred of them, at least five stations would program it.

As ruthless or underhanded as it may be, advertising as a patron of the arts also shows itself to be somewhat backward on occasion. While wealthy Avery Brundage was interrogating a few ski champions on how they made their living, the entire televised retransmission of the 1972 Sapporo games was sold to NBC, which then proceeded to get several advertisers to finance the operation. The result was that Winter Olympics as broadcast in the United States was vastly inferior to the programs in Europe (where there was live coverage of as many events as time differences permitted, including all of the trial heats). There was no direct coverage for NBC's viewers, though. All the technologically advanced satellites did was transmit pictures of the games to New York, where they were held until 11 o'clock at night in order to attract a large number of viewers at a time when most people start turning off their sets. No early bedtimes for America's sports fans. A second reason NBC did not broadcast direct coverage was that this would have complicated the insertion of advertising messages. The American public was therefore forced to settle for taped films interspersed with regular commercials. At the end of the games, sports enthusiasts could be easily spotted by their red eyes and continual yawning at the office. Millions of hours of national productivity were lost just so Chrysler and Texaco could sell their wares on NBC.

THE BILL OF INDICTMENT

Business Week noted at the end of 1971 that never had ad agencies been attacked from so many sides at once. Perhaps it is unfair to put the onus on the ad agencies, for advertising is no more than the handmaiden of industry. Advertising is the public language of business firms, practically the only one they have. The fact that it therefore plays the most visible role in the creation of the business community's image should come as no surprise to anyone. Though by its very nature advertising's aim is to mold people's desires, advertising is also a form of news, and one of its by-products is that, honest or dishonest, above board or deceptive, the ethics of business show through in ads. In this respect, even if the attacks to which the ad industry is subjected often seem unjust or disproportionate, they are inevitable, for advertising is by far the most conspicuous adjunct of the business world.

Little is known about the physiological workings of allergies. However, doctors have often noticed that certain substances with which an organism may have been in contact for years with no noticeable effects can suddenly, as if the organism had abruptly overreached its tolerance level, set off violent allergic reactions. Today's advanced societies are witnessing the beginnings of the public's allergy to advertising. After decades of intensive bombardment, doubts have surfaced, tempers have flared, and what was previously accepted as banality has suddenly taken on the aspect of near-dishonesty.

The cost to the public of advertising has often been questioned. It increases retail prices in amounts of as much as 20 to 25 percent for a box of Corn Flakes (according to the Federal Trade Commission's 1972 estimates). In its defense, advertising people claim, without citing figures, that, on the contrary, if there were no advertising, the turnover of cereal boxes on supermarket shelves would be far less rapid and per unit manufacturing and marketing costs would skyrocket. The huge advertising expenses for different brands of the same product are the result of desperate competition for which, whether he likes it or not, the consumer foots the bill. Some people claim that these expenses are futile, since advertising is not needed to sell basic products. If it were, how could one explain the fact that in the United States cigarette consumption has not declined in 1971, after the abolition of cigarette commercials on television? On the other hand, John Kenneth Galbraith, one of the most caustic commentators on advertising, maintains that it is effective in that manufacturers can condition the public into consuming exactly what they plan to produce. And Galbraith does not even reproach them on this point, for he considers advertising to be an unavoidable by-product of the industrial state.

However, these economic arguments are either contradictory or hard to prove. One cannot claim both that advertising outlays are ineffectual and a waste of money and at the same time argue that they enable business firms to hold the consumer in the palm of their hands. Nor is it any easier to settle the debate among those who maintain that advertising causes retail prices to rise and those who swear it lowers them, as long as controlled experiments with an advertising-free—but nevertheless capitalistic—economic system have not been conducted.

Advertising can be accused of just about everything, but there is no conclusive proof that such accusations are well founded (except in very specific and limited areas), and it is from this situation that the advertising industry derives its power: it knows how to take advantage of its critics' disputes with one another.

The unrest toward advertising today has subjective explanations unrelated to statistics and percentages. Principal causes include the saturation of individual consumers and the ever-increasing gap between society's educational level and the mass-appeal level of the advertising to which it is subjected.

Whether advertisements serve a need or are superfluous is beside the point for the average man, who, under the barrage of advertising he is subjected to, tunes out on the thousands of oral, written, visual, mailed, posted, mobile, colored, three-dimensional, commercial, political, public, national, local, new, worn-out, spoken, or sometimes even whistled messages which are thrust at him during the course of the day. Advertising comes in every shape and form imaginable— even toothpicks may carry ad messages—and recently it has even been foisted on the public in the form of postage stamps (there is no bottom to the American post office's unfathomable deficit). Since a high saturation level was reached some time ago, advertisers are compelled to make a bigger splash, create larger posters, and repeat themselves more often in order to retain the public's attention. And, even if this resort to excess does not necessarily provoke public furor (why wouldn't consumers be flattered by all this attention?), it is making the public increasingly indifferent.

While all this is going on, the country's most sophisticated minds have been avowing that advertising is an insult to their intelligence, aesthetic sense, and moral principles, and they claim (often despite evidence to the contrary) that they are totally immune to it. Criticism of this type has always been standard for the well educated. The difference today is that the massive increase in educational levels has swollen their ranks to such an extent that the highly educated now constitute a substantial minority. And, since businessmen and advertising people—even if they do make their living from advertising —pride themselves on belonging to this minority, they are that much more sensitive to rebuke.

The attack most often advanced these days is that every advertisement by its very nature is some form of lie. However, moral arguments are not enough to threaten the existence of advertising. Why, in a society where concealment has become an integral part of day-to-day living, should advertising alone be expected to meet evangelical standards of truth? The industry's real problem is that, like La Fontaine's fox, "it lives at the mercy of those who listen to what it has to say," and the public is now lending advertising a less and less favorable ear.

A REVERSAL OF PUBLIC OPINION

If advertising still remains one of the great success stories of the century, perhaps it is because consumers are on the whole quite responsive to the window it opens to their dreams of material possessions. If it did not strike a chord, advertising would not be able to manipulate and condition the public as it does. In a society where a family's prosperity rarely dates back further than the parents' or grandparents' generation, the need to rebel against the promises of a consumer wonderland does not appear to be very urgent.

In 1940, scarcely 40 percent of the Americans polled by Gallup had any criticism whatsoever of advertising and 51 percent of the readers of the *Ladies' Home Journal* felt then that advertising was honest and sincere.

One of the most thorough studies ever made on the attitudes toward advertising was conducted in 1964 by two Harvard researchers, Bauer and Greyser. Their research shows that, on the whole, the public has a favorable impression of advertising. Seventy-eight percent of those questioned felt that it played an essential role, 74 percent thought that it brought about improvement in products, and 71 percent were of the opinion that it played a part in raising the standard of living. Nevertheless, 65 percent estimated that, at the same time, it caused people to buy products they did not really need. Even 41 percent of those who answered that they were in favor of advertising recognized that it could lead to harmful consequences for consumers. As for the ads themselves, 36 percent said they found them enjoyable and 36 percent said they were useful, versus 28 percent who found them offensive. Thirty-eight percent of the respondents felt that television commercials were the most enjoyable and 59 percent felt that daily newspaper ads were the most useful.

Three years later, a control study showed that the percentage of people who favored unrestricted advertising had grown from 41 to 49 percent. Was this because the economic boom of the "fabulous sixties" had reached its peak during this period? Or did this study, financed by the Association of Advertising Agencies, simply present too rosy a view? Since then, however, public and governmental criticism has reached a point where it looks as though the advertising industry will have to conduct a public relations campaign on its own behalf.

At the beginning of 1972, *Business Week* published a survey conducted among the general public by New York ad agency Warwick and Legler in which 60 percent of those questioned said that the present criticism of the advertising industry was entirely justified. Half of the participants in the survey asked for stronger controls on advertising but at the same time held that this control should come primarily from the agencies and advertisers themselves.

As for advertising in each of the media, the Warwick study showed that its credibility was greatest in magazines and daily newspapers, followed, in descending order, by radio, billboards, television, and—ranking far behind the others—mail order.

A more precise survey made in 1971 for *Life* by the Harris Institute provided detailed information on the public's likes and dislikes with regard to advertising. On the positive side, 30 percent thought that advertising conveyed valuable information, 24 percent said that it kept the public informed of new products, and 20 percent felt that it had some entertainment value (curiously, this figure jumped to 27 percent among college graduates—which would seem to indicate that the educated are more susceptible to advertising than they generally pretend to be).

On the negative side, 44 percent accused advertising of making false or exaggerated claims, 29 percent felt that they were subjected to too much of it, and 18 percent said that it was either stupid or boring. On the whole, the study confirmed that the public has not yet turned *en masse* against advertising but it also gave evidence that its critics have substantial support among some segments of the population.

The most incisive criticisms, not unexpectedly, came from the youthful respondents, whose (sometimes simplistic) questioning of advertising can be summed up as follows:

—Is advertising necessary?

—Does it improve the quality of a given product?

—Does it contribute to lowering the price of a product?

—Does it present a true or trustworthy image of the product?

—Doesn't too much of advertising insult the intelligence of the public?

—Doesn't it encourage "conspicuous consumption" in order to "keep up with the Joneses" or out of fear of ridicule?

—Doesn't it have the effect of debasing the cultural level of the media?

—Doesn't it contribute to reinforcing monopoly control of certain products?

—Doesn't it limit consumer choices to the two or three products in different categories that are able to afford the greatest ad budgets?

—Doesn't it substitute buyer-persuasion techniques for hard product information?

—Don't too many of the ads elevate and encourage questionable taste?

—Aren't the ads slated for children socially harmful?

—Doesn't the omnipresence of advertising constitute, in effect, an invasion of privacy?

Two findings in the *Business Week* survey may be of some comfort to advertising agencies and businessmen: first, the survey revealed that, as a public service, advertising has a better reputation than Congress, the Pentagon, or trade unions; and, secondly, in response to the question "Should advertising be abolished?" 96 percent of those interviewed answered with a resounding "No!"

BECOMING AWARE OF THE DANGER

Businessmen who try to play on people's sympathy by claiming that they, too, are family men and consumers, bring to mind a routine of the French humorist Guy Bedos, who exclaims, "How can you say that I don't like babies—I'm a former baby myself!"

Yet, according to a study published by the *Harvard Business Review* in June 1971, businessmen's opinions of advertising are, surprisingly, hardly more favorable than those of the general public. To the question of whether money spent on advertising could on the whole be considered a worthwhile expense, 50 percent answered "no" and only 28 percent said "yes." And, although they still feel that advertising plays an important role in the economy, more than half of the businessmen surveyed nevertheless thought that too much money was spent on it and that the industry did not have a very commendable social influence. How can the advertising industry expect to find a general defense of its virtues when more than two-thirds of American businessmen feel that it does not give an accurate picture of the products it promotes?

In addition, even if the Nixon Administration succeeds in curbing their zeal, Washington officials have already begun to make trouble for the Madison Avenue crowd. From the beginning of 1970, the following measures have been put into effect in the United States as a result of their efforts:

—Since the discovery of the link between cigarette smoking and cancer, cigarette commercials on television have been completely abolished and tobacco manufacturers have been required to include a cautionary alert: "Warning: The Surgeon General Has Determined That Cigarette Smoking Is Dangerous to Your Health" on every package of cigarettes.

—Manufacturers of automobiles (including the makers of Chevrolets and Volkswagens) and of household appliances have been obligated to present conclusive evidence to back up the claims made in their advertisements.

—Networks have been obliged to "voluntarily" limit themselves to twelve minutes of advertising per hour (instead of the usual fourteen) at those times of the day when children make up a sizable portion of the television audience.

—Finally, and most important, certain advertisers have been ordered to broadcast advertising messages correcting exaggerated statements made in past commercials. For example, the reforms initiated by the Federal Trade Commission have forced the manufacturers of Profile bread to devote 25 percent of the product's advertising budget to televised messages explaining that Profile's purported qualities as a diet food are based on the fact that it is cut more thinly than competing brands and thus provides the consumer with seven fewer calories per slice. Under the F.T.C.'s edict, Profile has to go all the way by acknowledging at the end of its ad that a difference of seven calories is insignificant, and that eating Profile will not make one lose weight.

Faced with government intervention and the public right to challenge the claims of advertising, the advertising industry has reacted with extreme caution. Its greatest fear is that it will eventually find itself caught between the commercial requirements of its clients and the demands of the F.T.C. for accuracy and social responsibility. For this reason the advertising agencies have begun taking pains to verify the accuracy of their client's claims in advance. When Gillette brought out its new Track II two-blade razor in 1971, the manufacturer spent an entire day demonstrating the product to its ad agency physician, in an effort to convince the agency staff that the razor really was superior to its competitors. "Without their approval," explained one of Gillette's executives, "we would have had to cancel the whole campaign."

Once the validity of a product's claims has been established, the text of the advertisements themselves must be gone over with a fine tooth comb in order to make sure that it withstands accusations of exaggeration as well. The fees charged by lawyers who specialize in this area have doubled in the last few years. At the close of one of its ads, Avis, for example, stated that they could only guarantee reservations which had been properly received and processed, and ended with the P.S. "Our lawyer made us add that." Thus even meticulous compliance with the law has been turned into a sales pitch.

Agencies have begun to steer clear of campaigns that are essentially "aesthetic" in nature or that make direct use of such subconscious consumer feelings as the fear of being rejected or the need to feel secure. Advertisements have become more informative. In addition, advertising people have created their own National Advertising Review Board, whose purpose is to set up guidelines for the profession in order to obviate the establishment of government controls. The organization's major task is to examine complaints lodged against deceptive advertisements and, if an acceptable solution is not reached, to bring them to the public's attention.

Finally, realizing that by creating an image for its clients it had neglected its own, the advertising profession began doing ads for advertising. For several years now, French ad agencies have been conducting a campaign designed to strike back at or ridicule "those who do not believe in advertising" or are afraid of it (the *"publiphobes"*), thanks to space provided free of charge by the media which depend on advertising for their bread and butter. America is quickly picking up the trend with the help of Time, Inc., which in 1972 gave space worth $600,000 to the advertising agencies. Dan Seymour, president of J. Walter Thompson, the largest agency in the world, has been doing his utmost to find supporters for a national campaign on behalf of advertising on radio and television and in the printed press.

These efforts to adapt the industry to a period of transition will not be enough to appease advertising's critics and the public's uneasiness. But at least these measures are a more constructive response than the reactions of a number of traditionally minded businessmen who go no further than to announce, as did Gilbert H. Weil, legal council for the Association of Advertisers, that advertising has put its very existence in danger by vigorously supporting basic and functional changes which could easily lead to its extinction.

AESOP'S TONGUE

For the media, advertising, like Aesop's fabled tongue, is a force for both great evil because it has left a profound mark on the media's content and financial set-up; and for great good because, in capitalistic countries, it is the chief source of revenue which enable the press to operate without government subsidies and thus controls.

Even the Communist world recognizes the fact that advertising is indispensable. When the Chinese Communist Party asked its newspapers to become financially independent, it suggested that they advertise "public services and entertainment" and offer "classified ads for goods and services."

Neither the American public nor advertising's most virulent critics seem ready to abolish advertising altogether. It is essential to keeping the economy functioning smoothly. Also, as was evident during the newspaper strikes in New York in 1963 and southwestern France in 1972, it performs an important service in the everyday life of local communities.

As we enter the last third of this century, advertising expenditures and the industry's technical control and carelessness with regard to its social responsibilities have gone so far in the United States that the situation seems profoundly anarchic. It is not the idea of advertising as such that is being questioned but rather its volume and content: there is too much of it and it is too unrestrained.

Because the establishment of codes restricting freedom of advertising does not involve the same basic issues as restricting the freedom of information, it is predictable that the result of the current pressures to make advertising more socially responsible will be the institution of controls to tame its excesses. The days of "wild" or "no-holds-barred" advertising will become a thing of the past.

However, the media will probably never be any more satisfied with their dependence on advertising than Winston Churchill was with democracy when he said that it's the worst system there is, with the exception of all others.

45511

Chapter 5

The Press Empires

It is probably because the word "media" automatically brings to mind the idea of power that one speaks in terms of "publishing empires" as soon as some fortunate entrepreneur has managed to acquire three or four periodicals. Today in the United States, the expression "communications empire" would perhaps be more applicable to a press group that adds a book club and a few radio stations (since there are over 4,000 radio stations in the United States, it is not exceptional for a publisher to acquire one) to its newspaper and magazine interests. But in Europe newspapers and magazines will probably remain the central, if not the exclusive, concern of such empires, since radio and television stations are, for the most part, state monopolies or are—as in the case of the two private French radio stations, Europe No. 1 and Radio-Luxembourg—subject to heavy governmental control. Even in the United States, a company may, by law, own only a specifically limited number of local radio and television stations. Therefore, press lords infatuated with high sales and strong growth continue to devote themselves to the printed press, whose creation, purchase, and sale remains more or less free in all industrial democracies.

There are no precise criteria by which a publishing company is automatically considered to have reached the status of empire. The number of publications owned does not in itself have any bearing. Take the case of the Compagnie Française d'Editions, which controls nearly thirty specialized French magazines (which together do not reach even half the sales of *Le Monde* and which pull in an even lower percentage of its profits). Only its smallest competitors would go so far as to refer to it as the "Ollive Empire"—to give it the name of its owner. Nor is it simply a question of commanding both a large number of publications and high sales figures. The group created in Paris by the Italian mini-tycoon Cino del Duca, for example, is made up of a number of periodicals, several among them with circulations of over a million. Yet *The Wonders of Knitting, Tarzan,* and *Intimaté,* separately or together, do not have sufficient influence on public opinion to make the organization worthy of the crown of empire. In order to become a member of the envied club of "publishing empires" a firm must not only be big but influential as well. Only two or three companies in each country fit these somewhat vague criteria. In France, the two major organizations are Hachette, whose manifold enterprises include, among other things, a press empire, and the publishing holdings of Jean Prouvost, whose operations center around *Paris-Match.* The country's other groups rank not as empires but only as principalities. In Germany, the Springer and Grüner Jahr magazine groups are the dominant press enterprises; in England, Thomson and the International Publishing Corporation share top rank, along with Murdoch, an aggressive newcomer on the English publishing scene; in Italy the Mondadori group is the largest and most influential; in Sweden it is Bonnier; in Japan it is the three giant dailies: *Asahi, Mainichi,* and *Yomiuri;* and in the United States a dozen magazine groups and daily newspaper chains predominate. Most of these enterprises are among the 100 largest corporations of each country, even though they are almost exclusively based upon an ordinary product which lacks technological interest and is particularly perishable: printed paper.

Among the publishing empires or the groups which aspire to join their ranks, there are wide variations in character, depending upon the personality of the man who created them. For, more so than in any other industry, it is almost always an individual who is the founding spirit of a publishing business. And, more often than not, it is a man who started with practically no money at all; the majority of these fabulous corporations were begun with ridiculously small outlays of capital. No need for machines or funds to create newspapers or magazines—equal doses of talent, courage, and foolhardiness will suffice.

THE "COLLECTORS"

Essentially there are three ways to form a publishing empire. In ascending order of difficulty and rarity, they are: acquisition, imitation, and creation. The most frequent method, because it calls upon the talents of businessmen, which are found in greater abundance than the rarer talents of journalists, is acquisition. A businessman may buy journals that others have created. For this, two types of talent are required: financial ability (i.e., the "know-how" to negotiate a good price and to raise the necessary funds) and administrative ability (to assure the greatest possible return on the stocks that one has purchased).

Journalistic talent is unnecessary, and even somewhat of a handicap, for if a business genius starts trying to achieve editorial perfection in the publications he controls and needless expenses are incurred and absorbed in editorial perfectionism, he may be passing up other interesting acquisitions. By the same token, success is far more certain if one keeps as far away as possible from a political stance. It is far better if the editorial staff of acquired newspapers can be assured continued editorial control, while someone else gives his undivided attention to the yearly income statements. One of the best contemporary examples of this axiom is Sam Newhouse, who once said, "Anybody who loses money on a daily newspaper has to be crazy." For years now, Newhouse himself has been continuously buying up one daily after another with the aim of reorganizing its management and making it return 20 percent in profits before taxes, which in his eyes seems the one indispensable proof of mental sanity. In his stable, he has some ultraconservative newspapers and others that are boldly liberal, but he has never wasted his time trying to interfere with their political stands. Continuing on his money-making way, he also absorbed the Condé Nast group *(Vogue, House and Garden)* but has never become so involved in his operations as to personally choose his magazines' fashion photographs (an activity to which, on the other hand, the owner of the weekly magazine *Jours de France,* French billionaire aeronautical engineer Marcel Dassault, happily devotes weekends spent on his property at Villennes).

The world's most attractive acquisition-empire is without doubt the one put together by Roy Thomson, a Canadian who, in 1964, five years after his arrival in Great Britain, became Lord Thomson of Fleet. Born in Toronto in 1894, he began working when he was fourteen, but it was not until the age of thirty-seven, after several bankruptcies, that he opened a small local radio station in Canada—a move that was designed to help increase sales of sets for his radio business. In this roundabout way, he discovered that the news industry could be highly lucrative. Driven by a love for money, Thomson devoted himself from that point on to buying newspapers and radio and television stations. His approach was simple and direct.

Everytime he met the head of a media operation, he bluntly asked, "Would you like to sell?" He even approached the head of the Soviet newspaper *Pravda* this way, who was somewhat baffled and slightly irritated by the proposition. A remarkable financial wizard, he acquired his empire with money borrowed from banks and he was forever enlarging his geographical base, jumping from Canada to Scotland in 1952, then to London and the United States in 1959, ultimately extending his operations throughout the British Commonwealth. Today his fortune is estimated at some $300 million and is comprised of thirty-nine newspapers in Canada, twenty-four in the United States, fifty-three in Great Britain (including the *London Times,* a newspaper that is as deeply in the red as it is prestigious), twenty-four publications in South Africa, and a few in Rhodesia, Malawi, Liberia, Australia, and New Zealand. To this incomparable group of daily newspapers must be added nearly twenty radio and television stations (in practically every country of the Commonwealth); thirteen publishing houses, twenty or so printing shops, and several travel agencies, not to mention a slew of specialized magazines. He wanted to prove that a barber's son could become a multimillionaire (and a lord) in London. He achieved his goals. Not only does he never get involved in the contents of his publications (which is why few doubted his word when, on purchasing *The Times,* he guaranteed the independence of that venerable institution), but he has never even visited a great number of them. He is an insatiable and good-natured collector of businesses who just happened to specialize in publishing.

THE IMITATORS

The formulas for successful newspaper and magazine publishing are not limitless. Because most daily newspapers are quite similar as far as content and services are concerned, for variety one must turn to magazines. But even here, while on the surface there seems to be great variety, only a limited number of formulas have met with equal success in all free, developed nations. Large-format, weekly general picture magazines such as *Life* and *Paris-Match* have been imitated just about everywhere, as have news weeklies (such as *Time* and *L'Express),* women's magazines, and business publications. When an innovation succeeds in one part of the world (most of the time such ventures get their start in the United States), whoever is first to import it into his own country has an excellent chance of turning it into a success and making a profit. This is neither easy nor automatic, for it takes more than mere determination to be an imitator. Thus, forty years after the birth of *Time,* France still has no newsmagazine. A team financed by Edmond de Rothschild (and simultaneously by Thyssen in Germany) brought out in 1961 *Continent,* a magazine that used *Time's* formula and that was published simultaneously in French and German. In spite of its financial resources, it did not last five months and never surpassed the 40,000-copy mark. Somewhat hastily it was decided that the formula was not "adapted to the French market." This is probably what prompted Pierre Lazareff, dean of Paris journalism, to predict that *L'Express* "would fall flat on its face" when, a year after the failure of *Continent,* the former political weekly published as a newspaper in tabloid-format was turned into a weekly newsmagazine. *L'Express,* from the point of view of sales and revenues, was an instant success. *Continent's* short life span, in spite of the good idea and the huge sums of money that were behind it, was due to its weak editorial content and, above all, the total lack of effort to promote and market the new product.

A good imitation, therefore, must follow a number of simple rules. First of all, anyone seeking to try his hand at it must know his market well, must be a true journalist in contrast to the "collector" so that he can adapt an imported idea to local temperament, and, finally, he must have the qualities of an entrepreneur, for there is always a financial risk. One way to establish a publishing empire, then, would be to apply systematically the simple principle: "If it works somewhere else, why not here?" For example, over a span of twenty-five years, Giorgio Mondadori created Italy's largest press empire by successively introducing Italian equivalents of *Life (Epoca), Elle (Grazia), Time (Panorama), Historia (Storia Illustrata), Eltern (Duct)* and, *L'Expansion (Espansione).* Mondadori, who developed the press end of this printing and publishing empire, knew how to select the foreign ideas that best suited the Italian market at different times. The champion of quality journalistic imitation is unquestionably Jean Prouvost, a French industrialist who was attracted to journalism early and for half a century used his indefatigable energy (which he retained even after turning eighty-five) to unite his family textile fortune with his love for paper. Like Roy Thomson, Jean Prouvost did not arrive on the publishing scene until mid-life. In 1924 at the age of forty, he purchased a small daily, *Paris-Midi,* and used it to learn the newspaper trade. Five years later, he bought *Paris-Soir,* whose circulation was under 70,000 and, inspired by the methods of the mass-circulation British press, brought sales up to 2 million copies (a figure that has never been reached by any other French daily since) within ten years. Impressed by the success of *Life,* at the end of the 1930s he introduced *Match,* a photo-magazine which had reached a circulation figure of 1.8 million on the eve of the Second World War. The war was to bring Prouvost's empire back to zero. Having briefly served as a minister under Pétain, after the war he was obliged to lay low and keep out of public life for a time. In 1949, at the age of sixty-four—almost mandatory retirement age for many chairmen of the board—he started again from scratch with a new weekly picture magazine, now called *Paris-Match.* Five years later, in 1954, he launched *Marie-Claire,* a monthly women's magazine (comparable to *McCall's* and *Ladies' Home Journal*), and then in 1960 he brought out the French equivalent of *TV Guide, Télé 7 Jours,* which was to become (as is generally true of television weeklies worldwide) the largest circulation magazine in France. Always the successful imitator, often loosely adapting the ideas of others, he also introduced *La Maison de Marie-Claire* (a mixture of Germany's *Schöner Wohnen* and America's *Better Homes and Gardens*) and *Les Parents* and *Ambre* (the latter two modeled after two German publications, *Eltern* and *Jasmin*). True, he bought *Le Figaro,* a prestigious Paris daily, and breathed new life into Radio-Luxembourg, but his talents as a journalist-entrepreneur had, after the war, been dedicated to magazines. Of course, thanks to the family textile business, Jean Prouvost never lacked for money, but others as wealthy as he believed they were capable of buying themselves a place in newspaper and magazine publishing and failed. Even if he does not rank as an innovator, to succeed as an imitator he needed a tremendous amount of creativity.

THE CREATORS

In speaking of the press, perhaps it is a bit unfair to give the greatest credit to originators and innovators. Novelty is not necessarily a proof of creativity. For example, whoever introduces the computer industry's first specialized periodical that follows the format and approach of traditional technology magazines will probably have contributed less to the press than a man such as Rudolf Augstein who, inspired by *Time* magazine, launched *Der Spiegel* in Germany in 1947, incorporating in his imitation all the changes necessary for German readers' tastes. Every now and then somebody hits on a formula that sets a new precedent in publishing. Even if it is only a question of applying for the first time an already established journalistic technique to a totally different type of subject matter, the resulting newspaper or magazine still can be considered a new creation. In France, when Robert Hersant applied the techniques used by general magazines to the automotive press, he created *Auto-Journal*. When Wall Street's Gil Kaplan adapted the format of the quality monthly to the financial press, he created *Institutional Investor*. It would be useless to try to evaluate whether their contributions to the press demonstrated greater talent than the contributions of Mondadori or Prouvost, but there is no doubt that the former took an additional risk by introducing a combination that had never been tested elsewhere. This is precisely the chance that Jean-Jacques Servan-Schreiber took with the first issue of *L'Express* (in 1953) and Daniel Filipacchi (who is now a partner of Hefner in the U.S. with *Oui*) took with the introduction of *Salut les Copains* (in 1964). However, if creations such as these are to serve as the foundation for a press empire, the founder must have a great deal of luck in addition to a touch of genius. Consider the case of *Playboy*, which was introduced by Hugh Hefner as a competitor to *Esquire* in 1953, after *Esquire* refused to give its then-employee Hefner the raise in salary he had requested. *Playboy*'s formula, derived strictly from Hefner's personal ideas and tastes, arrived right at the moment of change in the American male's morality and dreams. In less than twenty years, Hefner not only produced a magazine with a circulation that ranked among the top ten in the world; he had also created one of the most lucrative publishing phenomena (measured by profits as a percentage of sales) as well. But if an award were given for the introduction of the best single idea it would certainly have to go to Lila and Dewitt Wallace who, in 1922, conceived *Reader's Digest* and launched it in a garage with virtually no funds. No other magazine or newspaper in the world sells (and none probably ever will sell) more than 25 million copies of each issue in fifteen languages. No other press empire is founded on a single publication (the organization's numerous other sidelines are not journalistic). The popularity of *Reader's Digest* is such that it bewilders many of the professionals in the trade who are unable to put the publication into any of the usual categories. They find its formula to be intellectually anemic and have trouble understanding the success of a magazine that they themselves refuse to read. It is the only magazine whose content has true mass appeal; with its extremely short articles (three to six digest-size pages each) and simple language, it has managed to put itself within the scope of what today is considered the average television viewer. The Wallaces instinctively created a magazine for people who are not otherwise readers. It was, and remains fifty years later, a true press innovation.

While it is relatively rare to find authentic creators of new types of publications in the contemporary press, it is almost unheard of for a single man to conceive, bring into being, and succeed with several such creations. To measure how difficult this is, one need only compare the press with industries in which the invention or creation of a product (be it a transistor or Frosted Flakes) and its manufacture, on the one hand, and its distribution and sales, on the other, are not under the control of different men. Once perfected, an industrial product can be reproduced and distributed without its originator ever having to participate. In newspaper and magazine publishing, however, a new concept or idea may be essential, but the idea can take shape only if its originator is also capable of putting the publication to press, making each new issue appealing, and constantly perfecting it. The inherent craftsmanship of publishing requires that the same person possess imagination, the ability to get things done, and of course some business acumen.

The man who totally synthesized these qualities left a greater mark on contemporary publishing than any other man and built the most powerful press empire in the world—Henry Luce, who died in 1967 at the age of sixty-eight. It was he who, with his friend Britten Hadden, came up with the idea for *Time* and introduced it in 1923, using a journalistic formula that today more than ever fills a basic modern need (to provide readers baffled by the confusing flood of daily news with a weekly round-up of current events). He was also responsible for the creation and introduction of *Fortune* in 1930 (the first in-depth and lavishly illustrated reportage of business news), *Life* in 1936 (the news of the week in picture form), *Sports Illustrated* in 1954 (sports treated as a serious subject worthy of quality reporting), and Time-Life books sold by mail throughout the world. For each of his magazines, Luce perfected original editorial ideas that assured content, writing, and illustration of a quality rarely achieved up to that time in the news field. The exact opposite of a "collector," he himself originated and built the immense enterprise that is Time, Inc., today (total revenues of over $600 million in 1972). Never have so few publications amassed as many readers and made so great a profit. Even *Life*'s recent demise must be seen in the perspective of a quarter-century of fantastic success. *Sports Illustrated,* which was in the red for the first twelve years of its existence, is now highly profitable. Luce's journals reflected his conservative politics, which his successors, in tune with a changing society, little by little have erased from the pages of his publications. All in all, Henry Luce probably will go down in publishing history as the most inventive journalist the profession has ever known and as a man who was able to do what most people believed to be impossible: achieve mass circulation without compromising editorial quality.

THE SUCCESSION CRISIS

Because, to a greater degree than other businesses, press empires are founded on a single individual's talents as a creator or entrepreneur, they are apt to go through a particularly delicate phase at the time of succession. Depending on the economic structure in different countries, press empires are usually passed on either to the family or, in the absence of a more-or-less competent heir, to the technostructure, i.e., a group of managers that appoints itself a monarch. The family produces both the best and the worst at the same time. The worst occurs when laws of capital and blood put power in the hands of either a widow (as in the case of a number of regional French newspapers) whose only knowledge of the business at the time of her takeover is what she has picked up during dinner parties, or an incompetent son who spends his life trying to equal the image his staff had of his father. All too often, the father has seen to it that whatever capacity for initiative his son may have had is exhausted by holding an iron grip on the empire until the age of seventy-five or eighty and keeping his heir in apprenticeship until he is in his fifties.

Keeping the business under family leadership is a good solution when the heirs have divergent but complementary talents which they can exercise freely while continuing to inspire mutual confidence through close family ties. This was true of the Bonnier family of Sweden, which has been able for almost a century to fulfill the duties of managing the family business and whose many activities include control of half the country's press. While his father Arnoldo was still alive, Giorgio Mondadori carved for himself a made-to-order niche by developing the group's press operations in Milan. As a result, when in 1969 a dispute erupted between Giorgio and his brother Alberto, Mondadori's operations as a whole were not deeply affected by it. Otis Chandler, heir to a line of *Los Angeles Times* publishers and directors, developed a passion for newspapers at the age of thirty and turned the publication into one of the highest quality and largest-circulation papers in the United States while his father was pushing for the enterprise's diversification into other activities. On the death of her husband, Philip, Katharine Graham took over the *Washington Post–Newsweek* group; hired competent, responsible people for key jobs; and closely followed the course of its growth. Handing down power in the press by inheritance poses few problems in the United States, but the practice is today often contested in Europe where journalists insist upon being directed by true professionals. (See Part 2, Chapter 2.)

The problems involved in succession to power are most evident when there is no heir and it falls to top management and the board of directors to designate a successor. As a rule, no single person in the company embodies all of the founder's qualities as a press entrepreneur—that is, an individual with both editorial and business talents. This is perhaps understandable, since men of this sort are rarely willing to work for others. In addition, by the mere fact of a press empire's having become a huge, complicated operation, the generally prevailing sentiment is that the management of the firm should be entrusted to a competent businessman who, by the very nature of his talents, is not in a position to judge, much less to direct, editorial operations. Consequently, succession for the most part leads to a lack of editorial dynamism and even a lowering of quality. Looking again at Henry Luce, one finds that he was well aware of the problem and, in a rare move among big bosses, wanted to organize and help put his successors into the saddle while he was still alive. Unable to find one man to fill all of his own roles, he developed a corporate structure that placed Jim Linen, president of the company, in charge of money-making and made Hedley Donovan the overall editor-in-chief of the magazines to whom the editor-in-chief of each separate publication was responsible. In 1960 Luce himself had abandoned his financial duties as president of the company and remained only as editor-in-chief. In 1964, at only sixty-six, he retired completely and Hedley Donovan took over the top editorial spot. Luce died two years later of a heart attack. Few transitions have ever been so conscientiously organized. Yet, despite the precautions he had taken, it was not long before problems began to surface. In 1969, less than two years after Luce's death, Time, Inc., was in difficult straits. *Life*'s ever-increasing losses, several investments which had cost the company $15 million, coupled with several years of poor advertising revenues for the American press as a whole, suddenly made it necessary to reduce expenses drastically. Jim Linen was replaced by Jim Shepley and authority for the entire company was put into the hands of one man, Chairman of the Board Andrew Heiskell, who had the advantage of having been a journalist early in his career. Dual hierarchies tend to show their weaknesses when hard times hit. In contrast to Luce's badly-rewarded foresight is the *"après-moi-le-déluge"* philosophy of Jean Prouvost who, at the ripe old age of eighty-five, still had not found nor truly sought a suitable successor. Paris high society is already anticipating the vigorous competition for the role of successor that is certain to follow when Prouvost leaves the scene—which is unlikely to benefit Prouvost's empire.

THE DIVERSIFICATION CRISIS

The principles of modern management demand that one avoid putting all one's eggs in the same basket, especially—according to the persistent warnings of financial analysts—in publishing. For the past twenty years, there have been dire predictions, repeated over and over again, that printed media will be totally displaced by the audio-visual industry. Even if such an event does not seem to be imminent, constant repetition of this absurdity has given rise to the belief that the press is on its last legs. Nevertheless, the prosperous press empires have shown themselves to be excellent money-making machines. Yet as soon as bank accounts start to fatten, management oracles rise again. "Contrary to what your immigrant ancestors believed," they explain, "having money in the bank is not a proof of good management." They claim that one should invest one's money and even go into debt in order to diversify and acquire companies which will produce independent profits. Such talk may strike a responsive chord among some heirs or successors of an empire who seek to distinguish themselves from the company's illustrious and intimidating founder.

For one reason or another, the crucial moment may come when a press empire feels that it is ripe for diversification—that is, ready to introduce or buy nonjournalistic enterprises. Those who seem most convinced of the necessity for diversification are the ones whose empires consist principally of a single large, powerful, and very profitable publication. They insist that the magazine's or newspaper's share of the company's sales and profits dwindle from the 90 percent it once represented to less than 50 percent. In any case, this is the goal young directors like Otis Chandler and Arthur Ochs Sulzberger, respectively head of *The Los Angeles Times* and *The New York Times,* have set for themselves. In keeping with this line of reasoning, Chandler purchased an important daily in the Long Island area, *Newsday* (which also gives him a chance to do some hunting on rival Sulzberger's stalking grounds), publishing houses, and even an aviation map company. As for Sulzberger, he acquired *Family Circle* (a very prosperous, practical women's magazine), Arno Press and Quadrangle (book publishers), and even some magazines for dentists and golfers.

The major difficulty, generally, is in the realm of profits. For, while it is easy to increase an empire's sales by adding the sales of the purchased enterprises to those of the principal publication, it is not rare to see a percentage drop in the earnings of the new group. This occurs because few businesses reach a profitability level as high as that of a daily newspaper or a magazine that is doing well. If the latter shows 18 percent in profits before taxes and the newly acquired operation only reaches 13 percent (which is not bad at all), the total yield will be lower and the apostle of the diversification will find that his reputation as an administrator has become a bit tarnished. But since the major reason for diversification is not, contrary to what most annual reports boast, to optimize profits but to enlarge the empire's holdings, the profit picture alone does not usually keep management from diversifying. In the case of Playboy Industries, *Playboy* Magazine, a superb money-maker, earns 21 percent in profits before taxes. Somewhat bored in his Chicago "electronic" mansion, Hugh Hefner decided to diversify his activities by introducing the Playboy clubs. Twelve years later there were seventeen of them, but their earnings do not exceed 10 percent. As for Hefner's more recent venture, that of the Playboy Hotels, they are still in deficit, and the construction of the one in Great Gorge, New York, has swallowed over $30 million in investments. When one thinks of the numerous magazines which *Playboy*'s excellent press team could have bought or launched with such a sum, one can only wonder if the best thing to do with a press empire's cash flow isn't to use it for what its directors really know how to do best: the publishing of magazines and newspapers.

THE BUREAUCRATIC EMPIRE

Once the crisis of succession has passed and diversification has been initiated with whatever degree of success, press empires tend to resemble any other enterprise. After a period of growth made possible by innovation and the tight control of the founder, the publishing firm finds itself in calmer waters, when each person in a responsible position, to avoid rocking the boat, carefully tries to pull his own oar and lets his counterparts in other jobs do the same. The new boss in most cases was chosen by his equals for his ability as a "co-ordinator"—that is, he knows how to preside over a business meeting without getting involved in embarrassing disputes. The watchword is no longer conquest, but endurance. If the stockholders are satisfied—i.e., the stock market price is rising and dividends are growing—they will allow the team in power to raise its salaries, fatten its expense accounts, and have its own way about who gets promoted to which position. At such times it seems advisable that no business risks or innovations be undertaken. A failure, even one involving a limited investment, would be detrimental to the company's image and injurious to the stability of its stock quotations. However, a refusal to grow at all—for example, failure to launch any new publication—is contrary to the very nature of an empire, which, by definition, involves spreading out. Thus, when creative young executives (and an empire's prestigious image always attracts a few) propose new projects, they are encouraged and their suggestion is presented for serious consideration to the development committee. In the next six months the committee will conduct a market survey, organize a budget for the project and put together a voluminous, usually favorable report (after all, the development committee *is* there to promote expansion) which is then transmitted to the financial committee. This group studies the profitability of the idea, looks over the projected quarterly earnings, anxiously scrutinizes mid-term projections, subjects cash-flow estimates to rigorous analysis, and three months later releases its own findings—frequently a few shades less optimistic than the original study. Finally, all of this is brought to the attention of the board of directors, the nervous and flattered young executive making detailed presentations supported by color slides and a three-volume report with appendices. The board may declare itself to be in favor of the proposed project, but insists that, because a tremendous effort must still be made to strengthen existing enterprises, it would be preferable to hold off adopting it until a to-be-announced date. The young executive, disappointed but still hopeful, quietly waits and in the meantime continues to contemplate his graphs. Six months later, still with no progress in sight, he borrows money from his uncle, leaves the company and launches the new venture on his own. At any rate, this seems to be the script whereby some magazines have in recent years made new competitors out of young men who found that the big houses had lost their taste for gambling.

However, sometimes the board of directors is correct in remaining steadfast. To succeed at launching a new magazine or newspaper, a business must know how to do so with a minimum of cash outlay and a limited number of men who are truly dynamic and willing to cut down on expenses and their own salaries while they wait for the returns to increase. This is the way press empires traditionally got their start, in fact. But today, in a world of wall-to-wall carpeted offices where one cannot possibly work without a secretary, a private telephone line, consultants, and market studies, "overhead" alone threatens to smother any newborn publication.

Yet from time to time the unexpected happens. Some particularly convincing and obstinate individuals have managed to obtain authorization for their schemes. There is no guarantee of success, however. The largest press enterprise in France, Hachette, introduced *Cinq Colonnes à la Une,* a weekly television magazine, in 1971—this, despite the fact that no other country in the world has ever been able to support several magazines of this type and France was a country that already had two, *Télé-Poche* and *Télé 7 Jours.* Also, Hachette itself owned 50 percent of the latter publication. In view of this, the odds of success were so slight they should have been evident without a market study. Hachette lost $2 million on the new magazine before it was forced to close it down, which seemed to sustain the company's wisdom in having previously discouraged such initiatives.

WHO PUTS OUT THE BEST PUBLICATIONS?

Not all newspapers and magazines are part of press empires. Many remain independent, created and directed by a loner for whom one crowning achievement is sufficient. Some deliberately refuse to capitalize on their reputations and financial means. For example, *Le Monde* has the strongest image of quality in French publishing and could use it with the assurance that every project introduced under its name would be exceptionally well received by potential readers and advertisers. In addition, *Le Monde* has at its disposal substantial financial resources and a remarkable (but too large) team of journalists. All of the elements needed for diversifying are present, except one—the desire to do so.

The reader who buys a journal at the newsstand generally is

not aware of whether or not it is part of a press group. Is the quality of what is read greater or less if the publication is part of an empire? Those who favor independence argue that the only true motivating factor for creating a press empire is increased earnings and therefore it is difficult to see how expansion would lead to higher budgets for any given editorial department. In fact, when economy measures are urgent, the empire's hierarchy calls for a 10 percent cutback in expenses, and it is generally the editorial budget that is the first to be hit. On the other hand, the proponents of large diversified holdings contend that if the same firm has several publications, each can benefit by pooling journalistic and graphic talents, computer resources, and the purchasing of paper, to an extent that no newspaper or magazine on its own can equal. Perhaps for the reader an ideal of quality reading may be found in a young publication that is still in the hands of its creator but has already met with financial success. It is at this time that the innovator has the means for editorial perfection at his disposal and has not yet been convinced by his bankers that his earnings would be put to better use if invested in a printing shop. As is true of all periods of grace, that of a newborn empire does not last long. However, fortunately for the reader, the world of publishing is constantly creating other prodigies.

Chapter 6

Printing Your Own Money

In the late sixties, Groupe Express in France, of which I was general manager, decided to reinforce its organization by hiring as executives young French graduates of American business schools. As things were, we had come to the conclusion that with perhaps two or three exceptions it was impossible to find sufficiently qualified press executives in France. They just did not exist. At best, one might come across an aging accountant, a senior executive who had once visited a printing plant, or a few former government officials turned businessmen, but not one experienced press specialist. I was therefore determined to hire some executives and to teach them the press business, so I asked our usual "head hunters" to find me a handful from among the few hundred ambitious young men who had decided to learn—at Harvard or Stanford—what the business schools in Paris were unable to teach them. During the first interview, every single one of them asked the same question: "If I enter the publishing business, won't I jeopardize a possible career in another business?" "Isn't there a chance that I might make a poor impression on bankers or industrialists later on by coming from—I don't mean to offend you—as unconventional a business sector as the newspaper world?" In short, their image of this profession was closer to Hollywood than to Detroit. "It must be fun, but is it serious?" I explained that several press groups, including ours, ranked among the first 300 French business corporations, that in tonnage of manufactured paper the press was not far behind steel as a heavy industry, that every day more papers were sold than quarts of milk. Individually, I succeeded in convincing a few of them, but their attitude on the whole reflected the general opinion that the press is not a "real" industry. This opinion is particularly true among bankers, who are much more willing to grant loans to a steel company which does not make a profit than to a magazine which can become a gold mine if it is well managed.

The results of a survey published in the United States in 1970 showed how little the public knows about the economic aspects of the periodical and book publishing industry: 24 percent of the people interviewed considered that they were reasonably well informed on the subject, but the figures rose to 37 percent for knowledge of banking, 43 percent for insurance, and 53 percent for the automobile industry. When questioned about the industries whose image was unfavorable or only half-favorable, 50 percent of the respondents listed the press and book publishing. Only cigarette manufacturers fared worse. Of course, in reflecting on these responses we must keep in mind that, during the last few years, American public opinion has become extremely conscious of the ever-increasing proliferation of pornography and of mail-order solicitations, both businesses that are often associated with publishing. The responses indicate that journalists and newspapers publishers ought to think twice before assuming that the public shares their own high opinion of their profession. Despite public response, the publishing industry is an important sector of the economy, and, though it may amaze outsiders, it is also one of the most profitable. However, before this fact is recognized, a few psychological obstacles must be overcome, which stem directly from the way this business is usually pictured.[1]

WHAT WORRIES BANKERS

In France, when a firm that employs a hundred workers closes down, it is hardly noted unless it is located in a village where it created jobs for half of the population. If, however, a French newspaper with a like number of employees stops publication, it is immediately considered to constitute a "press crisis." This expression has become an international cliché.

In the United States the folding of large magazines and the decimation of the number of dailies published in New York City

---

[1]The press (written, broadcast, and televised) is directly related to people's lives and affects them in immediate social ways. As we discuss later, and repeatedly, it constitutes one of the essential institutions of a democracy. But, to make it clear that the press can compete economically with the chemical or service industries, it is appropriate in this chapter to consider only its "economic" side.

opens a veritable floodgate of comment. In England, Fleet Street's problems provide the basis for a ceaseless flow of articles in the press itself. Even the professionals themselves feel it advisable to push the panic button periodically to attract state subsidies and retain tax concessions. But they should not be too surprised if they throw a fright into the financiers at the same time.

In France, where twenty-one dailies have failed since World War II, the high point was reached when *Paris-Jour* folded in January 1972. "Grave crisis in the press," the remaining Paris papers bannered in unison. And their cries of doom were reinforced by the spate of radio and television debates on the subject. Public opinion was aroused: 57 percent of Parisians, subjected to newspaper propaganda, considered that the state was responsible for the crisis (though it is difficult to explain how). In fact, *Paris-Jour* had been living on borrowed time for some years, and had *never* made a profit. The economic anomaly is not that *Paris-Jour* died but that ten dailies have survived in Paris. Most are losing money, more because there are too many for the market they feed on than because television is siphoning off their advertising revenues. In Paris—as in the other industrial capitals of the world (with the possible exceptions of London and Tokyo)—there is room for two morning papers (*Le Figaro* and one other) and for two evening papers (*Le Monde* and *France-Soir*), and *France-Soir* can keep going only if Hachette is prepared to inject a dose of business expertise before it is too late. Inevitably four or five of the ten Paris papers will find they have to close down.[2] With each passing the press will cry that it is on its last legs, reinforcing its public image as a hopeless invalid.

But though it is generally (and understandably) true, the rule that the number of daily newspapers will be reduced is proved by the exceptions. In 1969 in the United States, 105 more towns had their own daily newspapers than in 1945. And there is the startling resurgence of the London paper *The Sun,* which was sold by the International Publishing Corporation (IPC) to the enterprising Australian Rupert Murdoch in the conviction that

[2]Diversity of information and opinion will of course suffer, but we are no longer in the golden age of the daily newspaper, when it was the sole source of information. Now there are additional ways of keeping up with events: news weeklies, radio, and television.

its days were numbered. Today, revitalized by its new proprietor, *The Sun* has a circulation of more than 2 million and is the main threat to the *Daily Mirror,* the brightest monetary jewel in the IPC crown.

Studies in France have shown that it could be quite profitable to able to launch small dailies (in the 20,000-to-30,000 circulation range) in large towns where the powerful regional papers have grown complacent by virtue of having had a monopoly. By concentrating on the real sources of wealth in the towns themselves and practicing truly spartan budgeting, an enterprising entrant has an excellent chance of success. Under the noses of the lions, the mice may prove someday to run away with the profits.

As for magazines, thousands are spawned throughout the world each year. The infant mortality rate is high, but this is true mainly because these magazines are hastily thrown together by enthusiastic amateurs. Nobody would think of applying for membership to the bar without ever having opened a law book, but many an inspired amateur seems to think he carries a publisher's card as a birthright.

There are a few millionaires who feel this way. The press seems to hold some fatal fascination for them. When they have made their fortunes and have grown tired of their villas, yachts, racehorses, and starlets, there is still the ultimate status symbol, that fabled spokesman—a newspaper or magazine. It was not to make money that Marcel Dassault founded *Jours de France* and then *24 heures,* that textile tycoon Marcel Boussac bought *L'Aurore,* that business genius Sylvain Floirat sank a fortune into *Un Jour.* Secure in their business abilities, they are convinced that one day they will achieve success with their journals, just as they did in the aviation, textile, motor, or sanitation industries. But if they stick it out longer than they reasonably should, or even if they do not make it at all, these millionaires are not too hard hit. Being involved with a publication and seeing their name on the masthead gives them more pleasure perhaps than their first million. In the United States Jock Whitney financed the *Herald Tribune* beyond reasonable limits. Huntington Hartford had high hopes for the financially disastrous publication *Show.* Norton Simon keeps *McCall's* afloat long after hopes of profit are gone.

But though owning a publication—even a women's

magazine—can give backers a greater feeling of power than they get running a sardine packing-plant, it can also embroil them in political controversy. The business world likes to make its money quietly, and preferably anonymously, so such incidents as the besieging of Axel Springer in 1968 by German students angry over his domination of their country's press, the attacks by *Figaro* journalists on Jean Prouvost, and Spiro Agnew's invective against the news media all make bankers a little more cautious than usual. The press is a rowdy business with a flamboyant atmosphere that makes it a dubious prospect in oak-paneled board rooms. I know from experience that far too many French bankers (and not only those in nationalized operations) would prefer bypassing the lucrative returns of financing an opposition paper to risking displeasure in government circles.

There are factors that set the press apart economically from the large industrial sectors. First, its position on the financial market. Until recently most press operations were family and local concerns and the only publishing firms quoted on Wall Street were the magazine empires (Time, Inc., McGraw-Hill, Cowles Communication). Only since 1960 have daily newspaper chains been quoted on the stock exchange in the United States, after they bought up regional papers and reached the requisite financial size. In France, press corporations have been barred by law from the stock exchange since the end of the war. Of course there are exceptions—Hachette[3] is listed (all that is needed is for a corporation to have non-press holdings)—but the legal obstacle acts to discourage the formation of large press concentrations. Another inhibiting economic factor is the language barrier which makes it difficult to "export" a magazine abroad. This is a considerable handicap in a period when anything that cannot cross national boundaries suffers a financial disability.

The fact that the press is economically hemmed in in certain respects should not keep financial analysts from being aware that it can perform financially as well or better than many more traditional branches of industry.

[3]Hachette performed $600 million worth of business transactions in 1971 and represented 12 percent of the press market, 17 percent of the book publishing market, and 21 percent of their distribution. The biggest of Hachette press companies is FEP, which publishes *France-Soir*, *Elle*, and *France-Dimanche*, with a business volume of $80 million.

WALL STREET PREFERS DAILIES

The United States is undoubtedly the best country by which to gauge the economic importance of the media, not only because it offers the greatest variety and number of periodicals, newspapers, and broadcasting systems, but also because so many professional associations and economic analysts there regularly prepare readily available statistics and analyses for all fields and aspects of the economy.

First observation: though television is generally credited (perhaps a bit too hastily) with having the greatest influence on public opinion, the daily newspapers represent a weightier economic package. Overall they did business to the tune of $7 billion in 1970—twice the television figure. Newspapers were the tenth largest employer in the United States, with 350,000 salaried employees, and the fifth-ranking American industry in gross income. Their economic strength is not likely to decline, since their projected growth for the 1970s is 6.2 percent per year.

Since the 1950s their growth curve in advertising revenues has been the same as television's. What chiefly accounts for newspapers' advertising growth is the expansion of regional and local advertising, the strong point for the daily newspaper industry. By 1970 local pages and classified ads made up 82 percent of advertising revenues, as against only 18 percent from national advertisers. This is one of the fail-safes for the dailies; thus far no technological advances have enabled other media to compete with them on a local level. Another source of the dailies' economic strength is that they enjoy a monopoly in 97 percent of the towns where they are published, which gives both local advertisers and readers little choice but to accept their rate increases. The state of their economic health is reflected in their girth: in 1946 each edition averaged about twenty-seven pages; in 1968, it was fifty-five pages.

Thus, it is hardly surprising that their profits are on the increase. A daily in a middle-sized town with a circulation of some 55,000 and doing a $5 million a year business in 1968 was earning a profit of 28.6 percent before taxes—close to 14 percent after taxes. In that same year, the average profit margin on sales in American industry was 5.8 percent. With results like these it is easy to understand why the dailies are so highly valued for investment. Between twenty and forty of them change hands annually and their asking price goes up constantly. When Roy Thomson, the enterprising Canadian, bought twelve papers at one stroke in 1967, he paid something like $200 for each reader. Thus Wall Street brokers, scorning Marshall McLuhan's dire predictions of the twilight of the press, were advising their clients to invest in this flourishing sector. According to their estimates, local advertising expenditures would increase more rapidly in the coming years than the national advertising budgets, and the dailies should derive full benefits.

WHAT FRENCH NEWSPAPERS COMPLAIN ABOUT

The bustling health of the American dailies is in marked contrast to the rather sad state of their French counterparts, though the latter are in better shape than many of them are willing to admit, especially if we make a distinction between the Paris dailies and the regional papers. The Paris papers are indeed in trouble. In 1971, admittedly a poor year for advertising, they all lost money except *Le Monde*. But, as we pointed out earlier in this chapter, until their number is drastically cut down they have no prospect of prosperity. They simply have not adjusted to postwar realities. Before the war the Paris dailies were distributed throughout the country; they were, in effect, national newspapers. Today their national role has shrunk; they are nothing more than the local newspapers of the nation's capital.[4] Francine Amaury's study of the *Petit Parisien* (1876–1944) illustrates just how much the situation of a major newspaper has changed since the first third of the century.

1. In 1910 the *Petit Parisien* sold three times as many copies in the provinces as in Paris, thanks to its own distribution system.

2. Income from sales represented from 80 to 95 percent of the paper's total business. There were usually fewer than twelve pages in the paper. But the *Petit Parisien*, which sold more than 2 million copies across France at the end of World War I, was squeezed out by the expansion of the Paris evening press and by the growth of the regional dailies, whose production costs were lower.

But the Paris area still represents a market of 40 percent of the nation's economic potential. A more reasonable number of

[4]With the exception of *Le Figaro* and *Le Monde*, which have substantial national and even international circulations.

dailies could survive comfortably, particularly if they abandon their ruinous distribution policy. The evening paper *France-Soir,* which saw its circulation drop to below the million mark, is desperately trying to maintain its distribution wherever it can, despite the fact that only its Paris edition has a substantial share of advertising and its provincial edition, of much less interest to advertisers, operates at a steep loss. The road to profits for *France-Soir* would be to concentrate its efforts in the Paris area and to abandon its some 200,000 subscribers in the rest of the country. But its prestige would suffer. If *Le Figaro* really did lose money in 1971 it must have been the result of particularly serious mismanagement. Outside of television, *Le Figaro* is the major printed medium for advertising in France. It carries over $24 million worth of advertising each year. If under these circumstances a 5,000,000-circulation newspaper with healthy resources cannot make a profit, it deserves to be studied in business schools as an example of what not to do.

The French regional press is in better shape than the Paris press. Nearly all the small papers have been swallowed up by bigger ones, which now cover large areas. Right after the war there were half a dozen dailies in cities like Toulouse and Troyes. Today, everywhere except Lille and Marseilles one paper has a monopoly.

Profits on the American scale, 10 to 12 percent before taxes, are far from rare. Unlike their Parisian cousins, all the regional papers—except one—made money in 1971. However, many of the regionals are locked into suicidal financial battles with nearby competitors. *Nice-Matin* and the *Provençal* of Marseilles have spent who knows how much in vying for readership in the town of Toulon. Costly editions are maintained in virtually deserted rural areas on the theory of guarding against the possibility that a neighboring rival will gain an advantage. While American publishers realize that a specific local area is where the money is and the further away one strays the more one loses, French regional dailies have adopted a policy of trying to cover too much ground. This may boost circulation, but the cost is prohibitive. Despite certain poor business practices, most of the provincial dailies turn over a comfortable profit, which would seem to indicate that even in France the press as an industry enjoys an amazing safety margin.

In America, financial analysts are wary of magazines because in recent years these journals have suffered far more from television competition than have the daily papers. Their main source of advertising for magazines is nationwide advertisers, the very people who have the financial resources to spend money on television spots. The local garage or supermarket by its very nature gains far more by advertising in the local newspaper. In the second half of the last decade the growth of magazine advertising revenue was only 2 percent per year, and they garnered no more than 7 percent of all American advertising expenditures (compared with 30 percent for the dailies and 18.5 percent for television). Their average profit margins are about half those of the newspapers.

If we add to the advertising picture the number of sad deaths of magazines over the past few years, it is easy enough to understand why stockbrokers list magazines under the heading of "speculative investments."

But the overall income figures of magazines deserve more careful examination than an evaluation of their economic feasibility based on average profits, which mask wide financial discrepancies among the different journals. The range is from acute distress to decent prosperity. It is easy enough to point to the spectacular failures of the giants, but it is also worth noting that in the 1960s 123 more popular magazines were launched than were closed down, whereas the figure for 1950 to 1960 was eleven; and for 1940 to 1950, twenty-two. The dailies are quasi-homogeneous products which all, whatever their circulation, perform the same basic service: they provide information for the reader. On the other hand, under the rubric of magazine there are such mass-circulation products as *Reader's Digest,* sophisticated publications like *The New Yorker,* and specialized journals like *Ski.* It is the failing health of many of the largest magazines which makes the average profit figures for magazines look rather sickly, discouraging a realistic examination of the diversity and the vitality of the growing number of smaller and more specialized products.

Only three daily newspapers have a circulation greater than a million in the United States, whereas fifty-four magazines top this figure. But the most vulnerable are those magazines whose very size forces them to set advertising rates beyond the means of most advertisers except the very largest. While the shift of advertising budgets away from magazines and into television seems to have stabilized, a new and possibly more serious economic danger looms on the horizon for American magazine publishers. Postal rates will go up 150 per cent by 1976. The source of the strength of magazines, their huge subscriber lists, leaves them particularly vulnerable to this increase. For Time, Inc., the added costs would have represented $27 million (before the end of *Life*). *Newsweek* will be showing a loss along with many of the weeklies, which are harder hit than the monthlies simply because they have to mail out copies four times as often.

With a few notable exceptions *(Playboy, TV Guide, Reader's Digest)* the prosperous era of the giant mass magazines is over. This is far from true for the specialized magazines (see Chapter 3), which in the predictable future should be "where the action is" for the printed press.

Though the dailies are still able to attract financiers and large companies wealthy enough to add them to their holdings, they are well out of range of the average individual business-man. Their prohibitive cost makes the introduction of new dailies out of the question. The general interest magazines are on the whole financially weak, and, except for the *Playboy*-type periodical, they simply do not justify reinvestment.

But those magazines with a clearly defined reading public, a healthy economic structure (income almost equally balanced between sales per issue and advertising revenue), and a knowl-edgeably specialized editorial staff have the potential to per-petuate themselves. The operating costs are not always cheap. It cost only $300,000 to launch *L'Expansion* in France in 1967, but this was thanks to the parent organization *L'Express,* which in the early states of *L'Expansion*'s existence could help obtain both readers and advertisers. But it took more than $1.5 million to launch the weekly *New York,* which appeared at about the same time in the United States. *Ms.* apparently cost about the same amount when it appeared in 1972, even though it is only a monthly. The management of *Le Point,* a French magazine that aspires to be to *L'Express* what *Newsweek* is to *Time,* has asked Hachette for $6 million of credit backing, based on an antici-pated circulation of no more than 200,000 to 250,000. Happily, several publications appear each year with far more modest budgetary expectations. Magazines are one of those rare fields where one can still dream of a fortune—or a flop—with only a minimum of capital. And have a lot of fun doing it.

The virtual absence in France of the use of subscription sales (except for the *Express* group and *Sélection du Reader's Digest)* has prevented the magazines from attaining the relative circulation of their American counterparts. Nevertheless, the overall trends are similar. *Paris-Match* is doomed to the same fate as *Collier's* or *Look* sooner or later. But the future is rosy for the specialized publications. Women's magazines, however, are in the same situation as the Paris dailies—there are just too many of them compared to other countries. While it is difficult in the United States to keep even four large monthly women's magazines alive, France has a dozen with more than 500,000 circulation—and half of them are weeklies. Far more so than in the French dailies, the women's pages in the American newspapers are highly sophisticated and rich in advertisements, which accounts in great measure for the relative weakness of mass-circulation women's magazines. It is unlikely that all the French women's magazines will successfully tread their way during the next few years. Survival will most probably depend on the quality of their content, on the services offered their readers, and on their ability to adapt to the changing attitudes of women who are increasingly unwilling to accept the traditional roles to which women's magazines have catered.

WHERE TELEVISION PAYS

The association of profit with television is somewhat alien to most Europeans and downright funny to Frenchmen. Not only does the French state own television, but the network operates at such a loss, despite tax supports and advertising, that the deficit has become something of a national institution. In the United States, without government subsidies but through a combination of advertising revenues and efficient management—the importance of which should not be underestimated—all the TV channels make money: the local stations as well as the three giant networks (CBS, NBC, and ABC), which supply the bulk of the nationwide programs and which each own five of the 650 broadcasting stations (the law prevents ownership of more than five at once). On the average, over the last few years owners of television stations have earned a rate of profit ranging from 20 percent to 30 percent before taxes—and without huge outlays of initial investment. Return on capital invested varies from 70 percent to 105 percent (depending on amortization).

Though the profit picture for radio stations is less spectacular, it is still perfectly acceptable. There are far more of them than TV stations—4,000 in all. Many towns have several, each with very limited range and confined to the medium wave, and they are frequently "specialized"—e.g., confining themselves exclusively to broadcasting news, rock music, or classical music. Though television has virtually relegated the radio set from the living room to the automobile, the radio stations' operating statements are still very much in the black. During the 1960s the stations earned, on the average, more than 11 percent profit for their owners, and their growth potential is greater than the U.S. economic average. The high degree of specialization among radio stations means they can keep their personal costs to a bare minimum. Some stations, entirely automated, are no more than a vast electronic machine in a single room. Such a station can broadcast for half a day using prerecorded tapes of music, public announcements, and advertising, without human aid or intervention.

Compared to these enterprises, the only two privately owned radio stations in France, Europe No. 1 and Radio-Luxembourg, seem gigantic, with their hundreds of employees, their dozens of studios, and their luxurious accommodations. True, the state's broadcasting monopoly—to which these stations are the sole exceptions—has created a fabulous income situation for the two radio stations by concentrating on them all the available radio advertising budgets. For radio stations there are hardly any unanticipated running expenses. Once the equipment has been installed and the requisite staff has been hired, the costs tend to remain constant, whether there are 1 or 10 million listeners, and whether income is $20 or $40 million. In good advertising years, when all supplementary income can immediately be counted as profits, the total profit picture can be as high as 25 to 40 percent of sales before taxes. The economic boom in France over the past fifteen years has meant a substantial increase in advertising budgets, but the two private radio stations have reached the utmost limit of their capacity to accommodate additional advertisers. For, unlike a newspaper which can print more pages, a radio station is locked into the fact that there are only twenty-four hours in a day. Television's sudden draining off of $500 million worth of the total amount spent on advertising hardly touched Europe No. 1 and Radio-Luxembourg. In 1970, when television was making large inroads, Radio-Luxembourg's net profit *after taxes* was 14 percent and Europe No. 1's 25 percent.

CANADIAN REVELATIONS

The most striking study on the profit-making capacities of the media industries in a market economy was issued in 1970 at the request of the Canadian Senate. Here are a few of the sig‑ nificant findings.

> The publishing industry as a whole (as distinct from the printing industry) spends a much lower proportion of its revenues on outside goods and services than many other manufacturing industries. Despite frequent complaints by industry spokesmen about a "cost-price squeeze," the figures suggest that just the opposite occurred; during the period studied, revenues advanced somewhat faster than costs—not the other way around.
>
> One of press entrepreneur Roy Thomson's most memorable observations was that a television broadcasting permit is like having a license to print your own money. Ownership of a daily newspaper often amounts to the same thing. In 1965, which was a great year for the industry, after-tax profits of Canadian daily newspapers ran 17.5 percent of invested capital. The comparable figures for all manufacturing industries was 10.4 percent; for retailing industries it was 9.2 percent. Owning a newspaper, in other words, can be almost twice as profitable as owning a paper box factory or a department store.
>
> If you want to own a newspaper in Canada, it's better to own either a small or a quite large one rather than a medium-sized one. Companies that published newspapers with circulations below 10,000 or above 100,000 consistently earned after-tax profits of more than 16 percent from 1964 onward. Newspapers with circulations between 10,000 and 50,000 were less than half as profitable than the industry as a whole. Radio and TV stations do even better. The largest revenue-group of TV stations, for instance, earned a before-tax profit (on investment) of 98.5 percent in 1964. The big TV stations' worst year was 1967, when pretax profits declined to 40 percent. Thus we are confronted with a delicious irony: an industry that is supposed to abhor secrecy is sitting on one of the best-kept, least

discussed secrets—in fact, one of the hottest scoops—of Canadian business: their own operating statements.

Too many newspapers and broadcasting stations are delivering a product that is not as good as they could afford to make it, and are thereby short-changing the communities that make them rich. They don't try hard enough to improve their product because there is no economic incentive to do so—quite the reverse, in fact.

Newsrooms are chronically understaffed, the turnover in personnel is scandalous, and the best people frequently move on to some other industry, such as advertising or public relations, where talent is recognized and rewarded. In short, the owners of newspapers and broadcasting stations are making a great deal of money, but their employees are not.

CRITERIA FOR LASTING SUCCESS

To conclude this appraisal of the finances of the media industry, we will adapt the short list of criteria used by J. Kendrick Noble, a financial analyst who specializes in the press—which offers a fairly simple way of determining the most promising elements for financial success. Here are the things to study before investing:

1. Uniqueness. For example, the only newspaper in a city or the best magazine in a given field is most likely to be profitable.

2. Favorable demographic conditions. The publication should serve a growing and affluent audience.

3. General consumer orientation (rather than toward a technical field). This seems wisest, at least for the short to medium run.

4. Social utility. The publication is in a stronger position for the future if it performs a real and definable service for its group of readers.

5. Good employee relations. Costs rise faster in unionized operations and strikes can be damaging.

Here at least is a clear and concise way to consider the media when they are to be studied purely from their balance sheet point of view.

Chapter 7

Shock Treatment for a Hypochondriac

The printed press is not in its death throes, but no newspaper is invulnerable—not even the most powerful and most influential, not even the biggest profit-maker. Ten years ago *The New York Times* and *Le Figaro,* both virtually national institutions in their respective countries, seemed to be the epitome of solidity to newspaper publishers. Today, though there are no immediate worries, neither occupies its former top position. While it still adds up to a considerable amount, their advertising has stopped growing at the same time that operating costs—impossible to control—have cut deeply into profits. In addition, the clash of strong personalities and overstaffed editorial offices have produced an uneasy atmosphere which adds to the difficulties of decision-making by top management.

This is not to say there is an imminent threat to the survival of *The New York Times* or *Le Figaro,* but their present situations are so finely balanced that with a stroke of bad luck or a special drive by their competitors they could face a nasty crisis. *Business Week* also fits this situation. With the advantage to advertisers of the journal's readership being made up exclusively of industrialists and business executives, it has been the big money-maker for McGraw-Hill. Bursting with advertising—some 110 pages per issue, the highest figure in the United States—its gross profit on $38-million-worth of sales was close to 30 percent. But after a four-year period during which advertising expenditures were at their lowest ebb, the situation swung around. *Business Week*'s management thought at first that the advertising crisis was temporary and that its effects were being felt equally by other publications. But when in 1971 and 1972 the downtrend of other publications leveled off and even started to climb, *Business Week*'s ad revenues continued to drop. McGraw-Hill's management is still speculating on the real reasons. It is understandable that they should be puzzled, since *Business Week* is a publication of genuine editorial quality, it never offered cut-rate subscriptions, and its management seemed the very model of level-headed professionalism.

In France at the beginning of the 1960s, advertising men seemed to be focused exclusively on *Le Monde* and the women's weekly *Jours de France*. They both represented dream situations, their circulations increasing year after year without special promotion campaigns. Advertising increased proportionately, and their prosperity became legendary. But by the end of the decade the miracle disappeared as mysteriously as it had come. Probably for very different reasons the circulations of both publications stopped growing, spreading a certain malaise among a staff that had grown accustomed to effortless expansion.

There is nothing in this story to indicate that the entire information industry is threatened—it simply demonstrates that no publication is immune to difficulties. And one of the most delicate—but inevitable—moments in a press lord's career is when he has to turn his attention to a journal that has run into trouble.

A DIAGNOSIS

Increasingly it is in the area of diagnosis that a doctor displays his talents today—treatment depending largely on the skills of laboratory technicians and the efficacy of drugs and medications. Here the doctor has a considerable advantage over the publisher of a failing newspaper: the doctor himself is not ill, nor is a member of his family, so he can consider the case objectively and, for the most part, dispassionately. The publisher, on the other hand, bogged down in daily routine, only too aware of the character and vision of the men who work with him, a prisoner of his own past decisions, is probably in the worst position to make any penetrating analysis of his difficulties. Recognizing them is not the most problematic aspect of the situation, since they are probably all too obvious. The real problem is facing up to them. This simple but important responsibility is usually put into the hands of consultants and market researchers, those prestigious outsiders who are paid to report with solemnity what every insider already knows but has hardly dared to acknowledge. This is another example of the axiom that what is important is not what is said but who says it. When the circulation manager of a shelter magazine says for the twentieth time that sales are better when a room with exposed ceiling beams is carried on the cover, the editor smiles condescendingly at his obsession. But if a market research study that cost $20,000 or a consultant says that the readers prefer the rustic style, there will be quick enough action to assure that some changes are made in the fall issue.

Whatever the strategy used by a publisher to bring the facts home to his staff, he must first of all find answers to some basic questions. "If the paper didn't exist today, would we launch it?" And if the answer to that is not a categorical "no," "What kind of editorial formula, starting from scratch, would we choose to adapt the publication to present conditions?" And finally, "Since we can't start from scratch, how can we bring about as many of the necessary changes as possible in the publication as it exists now?" One has the general impression that these questions are asked and answered at the editor's desk at the start of each day, which means they are not studied seriously or worked through. And if the rest of the top staff has not been consulted, it is probably safe to say that no serious commitment has been made to effect changes. Still, it is a matter of some delicacy to involve the staff in the rethinking of a publication. Unless the urgency of the situation is impressed upon them, the employees are unlikely to be stirred by the need for change. If, on the other hand, the realities of the situation are presented at them in too dark a light, they may well panic, and the time that should be spent on analysis of the situation may well be wasted on reassuring the staff—in short, lying to them. Openly setting forth the basic problems has the virtue of demonstrating that no ideas are barred. Then discussion should focus on the two main areas: editorial policy and the fiscal balance sheet.

WHAT ARE THE EDITORS FOR?

Editorial judgments are fundamentally subjective. An article is "good," "bad," "interesting" strictly according to the criteria of the editor reading it, who puts himself in the place of the "average reader." But generally that editor, far from being an average reader, is a highly informed professional journalist, with his own prejudices and in all probability possessing some degree of cynicism. Of course, most great managing editors will maintain that the best newspaper is the one you produce as though you yourself were the potential reader, and that market research has never produced the right editorial mix for such a publication. It may be true that a really great managing editor can project beyond his own limitations, but the species is about as rare as the blue whale or the duck-billed platypus. It would be better for editors whose personal tastes and preferences are out of phase with the general public's—as is true in most cases—simply to try to ascertain whether their publication is necessary to its readership. One test of necessity is whether a journal provides a service that would be missed if publication ceased. In February 1972, *Sud-Ouest,* virtually the only daily in the Bordeaux area, was paralyzed by a printing strike. After a week, some assessment of the resultant havoc was possible. Turnouts at funerals were smaller than usual because the obituary column was unavailable; in some sections the town crier was back on the streets to provide the bare essentials of municipal information; movie attendance fell between 40 and 50 percent because program listings were not readily available; business in used cars and real estate was down by half because there were no classified ads. Of course some of these problems could have been overcome through the publication of information sheets listing movie programs, doctors available for emergencies, and birth, marriage, and death announcements as well as some classified ads. Local life did not suffer conspicuously from the lack of national and international news and the comic strips.

But there is more to a journal's function than its practical side; it provides a service that is psychological as well. One of the great advantages of market research is that it can shed light on the value of a journal to its readers beyond the basic and obvious purposes it serves. For example, less than two years after the launching of the monthly magazine *L'Expansion,* which I had conceived to function as a source of quality business information, we undertook to discover, through interviews with 100 readers, the real image of the publication among its readership. When the results of the "motivational" survey were given to us, managing editor Jean Boissonnat and I discovered that

L'Expansion's main function for its subscribers was to help them psychologically identify themselves with the management class they strove to be part of: it gave them some reassurance regarding their social status. We thought we were selling them information and found they were buying a tranquillizer. Of course *L'Expansion* was without doubt providing its readers with a very real service, but it did its management no harm to learn that the service was not necessarily confined to what we thought we were offering.

Another way of trying to measure the subjective elements of a reader's attachment to a journal was originated by John Peter, one of the few American press consultants (there are hardly any in France). The method is called the "editorial audit"—similar to a financial audit—and it aims to determine where the publication stands on the market in relation to its competitors. Though many publishers seem convinced that their publications are unique, in reality every journal is faced with direct or indirect competition. The research methods of editorial audits are on the whole fairly simple and not particularly costly, and the audit provides answers to such questions as what readers actually read and like, how the content compares with the competitors' in quantity and editorial performance, by what means do the editors keep abreast of the desires of the readers, and what can be done to increase readership.

It takes several hours to present the results with the help of charts and graphs (for certain editorial factors can be quantified). The procedure does not provide miraculous solutions but it does guarantee a more rational approach to the problem of meeting readers' real needs.

THE JOURNAL'S CHECK-UP

When a journal is having problems that indicate that it is far from healthy, there is no more useful practice than to scan closely all the tables and figures, and ask three simple questions.

The first is fundamental: is the present income structure viable? If, as was the case with *Life,* the product sold to the reader for 12 cents costs 40 cents to produce, the structure has to be changed as soon as possible. *Life*'s publishers took the first step in this direction in 1972 when they raised their average return on the selling price—to 14.3 cents. In itself, of course, this was not enough to save the publication. Since in most cases efforts to reduce costs have already been made, the key question remains whether the readers will agree to pay substantially more for the same product. If the answer is no, the journal has no future.

The other crucial question concerning income is the role played by advertising. If it amounts to more than 50 to 60 percent (the dailies can tolerate a slightly larger dose than the magazines), it represents a potential danger.

It remains to be seen whether it is possible to institute a policy in which income is more dependent on the reader (the journal's true customer) and less on the advertiser. This is not easy to achieve, but, if the conclusion is that it is impossible, it would be advisable to look for a job on a journal with a more promising future.

The second question involves costs. Are they tolerable? Can practices developed over the years and never really questioned remain unchanged? Obviously, it would be advisable to calculate very carefully the exact savings involved before announcing to the managing editor and the art director that the magazine's format has to be reduced by 25 percent. But if there is no refuting the figures they will accept them and comply.

After proclaiming for forty-two years that because of its format it was the only business periodical capable of providing quality layout, *Fortune* followed in the footsteps of many other magazines *(McCall's, Esquire)* and reduced its size in September 1972. Simultaneously it switched the emphasis of its publicity campaign, insisting that its format was now more practical—for instance, for reading in bed. Everything can and must be subject to change in a serious cost reduction study. Less luxurious offices can be found, printing can be done on out-of-city presses, a slightly lighter weight of paper could mean considerable savings without seriously compromising the quality of the publication, and it is also possible to reduce the number of pages of text without seriously depriving the reader. In general, it is probable that a skillful examination of the publication's sacred cows can lead to significant economies.

We turn, then, to the third question: does a large enough market still exist? And, if so, what is its predictable life span? The more specialized a publication is, the greater the likelihood that economic or social change will affect its readership and its advertising flow. For years there was a market for a partisan political press in France. Whether it represents a step forward or backward, the fact remains that readers' interest in ideological debates and party-line loyalties has waned to the point that most of these publications have become less and less viable. Even the Communists, who command a highly disciplined readership, have subsidized their official daily, *Humanité,* to keep it afloat (even though it is one of the few papers whose personnel is paid the minimum wage).[1] Twenty years ago in the United States there was a flourishing professional press devoted to the automobile. But the number of automotive manufacturers has dropped from twenty to four, proportionately reducing the number of advertisers. The automobile industry is still quite healthy, but changes in the economic structure of the industry have done in a sector of the press that lived off it. It does not usually require computerized research to foresee that changes of such a nature are imminent and to properly adjust the publication's focus. Nevertheless, the directors of many special-interest publications allow themselves to be caught unawares.

MOVE QUICKLY AND LET IT BE KNOWN

Once the basic situation has been assessed and the staff has been alerted and corrective measures decided on, the effectiveness of these measures will depend on how they are applied. Changes in content and in running expenses must be effected quickly. Those involving subscription and advertising rates, on the other hand, should be made gradually. Any sudden increase in the cost of advertising or in the price of the journal is bound to cause advertisers and readers to wonder if the publication is utterly indispensable to them. And who can be absolutely confident that the reply will be in the affirmative? The wisest course is a schedule of gradual increases punctuated by periods of stability.

[1]Its publisher, Etienne Fajon, wrote in an editorial on June 16, 1972: "The crisis of the press hits *Humanité* harder than other papers. . . . Our management is threatened with a deficit in the near future, a factor that is unacceptable for a paper that needs complete freedom . . . there will be gradual reductions in personnel, and operating costs must be cut." As we see, the laws of management know no ideological boundaries.

On the other hand, gradual improvements in the editorial content may well be ineffective, because the readers have to be notably affected by them if they are to have any positive impact. But reader attention is likely to be attracted only by obvious changes. Which publisher has not known the frustration of having a reader suggest, for example, "I like your paper but you should have a crossword puzzle," when the daily has been printing one for the last six months. And what about the journalist who gnashes his teeth when told, "I read your articles regularly in *New York*," when he hasn't written a line for the magazine in more than a year?

There is a great temptation to initiate small changes in each issue, since certain improvements are cheap and simple, such as changing the type face or size of headlines; other changes, such as the introduction of new features, need months of preparation. Staff impatience must be held in check until all the small modifications have been properly balanced, to increase the chance that they attract the attention of the reader. More important than the improvements themselves are their psychological impact. It is inevitable that in any series of changes some will be considered progressive and others detrimental. When the political weekly newspaper *L'Express* became a newsmagazine in September 1964, the change offended the political sensibilities and upset the reading habits of many of its subscribers, who thereupon stopped buying it. Such readers would never have acknowledged that the change constituted an improvement. But it is undeniable that the transformed *L'Express* became a real success, multiplying its circulation sixfold. On the other hand, in the final months of the existence of the *Saturday Evening Post*, several editorial changes improved the quality of the publication, but the magazine was obviously in such disarray that the advertisers did not believe the changes could salvage it. So the improvements achieved nothing.

Another reason for making the changes simultaneously is that readers do not like to be disturbed in their habits. My father, Emile Servan-Schreiber, founder with his brother Robert in 1908 of the financial daily *Les Echos*, used to say that "a newspaper is like a pair of bedroom slippers." He believed that the reader felt a bit lost when he could not find each section in its proper place. But there comes a time when the slippers are worn out and a new pair is needed. Nobody would think of replacing them one at a time to make the transition less painful. The reshuffling of the reader's expectations will be all the more acceptable if it gives promise of being stabilized once the basic change has been made. He will at least have the time to adopt fresh reading habits.

For the same reasons it is advisable to implement any necessary economies in a short period of time. Nothing is more likely to poison the atmosphere in any enterprise than uncertainty. "Who'll be laid off next? What's the next little petty rule they're cooking up? What's the next financial restriction?" Better announce all the bad news at one sitting, and then add, "That's it." Needless to say this advice is rarely taken by management, because there is a limit to the amount of bad news that even the most rational executives can summon up the courage to announce at a single stroke.

SURGICAL INTERVENTIONS

Two spectacular measures can be used as navigational aids through troubled waters. The first is a change of location. Even if the saving on rent is of no great significance, the fact of working in a new building lays the groundwork among the staff for wider-reaching changes. The relocation of offices provides an opportunity to put the less efficient employees out to pasture. Internal communications can be altered without resort to a series of tactless inside memos. The state of flux prevailing in the early days in the new premises will reduce resistance to changes that have been decided upon to reach new objectives and to introduce new methods.

The second measure involves a change in the frequency of publication. Like transplanting an organ, it may represent either the road to recovery or the hastening of the end. Increasing the frequency of publication generally results from the euphoria of success which the publishers want to make the most of. This was the case with *Veckens Affärer,* the Swedish economic magazine of the Bonnier group which initially appeared twice monthly, then became a weekly as soon as it had been established that its formula was successful.

The worrisome aspect of changing the number of issues lies in being forced to publish less frequently. A sudden reduction in the number of issues enables a pulication to reduce its staff, its newsprint costs, and general overhead, while retaining the same readership for a longer period of time, since this ploy pushes back the date for subscription renewal and gains desperately needed time when the number of readers seems to be falling off. There is, of course, also the hope that over half the advertising pages will be retained, improving profits in view of the reduced expenses.

Though many American local dailies first appeared as weeklies, then twice and three times a week, it is exceedingly rare that a daily tries, let alone succeeds, in reversing the process and becoming a weekly. *L'Express* managed this in 1957 because it had been a daily for only three months, after which it won back its previous weekly readers who had not had time to switch their allegiance to another weekly publication.

The McGraw-Hill weekly *Electronics* was flagging. Today it flourishes, appearing twice monthly. But the same switch could not save the *Saturday Evening Post*. Generally speaking, it is better to postpone major surgery until all other remedies have failed.

The most difficult decision a publisher will ever have to make is to stop publication. It is invariably painful, but it is common knowledge that in any large consumer industry one must stop selling when the profit line drops—and certainly before it reaches a dead loss. Unhappily there is often a tendency in the press to wait until huge deficits have piled up and several heroic and frequently uncoordinated efforts to stave off disaster have failed. Yet if studies reveal that there is no way out, it is far more sensible, and less painful and costly, to determine a specific closing date far enough in advance for the staff to find alternative employment or, better still, to plan and prepare other publications to fill the gap. It may well be that forethought of this kind is just too emotionally burdensome to pull off; thus far nobody has managed it successfully. Instead there is a tendency to act as though the journal were immortal and that its closing would be cataclysmic. When at last there is no choice but to cease operations, inevitably the closing notices hit the staff as a catastrophe—one they have been dreading but somehow did not believe would ever actually happen.

LANDMARK FOR THE FUTURE

There is really no reason why in the future the press should be more seriously subject to disaster than other industries. The foregoing chapters have tried to sketch in the broad lines of the economics of this rather attractive industry. We can now venture to suggest a number of simple predictions regarding the future of the written press.

—The press is a long way from death's door; it is not even a hopeless invalid. The printed word is not on the way out, if for no other reason than that it still remains the cheapest, most flexible, and most practical means of communication.

—Advances in secondary and higher education and the refinement of taste that comes with prosperity encourage reading. The written word no longer monopolizes information, but it is increasingly the pastime at the highest level.

—The boundary lines between books, magazines, and dailies are becoming blurred (e.g., books serialized in installments in newspapers and magazines; group journalistic techniques to produce books; magazine-style color pages in the dailies; paperback book and magazine prices becoming very close).

—The constantly increasing buying power of the reader means he can pay more per issue or subscription. For some papers this reverses a dangerously unbalanced situation (and provides others with huge profits).

—The thriving press business (dailies and specialized magazines) have a greater profit-making capacity than the industrial average. But the investment required is still heavy since the cost of dailies is being thrust upward by speculative buying, and it takes more capital now than formerly to start a magazine.

—The press is at the hub of a multiplicity of activities and services because it establishes a more direct link with its clients than any other industry and because the name of a newspaper is better known and more highly considered than most products. If it can resist the corruption of base profiteering, fresh and quite considerable profits are available to it. The reader will be seen increasingly as capital to be exploited (in the basic as well as figurative sense of the term) in a variety of ways.

—The profound modifications of the economic bases of circulation will continue. Cut-rate subscriptions, after being used for a century as one of the basic tactics for increasing readership, will have to be reduced or eliminated. The journal will either be sold at a realistic price or given away free. Free and selective distribution will become standard practice for some highly specialized publications. At the other end of the scale, expensive subscriptions and highly priced issues will be essential to the survival of general publications wishing to maintain at least partial independence from their advertisers. And the huge subscription lists will become a thing of the past.

—Advertisers obliged to secure the best possible results from their outlays will lean toward publications that serve a tightly concentrated market, even if the cost per reader is high. Direct promotional techniques—and mail order—will be used in conjunction with space ads in the press.

—A new kind of press, reflecting ideas and opinions, with very low production costs and entirely independent of advertising, will hit its stride. It will appear either in the form of short and highly condensed information sheets, or as the new underground "free" press—unorthodox and somewhat haphazard perhaps, but restoring the aura of freedom of the press and encouraging the emergence of fresh talent.

—Mergers, acquisitions, and concentrations will produce steadily larger financial groups, but these large and bureaucratic concerns will suffer from failing efficiency and creativity.

—Talent and business drive will tend to turn to smaller organizations, where individuals will have a greater sense of freedom, will be better paid, will make relatively swift capital gains and, very likely will subsequently bring their efforts to fruition by a transfer of capital.

—Furthermore, editorial quality (content, style, presentation) is singular and cannot be rendered obsolete by technological advances; it is one element that will stave off the possibility of the abandonment of newsprint (as a medium) by readers. The vast majority of publishers and owners of journals have still not recognized this, and their blindness is the sole serious and overall danger to the future of the press.

Part 2
Power Comes
from the Tip of a Pen

Chapter 1

Nobody Loves a Journalist

Early in 1963 it did not seem out of place for people to wonder what President Kennedy would do after spending eight years in the White House if—as everyone assumed at the time—he was re-elected. To what, indeed, could a man who had held the most important job in the world before he was fifty devote his untapped energy? What sort of position could still interest him? John F. Kennedy himself once gave the answer: he would probably enjoy running a newspaper. Fate decided otherwise.

Between World War I and World War II, two men played key political roles in France. Under the Third Republic, continually threatened by ministerial crises, these men's judgments and their positions had an impact on the solutions to the problems of the period. The two men were brothers: Maurice and Albert Sarraut. Albert often served as a minister in different governments. As for Maurice, all he did was to run his regional daily newspaper, *La Dépêche,* in Toulouse, the hotbed of radicalism at the time. But everyone agrees that during this whole period Maurice was the more influential of the two.

The press is recognized as the Fourth Estate and as such, in a free country, it is independent of the state. There are two reasons why its influence keeps growing today.

The executive, legislative, and judicial branches of government have tended to intervene more and more directly in the life and the organization of industrial societies. However, because of the increasing complexity of such societies, because of the greater gaps among social forces, their ability to modify a situation often decreases, even though their scope of influence seems to become wider.

On the other hand, the power to inform, through the written and spoken word, is increasing at the same rate that traditional political adhesions are breaking down. The media remain a synthesizing force. When both the Prime Minister of France and the head of the national radio and television system were replaced in July 1972, a number of French people considered the second appointment politically more important than the first.

The second reason for the media's increasing power is obviously the extraordinary instrument that appeared after the war: television. Many of the same reporters who maintained a dialogue with their readers in their written articles are now inviting themselves nightly to the viewers' living room (after having carefully chosen the color of their shirt). How could such intimate contact with the public fail to broaden their influence?

Who are these men who wield such great power virtually unchecked by any law? An examination of the privileges and problems peculiar to journalists will provide the answer to this question.

THE THREE POWERS OF THE PRESS

"I don't know who won the Battle of the Marne," General Joffre said in 1914 when people disputed his victory, "but I know who would have lost it." The publisher of a newspaper often feels the same sort of irritation when he gets angry phone calls from government officials, business executives, or celebrities upset by an article written by one of his reporters whom he himself has probably not seen more than once in the elevator. He certainly cannot reply—unless he is ready to have his status evaporate into thin air: "How am I supposed to know, much less control everything that's printed here?" When he receives the latest book of one of his friends, accompanied by a sycophantic dedication, he knows that the author naïvely hopes that, because of their long-standing acquaintance, the newspaper will give it an excellent review. The publisher goes to the limits of his editorial powers when he dictates a diplomatic note to the book review editor, the gist of which is: if this book is as bad as I think it is, you would be doing me a real favor by not giving a total pan. He can hire or fire the editor (even though, as we shall see later, this right is increasingly denied him) but for all practical purposes he has to apply friendly persuasion to prevent a cub reporter from playing havoc with his social life. At the same time, he has to take the responsibility for all the blunders that inevitably get printed in his paper.

The first lesson learned by the press agent for any organization—in government, the theater, publishing, or whatever business—is that in order to get something published he must get in touch with the editor of the department that involves his specific problem. It is much easier and more efficient than playing golf with the newspaper's owner.

But this was not always the case. In the past, when newspapers were smaller (because there were more of them), when the publisher was at the same time founder, owner, director and editor-in-chief, when journalism had only a few real professionals, when the rights attached to ownership still meant something—the owners were virtual dictators. It was their Golden Age.

In relatively unsophisticated areas—a French provincial city, for example—this is often still the case. Whenever someone in the area has incurred the publisher's disfavor, the malefactor's name is never allowed to appear in the paper again. One such owner has even gone so far as to touch up a group photograph when the unfortunate person appeared in it, in an effort to blot out his very existence. This can become a difficult policy to stick to when one of the names on the blacklist is the local prefect, who happens to be the most powerful state official around.

But with a national publication, whose journalists have taken on a particular personality in the eyes of the public, whether as a political columnist or a restaurant critic (who had greater influence on New York life: James Reston or Craig Claiborne when he was writing his food and restaurant columns?), the legendary power of the publishers has become more symbolic than real. They represent the Fourth Estate but are no longer its major power brokers.

To better understand the division of power between those who own or manage newspapers and the journalists who write for them, we can try to take a closer look at who controls different functions of the press, which are to investigate, to publish, to set priorities.

The power to investigate and to write belongs indisputably to the journalists rather than the managers. Finding a story, researching it, doing the legwork, and presenting the results clearly and readably—that is the journalist's job. More often than not the journalist has nothing to start with but raw facts which he must transform into an authoritative column or news story. He does not have the time to carry out public opinion polls or to undertake certain kinds of research that can involve months or years of study. Universities, foundations, or the government produce these facts. But in most cases the style of these official reports is so convoluted that it defeats the nonspecialist. This is where the journalist comes in. He translates the facts into understandable language, condenses material, and brings out its significance.

A good journalist knows there is no subject or event which, after patient and systematic investigation, will not yield new facts. Yet one of the greatest weaknesses of the press is that its ability to investigate is used too little. Most of the "news" in a newspaper is about what happened the day before as dispatched by a wire service. Creating "new" news through investigative reporting is still the exception to the rule. From time to time, the great American tradition of the crusading journalist denouncing scandals or social ills does reassert itself. *Life* Magazine exposed big-city corruption; *L'Express* revealed the actual role of the police in the "kidnapping" of the Algerian Ben Baraka on a Paris street; Jack Anderson published the secret minutes of the National Security Council meetings on the India-Pakistan war, and Woodward and Bernstein of the *Washington Post* compelled national attention to the Watergate affair.

This power to investigate is the least restricted of all. With enough talent, any determined individual can exercise it. He does not need the blessings of a newspaper, because a book can be just as effective. One of the most impressive pieces of investigative reporting in recent years—Ralph Nader's *Unsafe at Any Speed*—was first published in book form. Yet it is an example of truly effective journalism.

The second power of the press is the decision on what is published and how. This power is, in principle, held by the owners and publishers of newspapers, who in France, for example, are legally responsible for everything that appears in their publications. But the day-to-day decision of to print or not to print a given story is made by the editor-in-chief or managing editor. Though the top editor rarely writes anything himself, he does choose the subjects and the writers, and reads, evaluates, corrects, and finally sends the copy to the composing room or into the waste basket. His simple "yes" or "no" plays a key role in the lives of journalists. In a great number of newspapers many more pages are written than printed. Every day *The New York Times,* with its large staff of writers, could easily print a second newspaper made up of the articles that did not appear in the regular morning editions.

Under certain circumstances the power to publish is exercised directly by the chief executive of the paper—for example, when the article could harm the reputation or the vital interest of the publication. The most commonplace decisions concern news that could be harmful to the advertisers whose ads provide an important source of income. The big newspapers or magazines claim to be above such considerations and boast of the independence of their editorial staffs. Before Ralph Nader appeared on the scene, when General Motors still believed that it could keep the press in line, *The Wall Street Journal* published an article which did not please the largest industrial company in the world. In reprisal, General Motors instructed its advertising agency to kill all ads in the *Journal.* The editor-in-chief then sent his best reporters to Detroit to expose GM every day in the paper. Each morning thereafter, when the GM executives picked up *The Wall Street Journal,* they learned—as did their competitors—what was happening in their factories, even before their own personnel could tell them about it. GM ended up by calling off its boycott and resuming normal relations with *The Wall Street Journal.*

But for the local or specialized—therefore smaller—newspaper that depends on a handful of large advertisers, it is heroic to publish an offensive article. Practically speaking, even editors-in-chief who are jealous of their powers prefer to clear with higher-ups stories which might upset advertisers. They have nothing to lose. Either the publisher takes responsibility for printing the article, and no matter what happens the editor-in-chief is off the hook, or else the publisher refuses to print it and the editor can crow that the moneymen are interfering with his editorial freedom.

The publication of the Pentagon Papers in 1971 is one of the most famous examples of the scope of the right to publish. Investigative reporting as such was not involved. The crucial issue was the decision, despite the risks, to publish the documents classified as secret which Daniel Ellsberg turned over to the *Times.* The *Times* staff showed its mettle in checking the genuineness of the papers, in selecting and arranging the material, and in coming to the decision to publish them. The final decision naturally had to be approved by the paper's publisher, "Punch" Sulzberger. When *The New York Times* was temporarily enjoined by the government from publishing the documents (pending a hearing in the Supreme Court, which ruled in favor of the *Times* on narrow legal grounds), other newspaper publishers—Kay Graham of the *Washington Post* and W. Davis Taylor of the *Boston Globe*—published additional selections from the Pentagon Papers, circumventing the White House's attempt at "prior restraint." In so doing, they risked going to jail themselves. Such cases involve the broadest questions of freedom of the press versus the rights of governments to protect data stamped "secret," and they require the newspaper publisher to be something more than a businessman. In the spring of 1972, when the Pulitzer Prize, the highest American journalism award, was given to *The New York Times* for the Pentagon Papers and to Jack Anderson for his revelations about the India-Pakistan war, there was a fresh political uproar from the White House, which took the awards as an affront.

The impact of the news does not always depend on gutsy or bravura reporting. In TV broadcasting, there is a tradition of presenting the news impartially. When listening to, for example, Walter Cronkite or John Chancellor, one does not have the feeling that they are trying to influence the viewer. Only very rarely do they make judgments or pointed comments. They tell what happened and present the various filmed reports their photographers have shot. There is nothing political or partisan about it. What, then, is the basis of the great power they are supposed to have and for which they are often criticized?

The fact is that the average TV newscast lasts less than twenty minutes (the rest of the half-hour program is taken up by advertising), which drastically limits the number of news items that can be presented. Because of the immediate emotional impact of television, the twenty minutes presented by CBS, NBC, and ABC every evening determine the order of importance of the news of the day for the American nation. These twenty minutes can alter the mood of tens of millions of people. Selecting a few items from the ocean of news, the TV editors exercise a prerogative that many consider excessive. Newspapers, too, simply by choosing the front-page headlines, also establish an order of news importance. But few of them have the influence of televised newscasts.

Others, less conspicuous to audiences, have as heavy responsibilities as TV newscasters in the system of news distribution. Richard L. Tobin wrote in the *Saturday Review* of May 13, 1967, that the most powerful man in the United States was not the president of A.T.&T. or of Harvard University, but the desk chief at AP or UPI. Every radio station depends for its news on that man, on his integrity to pick out news that is then sent out over the wires. And only the very best among the 1,754 dailies depend on their own journalists rather than the wire services for all the information that does not directly concern their city. Tobin concluded that the wire services had a formidable responsibility.

JOURNALISTS IN THE THICK OF IT

The exercise of power is bound to generate crises, and the press has never been an exception, but recently in the United States journalists have found themselves in the middle of two conflicts of unprecedented magnitude. The first is the traditional one that opposes them to the government. The only thing new about this is its present intensity. The second, more surprising and less talked about, is a growing credibility gap.

The war against the press was declared by Vice President Agnew in November 1969, one year after his election, in the first of a long series of speeches against the press. He accused the press of partiality toward liberal ideas. According to him, a "silent majority" of Americans did not share the prejudices of the journalists, especially those working in television, who exerted an "excessive" amount of power. He hinted at a conspiracy aimed at deceiving the public about America's true image.

What is so unusual about these attacks? Certainly not the fact that the government is unhappy with the press. During the Civil War, Lincoln did not hesitate to use his emergency powers to shut down newspapers and to arrest journalists. Up until the start of World War II, Roosevelt was opposed by most of the press, and he counterattacked with verbal gusto. After the Bay of Pigs fiasco, Kennedy exhorted the press not to print articles that could threaten national security.

The new element in Vice President Agnew's attacks was the

implication that the press needed to be controlled and the singling out of specific journalists, with no holds barred. The press was deeply shocked. Since the charges came from the Vice President of the United States, the broadcasting journalists particularly—who cherish their reputations for impartiality—were increasingly embarrassed by these repeated denunciations, all the more so because they were obliged to report calmly each new assault against them to the public. A kind of moral crisis developed, and some newscasters seriously questioned whether they had done enough to present opposing viewpoints.

For a European, who remembers indictments and seizure of entire issues of *Der Spiegel* in Germany or *L'Express* in France in the early sixties, the reaction of the American press to mere verbal attacks is surprising. Then again, the respect generally given to the press in the United States is just as unusual to Europeans. Journalists in the United States have a virtual right to call politicians to account; a correspondent of *The New York Times* or *Time* stationed abroad has a status that is in some ways comparable to that of the American ambassador. It is so rare for the police to beat up reporters in the United States that the Chicago Democratic Convention riots of 1968 were the subject of scandalized commentary in the press for a long time afterward. In view of that enviable respectability, one can understand how American journalists came to regard the unbecoming remarks of a Vice President as more threatening than the sharp reproofs addressed by de Gaulle to their French colleagues.

Now a new element began to emerge: the public itself was beginning to question the credibility of its sources of information. The notorious "credibility gap" stemming from government lies about Vietnam helped to topple President Johnson and cast permanent doubt on the intentions of the Nixon Administration, but the press felt above suspicion.However, when Bill Moyers, a former spokesman for President Johnson, then head of *Newsday,* and later associated with a Public Broadcasting Service television news show, heard one of his listeners remark after one of his talks that because Moyers had been both in government and journalism there were two reasons to doubt what he said, Moyers shared a growing disquiet among journalists: public opinion, after having toppled a President for lack of credibility, was pulling the press off the referee's stool where it had thought it was firmly entrenched.

One month after the first attacks by Agnew, a Gallup poll showed that 42 percent of the American people thought that television did not provide them with impartial news (40 percent thought it was objective and 18 percent had no opinion). Forty-five percent thought the same thing about the newspapers. The poll showed further that, of those people with a college education, 53 percent did not have confidence in what they saw and heard on television and 60 percent did not trust the newspapers. These figures confirmed in a disquieting way what newsmen had been hearing from their barbers and taxi drivers. Had the public fallen in line with the Nixon Administration? What did they have against journalists?

Ever since Cleopatra put to death the messenger who brought her the news of Mark Antony's death, journalists have realized that they run certain risks when they report bad news. But the basic rule of their profession remains: "Good news is no news." Going against this axiom, a newspaper in Fair Oaks, California, *The Good News Paper,* decided to print nothing but good news. It has been in financial straits ever since.

Starting with the great shock of the assassination of John Kennedy in November 1963, America has been suffering from what strikes this European observer as a collective nervous breakdown, deepened by a continued barrage of bad news: assassinations, the Vietnam War, racial turmoil, student revolts, drugs, pollution, unemployment, decline of the dollar. Is it any wonder, then, that the citizen has been quick to blame those whose job it is to give him daily reminders of these problems? The process was sharpened when, in reaction to Agnew's attacks, the press did its utmost to prove, by publishing secret reports and confidential documents, that the biggest liar, the one that really deceives the public, is the American government. In this respect, the Watergate scandal, perhaps more than any other event in American history, has helped the press make its point and has reversed public response to the Agnew-type attack for quite a while to come.

But the shock of bad news is not enough to explain the tensions American media are undergoing. The crux of the problem is the increase in the power of the media to make or break a man and to highlight or play down an event. During the 1967–1969 student revolts, in many instances the scuffles only started for real when the television cameras arrived on the scene. Afterward, the participants who had not been arrested hurried home to see what had happened—in other words, to see what the American public was going to be told about it. It is no exaggeration to say that whatever is not reported by the press simply has not taken place.

It is true that those who exercise these immense powers are not elected by the people, but are businessmen—the owner–publishers—or professional journalists. Without an elective mandate, members of the press hold the broadest rights of investigation, which has provoked uneasiness on the part of the public. Add to this the fact that among the tens of thousands of journalists, the famous as well as the obscure, there is, as in any system, the usual proportion of the third-rate, the lazy, and the irresponsible. Because their words appear in print or are heard over the public airwaves, their faults will show up much more than if they were working for an ordinary business enterprise.

Finally, the limited means of investigation at the disposal of journalists (number of hours available, traveling time, or documents or records at hand) would terrify the public even more if they knew just how meager those means are. The journalists are the first to understand (and to suffer from) this.

FRUSTRATIONS AND DANGERS

The man in the street never tires of learning that celebrities can be just as unhappy as he is. The neurotic billionaire, the grief-stricken movie star or the troubled princess are the raw material, continually rehashed, of a specialized press with a tremendous following all over the world.[1] The public seems

[1]When the Queen of England visited France in May 1972, a former managing editor of the scandal sheet *France-Dimanche,* published the following statistics (no doubt trying to make amends): Since 1958 the French press has printed twenty-nine times that Elizabeth's life was in danger; eleven times that she was taking the pill (which did not prevent her from having ninety pregnancies and nine miscarriages); she had had 149 accidents, forty-three anxiety-ridden nights, twenty-seven nightmares, and narrowly escaped nervous breakdowns thirty-two times. She was close to abdicating sixty-three times, on the verge of breaking up with Prince Philip seventy-three times; showed a lack of consideration for Princess Grace six times and eleven times for Farah Dibha. Finally, she banished her brother-in-law Lord Snowden from Court 151 times.

unaware of the woes of the journalists themselves; these powerful, well-known, and envied people nonetheless have their own crosses to bear.

Like everybody else, journalists would like to be liked. Yet their notoriety can be compared to that of well-known politicians or great artists, because their bylines or faces appear everywhere. It may take a public figure years of work to become well known, but a new TV weatherman is instantly recognized by the waitress in a neighborhood restaurant. Nevertheless, while politicians and artists can evoke very positive emotions in the public, the best journalists can only arouse interest. Their job is to confront the public with reality; how can they be loved?

Newscasters are stars, but since they are wage earners, they can be fired and consigned to oblivion. This is what happened in French television after the events of May 1968. A great number of journalists, among them some of the most famous, had taken open anti-Gaullist positions. Fired after the General's triumph, they were no longer stars and had to make do with minor jobs in less-prestigious areas of media, and the public quickly forgot them. The same thing happened—to a lesser degree—in 1972 when a dozen or so journalists followed Pierre Desgraupes, a news director of the main channel of ORTF into exile. Unlike French newspapermen, television employees do not receive severance pay.

Fear of finding themselves out of a job no doubt contributed to the sensitivity of American journalists to Agnew's tongue-lashings. Although they cannot be brought into court, the businessmen who own the newspapers and TV stations may be cowed by administration pressure and take a second look at the independence of their staff writers.

These are frustrations inherent in the profession. A journalist's job is to produce ideas and words, but he enjoys less prestige than writers, who are considered "artists." Nothing pleases a journalist more than to become known as "a man of letters." Even though such great writers as Ernest Hemingway or Joseph Kessel started out as reporters and never looked down upon journalistic reporting, journalists are quite aware of the difference between great writers and themselves. The real writers are those *about whom* articles are written; journalists merely write the articles. For every superstar journalist such as James Reston, Theodore White, or Jack Anderson, there are thousands of unknowns. Reporters might accommodate themselves to obscurity if everything they wrote was printed. But generally lack of space prevents the bulk of their writing from appearing. In some overstaffed newspapers—*France-Soir,* for example—a good newsman can go for weeks without seeing one of his articles in print. The articles that do appear are cut so much that the writer always feels that he has been personally wounded. In newsmagazines the original text is drastically rewritten to fit the house style. Even the most experienced journalists never get used to this blow to their pride.

Outsiders don't understand the assaults constantly made on the professional ethics of newspapermen. Public relations men try to buy them with gifts or free travel; politicians do their best either to charm or to intimidate them; the publisher and even the managing editors pressure them into toning down frank opinions which might get the newspaper into trouble. Finally, there are the physical risks—at demonstrations, protestors and police alike often unleash their collective fury on reporters.

And then, professional adventure can turn into tragedy. Although not elected by the people, not serving in the army, not appointed to official missions, but doing their reporting job, journalists are killed in all sorts of wars—Vietnam, Biafra, Algeria, Ireland. Correspondents tend to believe that their exposure to danger and risks is one of the great differences between them and an accountant or a grocer.

A FASCINATING JOB ALL THE SAME

The real danger to a newsman does not come from stray bullets, but from the life style the job demands. Demanding hours, continual travel, deadlines, countless cigarettes, and a lot of drinking—all combine to build up tension. Contrary to popular belief, the highest incidence of heart trouble is not among executives (who statistically come only after priests) but among journalists.

In the last few years, despite the prospect of professional frustration and physical danger, the greatest increase in enrollment in American universities has been in schools of journalism, and there are far more candidates for the profession than jobs. The number of dailies and magazines remains static at best. Something about the profession attracts young people who will only be fifty by the year 2,000.[2]

Why do billionaires so often think of buying a newspaper as a present to themselves? After years devoted to building his fortune, the billionaire suddenly decides to try his hand at the newspaper business, just for the fun of it. Money is no concern. By launching a publication or buying an existing one, he hopes to mix power and intellectual excitement—even when the newspaper he chooses is unsuitable for his ambitions. Thus the richest man in France, the aeronautical genius Marcel Dassault, also a member of the Chamber of Deputies, is delighted with his title of editor-in-chief of *Jours de France,* the women's weekly he created. *Jours de France* is a run-of-the-mill women's magazine, but it makes no difference to him—it is his hobby. He has installed its offices in a mansion on the Champs Elysées, opposite *Le Figaro.* Marcel Dassault thus considers himself to be a "press lord." Has a billionaire ever bought a paper mill or a supermarket for his own pleasure? The press obviously has its own special appeal.

First of all, the press opens a route to fame. Any young reporter who gets his first byline has the irresistible desire, going home on the bus, to tap the shoulder of the stranger reading his newspaper and say: "That's my article you're reading there." The first working day at IBM or the Renault auto plant offers nothing comparable.

Whoever invented the masthead—that column in magazines (most dailies do not carry one) where the names of the major editorial and administrative people appear—created one of the most efficient and cheapest gadgets for recruiting talent. Most journalists can count on having their byline appear above an article (except in news magazines), but even the advertising manager, the business manager, or the circulation manager is bowled over by the knowledge that their names appear in print on millions of copies every year. Their families and acquaintances treat them with more respect simply because they work on a magazine instead of in a factory or advertising agency.

Journalism can satisfy the lust for power, even in a modest way. When Jean Ferniot, a French political journalist on good

[2]In Japan, journalists are recruited annually through an extremely difficult nationwide competitive examination open only to university graduates. There are 8,000 candidates for 500 available jobs.

terms with men in power, wrote for his own amusement a restaurant column under a pseudonym, he would receive letters from restaurant owners saying: "I was practically bankrupt, but since your article appeared, I have to turn away people every night." Who does not like to play Santa Claus? He stopped writing restaurant reviews because, of all the forms of journalism, restaurant reviewing is the most detrimental to one's health.

Among other rewards of the profession are the relationships maintained with important or famous men who know how to deal with journalists. Newspapermen can satisfy their own curiosity about various things (since the subject matter of their articles changes constantly), or they can indulge a creative urge while being part of a team. Perhaps they can even succeed in achieving social ends, provided they are not too eager or impatient for results.

Finally, every journalist considers himself almost an intellectual. He is a worker whose tools are in his head; his style, his byline—when he becomes well known—and especially his friendships and contacts enable him to dig out facts to pass on to his readers. Even if he is fired, he still has his tools. Of all the salaried professions, journalism is the one which provides the most incentive, creative possibilities, and freedom.

Chapter 2
The Revolt of the Journalists

"Hello, Jean-Louis? Well, it's happened. The editorial staff delegates have just left my office. They gave me the statement they want printed in tomorrow morning's edition."

"What does it say, Pierre?"

"That the agreement you just made with our competitor *La Montagne* jeopardizes the political freedom of the *Journal du Centre*. They want to tell the readers that the contents of the paper are no longer their responsibility."

"But that's the same thing as telling our readers to stop believing the paper. That's not possible."

"But if we refuse to publish their statement they're going to go on strike."

"Are all the employees for it?"

"No. Just the editorial staff. What should we do?"

"We must explain to them once again why this statement doesn't in the slightest way affect the paper's editorial independence. I'll come to Nevers this afternoon to go over it once more. But for us to print such a statement is completely out of the question."

Such was the conversation I had on March 22, 1971, with Pierre Janrot, publisher of the Nevers daily *Le Journal du Centre*. I was president of the company at that time. This was the beginning of a showdown, characteristic of the new, testy relationships between editorial staffs and publishers that was to surface throughout.

What was the problem? It was not a matter of wages or firing people. In fact, the marketing and technical co-operation agreement with *La Montagne* had detailed provisions guaranteeing both political freedom and job security—good news for the personnel of a newspaper with a circulation of 48,000 readers and which was in financial difficulties. Under the new arrangement, the *Journal du Centre* could find assistance from its associate *La Montagne,* with its circulation of more than 240,000 and excellent profitability. However, there was a big "but." *La Montagne* was Gaullist, while the editorial staff of the *Journal du Centre* backed the Socialist party. The strike started that very night. It lasted seven days before petering out for lack of support.

Anyone familiar with the French regional newspapers knows that their political allegiances have little influence on their editorial content.Newspapers that can afford the luxury of expressing strong editorial opinions are few and far between. Therefore, this strike—which collapsed because no concrete demands were ever put forth—stemmed from little more than emotional mistrust. Backed by the Socialist City Council of Nevers, the newsmen demonstrated in the streets. Several hundred citizens, convinced that their daily newspaper was seriously threatened by the very fact that it was not on the newsstands, rallied to the support of the strikers. *Le Monde,* the great Paris daily which steadily airs the gripes of journalists, reprinted word for word the releases issued practically every day by the strikers. But, as it became apparent that the strike was based on subjective views of the editorial staff, its leaders became isolated. The newsmen made up only one third of the personnel of the newspaper. From the beginning, the printing shop workers and administrative employees let it be known that they did not support the strike and were idle against their will. The strike collapsed when all but six of the journalists changed their minds and went back to work. In the six months that followed, the six holdouts left the *Journal du Centre* one after the other. A year later, when I decided to sell the shares I owned in the *Journal du Centre* to *La Montagne,* the two workers' representatives who sat on the executive board voted in favor of the sale.

This was not an isolated incident. In the same year, 1971, there were other strikes in which employment and wages were not at issue. Throughout France, Germany, Italy, and even Spain, editorial staffs are in a continual state of readiness to challenge the management or policy of their papers. This attitude, which has been developing over the past ten years, is gathering momentum in Europe and, in a different form, in the

United States as well. More than television or technological change, this journalist revolt could be the instrument for changing the role of the press.

EUROPE—CRADLE OF THE MOVEMENT

It is no accident that a protest movement of newspaper editorial staffs has started in Europe—first in France, then in Germany and Italy, countries with newspapers operated by private enterprise in which the effects of recent history still reverberate. The memory of fascism within their own countries is engraved on the conscience of the current generation of these European journalists, which sets them apart from British and American colleagues. Democracy and freedom of the press are not taken for granted. In Italy, Germany, and Spain, and then in France and the other countries occupied by the Nazis, journalists were muzzled and censored when they were not thrown into prison, persecuted, or killed. In Germany, the Nazis appropriated the press. In France, all journalists who did not swear allegiance to the Pétain regime were purged. During the fascist period in these countries, the press was an instrument of totalitarian propaganda. Anyone who lived through that period or saw his father go through it knows how fragile freedom of expression is.

The reputations of most newspaper owners were severely damaged during this time. Those who ceased publication to keep their newspapers from being of service to the fascists were few and far between. Some who were finally ousted or arrested by the fascist authorities had tried to compromise in order to hang on a bit longer—often in the hope of keeping their employees working. As was to be expected, the retaliation at war's end was severe. In France, almost all the papers that appeared during the Occupation were banned; their assets were expropriated, their publishers taken to court and sometimes sentenced to death; presses were turned over to Resistance groups, which alone were permitted to bring out new publications. Throughout Europe, while most industries remained in the hands of their old owners, the press had to start up again from scratch. What was clearly demonstrated was that behind the sacred myth of independent ownership lurked a group of servile men and a handful of scoundrels. Under these circumstances, it is not surprising that journalists have little respect for the traditional rights of property.

Nevertheless, the high-minded idea of a "Resistance" press, with traditional capitalists replaced by socially aware journalists, collapsed within a few years. The new owners simply couldn't manage the business end. One after the other, the new dailies folded, without ever balancing their budgets, despite the exceptional headstart offered by the government's gift of printing presses. Of the papers that survived, the publishers were replaced by businessmen, in whose eyes political ideals meant little compared to increased profits. The return of the press to the realities of the system was a new source of frustration for the journalists then, most of whom are in their fifties today. Now many of them are nostalgic about the euphoria of the Liberation, when it seemed their profession could be practiced in a state of weightlessness. The most bitter among them still do not acknowledge their own failure and blame it on some sort of sell-out.

The weight of recent history, then, explains why the new conflict began in France and Germany. But certain tendencies of contemporary society relevant to the journalistic profession make similar confrontations likely to occur in other advanced industrial countries. One of these is mounting criticism of profit-making and advertising. Most notably, this criticism no longer comes only from Marxists. The critique of private ownership and business methods has emerged from the political ghetto and achieved a good measure of respectability.

Another aspect is the gradual "proletarianization" of white-collar workers, whose numbers have grown to such an extent that they can no longer feel privileged and who are increasingly alienated by the bureaucracy of big corporations. Perhaps this situation leads quite to a sense of solidarity with others in the same situation. Today in Europe it is no longer exceptional to see management personnel joining a union. Among journalists, many consider themselves intellectuals exploited by publishing firms that have grown from small family businesses to large corporations. They are alert to the implications of these tendencies and respond strongly to them.

In a publication, the editorial staff lives in its own world and suffers a double complex. First, journalists feel inferior because, even though they have privileged status, a barrier exists between them and the business end of the enterprise. One way or the other, they realize they have no say in the management of the firm. At the same time, however, they feel superior to the businessmen, who, incapable of abstract ideas, understand nothing more than profits and losses.

Moreover, the press has always been vulnerable to strikes because in every country the printers have been among the first to build powerful unions. This fact has been a challenge to the new generation of newspapermen who, in their desire not to be outdone by the hostility of the working class to management, often seem obsessed by the need to prove their rebelliousness even on the flimsiest pretext.

One other factor contributing to the conflict between the editorial workers and owners is that a decrease in the number of publications has coincided with the arrival on the labor market of many more aspiring journalists. Since the middle 1960s this has resulted in chronic unemployment in the profession.

THE UNIQUE CASE OF *LE MONDE*

The revolt of the journalists in France began with the founding of the Journalist Association of *Le Monde*. Although eventually there would be more than thirty such associations among various French publications, fourteen years elapsed between the founding of the *Le Monde* association and the formation of one at *Le Figaro*. Today *Le Monde* is the only newspaper in France where the aims of its association have been completely attained: a voice in running the paper backed by the association's owning a substantial share of the paper.

Le Monde first appeared in December 1944, headed by a thoroughly honest and serious journalist, Hubert Beuve-Méry, then forty-three years old. A scrupulous concern for quality and absence of sensationalism, even to the extent of refusing to carry photographs, quickly made *Le Monde* the indispensable source of information for political and intellectual circles. In 1949, two years after the beginning of the Cold War, *Le Monde* started publishing "neutralist" articles which dared to question the validity of NATO and the Atlantic Pact. Hubert Beuve-Méry, criticized on this issue by the company shareholders, resigned during the summer of 1951, but the editorial staff threatened a work stoppage and obtained his reinstatement as well as a share of the company stock which assured them a say in subsequent important decisions.

Since the original *Le Monde* shareholders had some affinity to the ideals of publishing at the time of the Liberation, they were willing to reorganize the company and allot a minority interest with veto power (28 percent of the stock) to the editorial employees. The Journalist Association of *Le Monde* was thus formed in October 1951 to obtain the employees' shares. Since then, the employees of *Le Monde* have gained control of more than half of the company's stock, making them masters of an enterprise which has become, for all intents and purposes, a self-managed co-operative.

The *Le Monde* affair had far-reaching repercussions, and its features were to be repeated elsewhere on numerous occasions: conflict erupting over the departure or demise of a respected executive; guarantee of political freedom in editorial matters; blocking the choice by regular stockholders of a publisher whose job would be to keep the editorial staff in line; demand for a journalist association to participate in decision-making and to control part of the stock, giving the journalists a privileged status relative to other wage earners on the publication.

THE MOVEMENT TOWARD JOURNALIST ASSOCIATIONS GAINS MOMENTUM

It was years before the example of *Le Monde* was repeated. The situation was again ripe in 1965, when Pierre Brisson, publisher of *Le Figaro,* died. Though Brisson did not have the professional distinction and moral authority of Beuve-Méry, he had been the undisputed top man of his paper since the Liberation.

The bloated editorial staff of *Le Figaro*—numbering 300 journalists—was threatened when Jean Prouvost, the major shareholder of the company who was a journalist but also a textile industrialist, announced his intention to succeed Brisson. The journalists formed a association, setting off a complex conflict which lasted five years before being settled through compromise. The year 1965 also saw the retirement of Paul Hutin as manager of *Ouest-France*—the largest-selling regional newspaper in the country. The editorial staff, wanting a voice in picking his successor, founded an association and took their case to court.

From 1965 on, whenever there has been the possibility of a publication's being sold, when the owner has died or there has been a prospective change in management, the ritual of organizing a journalist association has been repeated. More often than not, this is as far as it goes, but no detail remains unprinted in *Le Monde,* which is the sounding board of the movement. The guiding spirit of the revolt is one of *Le Monde*'s staff writers, Jean Schwoebel, who spends most of his time spreading the good word in the provinces and abroad. In his 1968 book, *La Presse, le pouvoir et l'argent* (Press, Power and Money"), he listed the major demands of the insurgent journalists:

1. The right to veto the nomination of publisher and editor-in-chief, particularly when a newspaper is sold or the posts fall vacant.

2. A special status, distinct from that of the other personnel of the newspaper—which would prevent management from tampering with articles.

3. Control of 35 percent of the paper's stock by the journalist association, enabling it to block major decisions to which it is ideologically opposed.

4. Eventual transformation of the press into nonprofit enterprises, making newspapers a public service, largely subsidized by the state.

Corollary to these is one other demand: to grant a kind of tenure to journalists. To an extent this has been achieved, in that no matter how inept a newsman may be, anyone who wants to fire him will run into the resistance of the unions or the journalist association. In France today, newsmen are fired only when they have been convicted of a crime or their newspaper is on the verge of bankruptcy.

Thus the insurgents would have it that the journalist is an unimpeachable professional, entrusted with a mandate as sacred as that of a judge or professor. Moreover, the journalists demand the privilege of choosing the person to direct their paper who, once elected, cannot interfere with what they write.

Except for *Le Monde,* at the thirty other publications where journalist associations have been formed, they are indistinguishable from any other union except for their more elitist characteristics. What they have obtained is a widespread awareness of the problems on the part of all journalists, newspaper publishers, and the government. The *Figaro* compromise, in fact, was not negotiated by the paper's journalist association. And there was no journalist association at *L'Express* during a major conflict there in 1971 between the owner-founder Jean-Jacques Servan-Schreiber and the top editors. Nevertheless, the new climate in French press circles prompted the publishers of *L'Express* is experiment with having *all* the personnel of the magazine, not just the journalists, participate in appointing the executive director.

STATE OF UNREST

The conflict between journalists and publishers is not limited to France. In other European countries, and recently in the United States, journalists are making similar demands.

In Germany, the *Stern* affair of the spring of 1969 is reminiscent of the upheavals at *Le Monde* and *Le Figaro*. This influential weekly picture magazine, with a circulation of 2 million, has become a political force thanks to its truculent editor-in-chief, Heinrich Nannen. A major stockholder, Richard Grüner, wanted to sell his 39.5 percent share to a publisher of pulp magazines, Heinrich Bauer. As soon as this was known, a majority of the editorial staff threatened to go on strike if the deal was concluded. Bauer withdrew his offer and Grüner was forced to sell at a lower price to his partners, who in turn granted privileged status to *Stern*'s editorial staff. Since then, a seven-member editorial board has been elected every year from among the journalists, and an editor-in-chief cannot be fired or appointed without the consent of at least two-thirds of the editorial board. The agreement stipulates that no journalist can be forced to "write anything that goes against his own beliefs," and that employees will be consulted before any changes are made in the ownership of the magazine. Here, too, the newsmen have taken a decisive step toward autonomy.

Rudolph Augstein, the founder-owner of *Der Spiegel,* the well-known German newsmagazine with a circulation of nearly 1 million, is a man receptive to new ideas. He no doubt thought he would be fully gratifying his journalists' desires when in 1971 he proposed to sell them the majority of the magazine's stock. There was difficulty in concluding an agreement because the editorial staff considered the arrangement—scheduled for

1973—too far off. They wanted the immediate right to veto any and all decisions of the publisher.

In March 1972, the journalists of the largest Italian daily, the *Corriere della Sera,* went on strike to have a say in the appointment of the newspaper's executives. They invoked the example of *Le Monde.*

In June 1972, the editorial staff of the Milan daily *Il Giorno* declared a "state of unrest." This newspaper is owned by the state-controlled petroleum company ENI (just as Turin's *La Stampa* belongs to Fiat) and had just changed publishers. The newsmen immediately condemned "the way the new publisher has been appointed without consulting the editorial staff." They demanded "the problem of more democratic and correct relations between the editorial staff, the political management, and the owner be resolved once and for all."

In Denmark, the editorial staff of a small daily, *Information,* rose up as one against the owner when he tried to fire the editor-in-chief. Since the paper was losing money, the owner sold it to the employees for a nominal sum, and it has been self-managed ever since.

In Britain, when Richard Grossman left as publisher of *The New Statesman,* the editorial staff demanded and were granted the right to participate in nominating a replacement. The staff's own candidate, Anthony Howard, was appointed in April 1972.

Even in Spain, where the press is under constant pressure from the Franco government, the journalists of the daily *Madrid* formed an association in October 1971 to oppose the appointment of a new publisher, who was backed by the Ministry of Information. Eventually the paper was closed by the authorities.

The common feature of all these cases has been that a change in publisher or editor-in-chief sparks a crisis. In each, the journalists have challenged the right of the owners to make their own changes.

PROTEST AMERICAN STYLE

In May 1969, in Williamsburg, Virginia, I addressed the American Magazine Publishers Association on "Journalists against Owners," describing the situation in Europe at the height of the *Figaro* and *Stern* battles. After the talk, my American colleagues, dumbfounded by these infringements upon the rights of owners, told me that nothing similar could ever happen in America. Yet even at that time a few incidents had already occurred which indicated that not everything was going smoothly between American journalists and their employers.

In February 1968, Arthur Ochs Sulzberger, publisher of *The New York Times,* wanted to change his Washington bureau chief because he felt that that office had become too autonomous. The Washington bureau counterattacked with the support of superstar columnist James Reston, forcing Sulzberger to back down. In October of the same year, a group of disgruntled journalists launched the *Chicago Journalism Review* as a vehicle for criticizing newspaper publishers as well as the content of their papers, which they considered conformist.

Since then, these trends have gathered momentum. Clashes have broken out between top editors and publishers. In March 1971, Willie Morris left *Harper's* (circulation 300,000), followed by some of the best members of his staff. Morris declared that the conflict reflected the old argument between the moneymen and the editors and that, as usual, the moneymen had won. In November of the same year, Norman Cousins resigned from *Saturday Review* (circulation 600,000) after thirty years, because he was in "philosophical and professional disagreement" with the new owners, John Veronis and Nicholas Charney; six months later he launched his own magazine, *World.* A year after that, in the wake of the economic and editorial catastrophe that followed *Saturday Review*'s attempt to become four different magazines, Cousins' original concept had triumphed. The revamped *Saturday Review* folded and Cousins had access to its subscription lists. The magazine now carries on its cover the titles *Saturday Review* and *World,* each title differentiated (at the time of this writing) by a different type face.

At another level, a significant clash took place in Chicago at the time of the municipal elections of 1971. The owner of the *Chicago Sun Times* and the *Chicago Daily News,* Marshall Field, decided his papers would endorse the powerful conservative democrat Richard Daley for re-election. Most of the editorial staff of the Field papers were against Daley, but they did not react in the same way newsmen in Europe might have. Instead of threatening to strike, they collected enough money to buy ads expressing their disagreement with the papers' views. Marshall

Field agreed to print the ads in order to avoid making matters worse.

Most significant is the growing number of militant anti-newspapers—following in the steps of *The Chicago Journalism Review*. In Denver, Philadelphia, Saint Louis, Providence, Honolulu, New York, California, and Connecticut, journalists have opted for this way of letting off steam. They keep abreast of developments in Europe. The Philadelphia publication has stated "we will no longer agree to the authoritarian concept according to which an editor-in-chief has the right to ask us to put his demands ahead of our principles . . . control of the press by economic means is anti-American . . . boss-type journalism is coming to an end." Support has come even from the craft unions. Bertram Powers, the powerful leader of the typographers union, declared in June 1972 that the time was past when publishers could reserve for themselves the managerial decisions.

In April 1972 occurred what *Time* Magazine called the "Woodstock of Journalism." While the annual convention of newspaper publishers was being held in New York, the protest magazine *More* organized a "counterconvention" attended by 2,000 journalists and students. Here, for the first time, obscure journalists as well as such famous ones such as Gloria Steinem, Tom Wolfe, Murray Kempton, and Tom Wicker aired their grievances in public: too strict control by editors; excessive credit given to official sources of information; not enough blacks and women in the newsrooms; not enough staff participation in policy matters; low salaries. Meanwhile, at the other end of the city a newspaper publisher was grumbling: "I'm responsible for what is printed in my paper and have no intention of submitting my rights to a vote. We're headed for disaster if we give in to these crackpots and perverts." The antagonism between staff and management has not yet run its course. A second counterconvention was convened in 1973 in Washington.

Nevertheless, American newsmen are far from mounting European-style confrontations; for the time being their protest is limited to words. But the frustrations and basic demands are the same on both sides of the Atlantic. The dissatisfaction of journalists is bound to deepen now that sharp-tongued criticism of the "system" has become a permanent fixture in the United States.

ONLY THE BEGINNING

The various demands being put forward by journalists in different countries are only the spearhead of a growing movement. First of all, journalists work in conditions similar to that of any normal wage earner, yet exercise special social and political responsibilities. They are often prosecuted, sometimes beaten up by the police, killed on the job,[1] and, in certain countries, even tortured. They can legitimately wonder what entitles a widow or a son of a millionaire to interfere with their job merely because they have inherited a newspaper.

But journalists commit the sin of pride when they claim privileged status for themselves. The other employees of a newspaper are just as indispensable to the spreading of information as the editorial staff. Shouldn't the others have the same right to participate in the decisions that affect their future? Furthermore, shouldn't stockholders of newspapers have the privilege of not being stripped of their property rights? It can also be said that consumers have even a greater right than newsmen to be protected from the excesses of advertising.

Journalists are naïve if they think that a press not dependent on advertising revenues would become freer by being subsidized by the government. It is unnecessary to cite the examples of the authoritarian rightist regimes of the Third World and the leftist regimes in the East, for we have the example of the state-run French television and radio. Newsmen would do well to put the question to the managers of the American Public Broadcasting Service, which does not accept advertising. They already feel too dependent on the minimal Congressional subsidy supervised by the Corporation for Public Broadcasting. Consequently they feel direct pressure to tone down controversial programming for fear of government regulation. Four public affairs programs— three "liberal" and one "conservative"—had been threatened with discontinuation (including Bill Moyers' and William F. Buckley's programs). Nevertheless, interestingly enough, the PBS's live coverage and nightly complete and unedited rebroadcasting of the Senate Watergate hearings was funded in part by the Corporation for Public Broadcasting (and in part by a grant from the Ford Foundation).

---

[1]From 1964 to the time of the Paris peace agreement, forty American reporters had been killed in Indochina, twenty were missing, and 167 had been wounded.

136

Journalists are short-sighted if they think the revolt of the journalists is not a passing fad. The reasons behind the conflict are too real and too deep-seated to disappear by themselves. It seems likely, however, that changes will be made at a much slower pace than the journalist associations would like, but faster than newspaper owners (especially in America) think.

The revolt has not attained epidemic proportions anywhere—not even in France. The majority of newspapers function smoothly, their control uncontested, and the problem of power rarely comes up in periods of prosperity or among the most qualified professionals. But as soon as the paper has to tighten its belt those who feel the least secure in their jobs are the first to take refuge in attacking the status quo.

This does not mean that management should reject staff criticism outright. If the initiative is not taken to meet reasonable demands, a form of cold war can spread throughout the press in a few years. The consequences could be lowered productivity and less and less appeal to investors. Even more important, it would become difficult to attract qualified personnel.

If the owners and publishers want to avoid being saddled with a depreciated investment in the future they would do well—whenever the structure of the firm allows it—to allocate a portion of the shares to all the personnel, not merely to the journalists. Above all, if they want to avoid the day when their own position is directly challenged, they should put forth realistic proposals for the participation of the staff in certain forms of decision-making. If these prospects do not seem very enticing, the owners can console themselves with the fact that other industries sooner or later will undergo the same traumas.

Chapter 3
Journalism, Old and New

The highest paid journalist in the world does not tell his readers what happened the day before. Nor does he do any reporting. He hardly ever travels. He does not appear on television. He does no interviewing. He does not pore over files or rewrite other people's articles and has never headed an editorial staff. He is content with writing three short articles a week, which are published in hundreds of newspapers throughout the United States. This unusual journalist lives in Washington, but spent more than ten years in Paris. His name is Art Buchwald and he earns $3,000,000 a year, half of which comes from his articles, the rest from lectures and royalties. His income has reached this astronomical figure because he sells a rare commodity in great demand: humor. Art Buchwald is funny, sometimes very funny, because he makes the most out of a simple journalistic gimmick: taking an event from the news that everyone has read about and telling it in a different way, exaggerating the characters and the circumstances in order to highlight their oddities, their absurdities, and their ludicrous side. With his three short articles a week, Buchwald has become a formidable critic of social and political mores because he spares no one. Besides, he is invulnerable because his not-so-secret weapon is laughter.

In his way Art Buchwald is the most modern of journalists, since he leaves to news agencies and television the task of providing raw information. What he does is skillfully trace the inner logic of an event and thereby bring out its absurdities. In this sense, he exemplifies a new era in journalism, where reporting in the old sense is losing its overwhelming importance.

THE LONELINESS OF THE CUB REPORTER

In the beginning was the reporter. He is to a detective what a photo-safari is to a real one: the same thing without the gun. His major goal: to collect news and facts. His method: solitary research. His working tools: a notebook and a good pair of shoes. This is what is offered to beginners by the daily press. They start by being legmen, in the hope that this will eventually lead to a byline or an editorial desk. Whether research on a particular story lasts two hours or two weeks, the work methods are the same no matter what the area to be covered. First stage: the editor selects a newsworthy event—for example, a drilling site has just yielded oil in the Pyrenees—and puts a reporter on it. Before he leaves for the site, the reporter, who has never seen a derrick in his life, makes a feverish attempt to become a specialist in oil. He goes through Agence France Presse releases which the teletype has piled up on the floor during the night. He asks the reference library for the "oil" file and gets from it, say, ten clippings from *Le Monde* dating back six months or a three-year-old Shell annual report. Realizing that all of this background material has a slight tinge of staleness, he calls up the public relations officer of the drilling company and asks for more information. He is promised a stack of press releases and a more recent annual report. Second stage: now that he is able to tell a rack drill from a gas pump, the journalist gets into his own car and heads for the Pyrenées. He has to have some means of getting around but the newspaper is not all that fond of paying for a rented car. On the other hand, since his boss is not too stingy about restaurant bills (this is France, after all), he has a copious lunch at the famous Hôtellerie du Moulin in Angoulême. That night he arrives at his appointed destination. In the morning he discovers a small, ordinary-looking metal scaffold which is being used as a temporary well cap. He talks to some workers, the village mayor, and of course a gas station attendant. But he cannot find any of the company's executives—since the home office is located in Paris. So he takes notes that will later supply him with a few touches of local color and a description of the geological cross-section of the drillsite. The economic dimension? Not a clue. No one at the site can give him any information on this point. Back to Paris. Third stage: the public relations man at the company's headquarters talks to him seemingly without any qualms but remains quite vague in response to two key questions: "How much oil do you think is there?" and "Will the price be competitive with that of Dutch Gas?" The reporter tries to learn more, first from the Ministry of Industry (where, after having been sent from one office to another at least five times, he finally finds a civil servant who is even willing to state his name) and then from a competitor's spokesman who replies with a few courteous noncommittal remarks. Fourth stage: it is now five o'clock in the afternoon, and his article is slotted for next morning's edition. He sits down in front of his typewriter in the newsroom where three fellow newsmen are sipping whiskey, two others are on the telephone, and a sixth one, just back from Brussels where he was up all night covering a Common Market story, is asleep at his desk, his head on his arms. Seven pages later, at 7:30 P.M., the oil story is given to the managing editor, who rewrites the lead sentence, asks three questions, and insists that forty lines be cut. Back in the newsroom, the journalist gets on the phone to track down the answers to his editor's questions while furiously crossing out lines in his copy in order to shorten it. At 9:00 P.M. the article goes to the composing room. This is the classic way that an article gets into print: on-the-spot investigation, background research, writing, polishing. All of this is accomplished by one man. This system, which has been the practice since the beginning of journalism, is the one used by most dailies for any article that is more than a slightly rewritten press agency dispatch.

ASSEMBLY LINE STORIES

For reasons completely opposite to those of Henry Ford, Henry R. Luce decided one day to apply to journalism what had been such a boon to the automotive industry: the assembly line technique. Ford installed the assembly line in order to produce more cars in a shorter time. Henry Luce, on the other hand, when he started the weekly newsmagazine *Time,* had more time than the dailies to track down a news event. In order to differentiate *Time* from the dailies, he had to produce better quality articles. Therefore it was not to produce more and more faster and faster but to fight against the scarcity of writing talent that he decided to break down his publishing operation into its component parts. The perennial problem of any quality-minded editors is that there is no lack of legmen, but good writers or rewrite men can be counted on the fingers of one hand. To achieve his goals, Luce was adamant about bringing each article up to the level of a short literary essay. At the same time he insisted that all facts stated be scrupulously exact. This meant they had to be checked out more thoroughly than is the practice at a daily. Thus, Luce fashioned "group journalism," a revolution in work methods. To accord with this technique, our cub reporter's assignment above would be as follows. First stage: On Monday morning the business editor finds a "story suggestion" on his desk from his correspondent in Toulouse concerning new oil findings in the Pyrenees. This twenty-line memo came in by Telex over the weekend. At the story conference that morning, it is decided to schedule an article on the subject for the next issue. The department head responsible for the article then assigns it to one of the three "writers" (as opposed to fact-finding reporters) who work for him. At the same time he assigns a researcher who will assist the writer. (Traditionally at Time, Inc., writers were men; researchers, women.) Second stage: the writer cables the Toulouse correspondent to tell him what angles to cover in his investigation. The correspondent then leaves Toulouse for the drilling site. Meanwhile, the researcher assembles all recent press clippings, releases, reports, etc., published on the subject, reads them, and writes a summarizing memo. The writer goes home early in the afternoon to rest up for what could be a slightly hectic week. Third stage: the next day the writer starts sifting through the researcher's report and the background material she has accumulated. The Toulouse correspondent writes up his report and cables or phones it to the head office. Either the writer or the researcher makes a few phone calls to the home office of the company, to rival firms, and to relevant government agencies. Fourth stage: all the elements of the story are on hand and the writer, who has not left his office, settles down in his chair, deploys his favorite stimulants (coffee, cigarettes, whiskey), and begins to write the story of the oil find. He incorporates a good deal of the correspondent's report, rewriting it in his own style, a few bits of information the researcher has gleaned from the press, the statistics the government has supplied, and a few personal impressions he remembers from last year's vacation in the Pyrenees. At 10:00 P.M. on Wednesday he has finished his first draft; he gives one copy to the department head and another to the researcher. Fifth stage: while the department head is making his own—often substantial—changes in the style or the length of the article, the researcher checks it for accuracy, indicating the origin of each fact (correspondent's report, quotation, press clipping, etc.). At last, a final version is cabled to the correspondent, who is invariably floored to see how radically his text has been changed; he gets his revenge by pointing out all the errors of interpretation made by the writer and his department head.

The article is finished, a collective work that no one will sign. This way, all who contributed to the various stages of the article are slightly frustrated because, even though they have given it their best, the result is really not their work. The person most victimized is the correspondent, who feels he has done the investigating yet recognizes very little of his own in the final product. The most satisfied of all should be the writer, since it is more or less his version that is printed. But in his eyes, the most important thing of all—his byline—is missing. It was not long before Luce realized these problems: thanks to *Time's* success he was able to compensate for the lack of fame (which is a serious matter for a journalist, whose name is his only stock in trade) by paying the highest salaries in the business. This does not entirely eliminate suffering, but it silences it.

For the publication, group journalism means substantial expenses. For the reader, it may have a comforting consistency of tone. Each article gives him a wealth of facts and entertainment as well. Many journalists however dislike this formula and consider the final product homogenized hamburger. Nevertheless, most magazines have one way or another adopted one or more features of the Luce method (be it the rewriter or the researcher). According to Otto Friedrich, a critic of group journalism who was the last editor-in-chief of the *Saturday Evening Post* (before the journal attempted its current revivification), the obsession with facts ends up taking the place of reality. What counts much more than the meaning of an event is precise detail—the exact size of a prize poodle, the color of Prince Juan Carlos' eyes. Friedrich tells how one writer put the following in his copy: "There are 000 trees in Russia," relying on the researcher to supply the missing figure. This obliged the young woman to make the futile effort of multiplying the area in square miles of Siberia by the density of trees per square mile and come up with a hypothetical figure which will remain unverifiable unless the Soviet government itself undertakes an exact count for some unfathomable reason.

Any formula taken to its extremes ends up in absurdity. But the fact is that, twenty-five years before television, Luce ele-

vated journalistic form above news content. He had thus discovered the only response the press would be able to make to the
superior data-transmitting power of the electronic media: to
offer style and ideas.

FROM DIGGING TO PROCESSING

The journalist's role differs depending on whether his job is to
get new information or to present and interpret information
already at hand. In the heroic old days (nostalgia always seems
to transform the old days into "heroic" or "epic" proportions), a
newspaper had to get as much news and print it as fast as it
could. Thanks to reporters who really had a nose for news,
primitive but clever means of communication, and a fast rotary
printing press, a paper could make it to the newsstands one or
two hours earlier than its competitors and increase its readership. Before the transatlantic cable, New York newspapers
would send speedy vessels out to meet the clippers arriving from
Great Britain and bring back post-haste the latest dispatches.
When important events took place, special editions were rushed
out to the stands. By the grace of the ocean spray, news chiefs in
those days had much better complexions than now, when their
only on-the-job exercise consists of going from their desk to the
teletype room and back.

The newspaper's major function—as with any other mining
industry—was to bring raw materials to the surface. These
materials were provided by the local reporter who described the
school's bake sale, by the journalist assigned to a government
agency who would camp out in the hallways and occasionally
get a piece of news, by the editor-in-chief just back from a trip to
South America, or by the columnist-about-town who picked up
gossip at parties and dinners. The entire editorial budget of the
newspaper was invested in tracking down news to be published
in more or less the same state that it was received.

Today the investigative journalist is still much admired, as is
the journalist-commentator who may be as adroit at digging
up news as he is at analyzing it. Nevertheless, most of the
digging up of news these days rests less with the obscure legmen
or star reporters than with press agencies or wire services,
which are directly linked to newspapers via teletype and which

daily flood the newsrooms with more news than the papers have space to print. Another important source of news is local correspondents of regional newspapers and stringers for the larger papers who phone in local events that may be of interest to a broader readership.

By the time the editor-in-chief goes to the office, he has already heard over the radio what he is going to find in the yards and yards of agency copy waiting for him at the office. He knows his counterparts at other publications have the same news. So what is he going to do with all his newsmen waiting for assignments? He could actually put out a newspaper without them. The *International Herald Tribune* (the American daily published in Paris and considered quite a good newspaper), for example, only uses one newsman-reporter. All the rest of its news comes from sixteen teletypes, whose stories are rewritten or cut by staff writers.

In all sectors of the economy, when product scarcity is replaced by plenty, consumers are offered a greater variety of the same basic product, the packaging of which may be as significant in generating sales as the quality of the product itself and the consumer need it fills. In an era when news gathering has been transformed from a digging operation into a processing industry, successful competition for readers does not depend on quantity of information or the speed at which it is published (since all papers have access simultaneously to more than 80 percent of the news), but rather on the ways in which the news is adapted to suit various audiences. The person whose only source of news is television knows he can find detailed information and greater variety in the *New York Daily News,* to say nothing of *The New York Times.* The reader of *Time* Magazine certainly does not expect to find many new revelations if he has read a good newspaper carefully during the previous week. The "new" news appearing in a weekly magazine would not in itself justify anyone's buying it. But perhaps the reader has only glanced at the headlines of a daily paper and skimmed a few articles here and there. He may prefer *Time*'s easy-to-read style, its more compact and uniform presentation—in short, the magazine's characteristic packaging of a basic product that is available elsewhere.

The example of the "News in Brief" page of the French business newspaper *Les Echos* is significant. This back page sums up in about twenty small items of ten lines each what is going on in France and in the world. At the time I headed the editorial staff of the daily, the "News in Brief" topped readership surveys and some people insisted the only reason they subscribed to this financial publication was to read this page, where business and finance items, dealt with elsewhere in the paper, did not appear. The "News in Brief," moreover, was consistently late in reporting the news. *Les Echos* was put to bed around 10 P.M. in order not to miss the mail trains going to the provinces, whereas all the other Paris papers waited for last minute news up until 5 A.M. The "News in Brief" was written about 8 P.M. and contained the gist of the news that had appeared in *Le Monde* that evening. Therefore the sole service rendered to the reader was to give him in a nutshell what *Le Monde* had offered by the bushel. It did not quite satisfy the traditional journalists' canon of having a scoop, but for the readers of *Les Echos*—businessmen who only had a few minutes to keep themselves abreast of daily events—it was ideal.

FROM JOURNALIST TO COMMUNICATOR

At the risk of adding to the semantic inflation that frequently impoverishes languages, I want to propose using the term "communicator" to highlight an evolutionary trend in journalism. Journalists have always hunted for news. The communicator, on the other hand, finds on his desk all the information supplied by the news agency supermarkets. He is flooded by news and knows that his readers or listeners would be similarly inundated if he passed the news on to them in the same form he receives it. The role of the communicator, then, can for practical purposes be summed up in four points: to select, to condense, to simplify, and to synthesize.

To condense means to adapt material to the reader's capacity for absorbing it. The same number of items can take up a "News in Brief" page of *Les Echos,* a half-hour telecast, or twelve pages of fine print in *Le Monde*. Condensing implies choosing. It is the most subjective operation of all, because one puts oneself in the reader's shoes and selects for him what he should know. A good communicator knows his audience well and senses immediately when its interests are beginning to shift.

To simplify means to replace the jargon of experts with everyday words. (A French radio meteorologist became a minor celebrity by translating into simple language what the national weather bureau called "milibars," "disturbances," etc.). It also means to make comprehensible what inarticulate politicians, union leaders, and other public figures are actually talking about where they are fumbling for words or using verbal "overkill."

The most creative function of the communicator is synthesizing: grouping divergent items, linking up related facts, explaining the material and conveying its significance to the news consumer. Obviously it takes more talent to write an analysis than to produce a short digest. That is why the range of journalistic functions remains very wide: from the simple newsman's job to the prestigious role of columnists.

The communicator, much more than the traditional journalist, has to know how to handle language smoothly and accurately. Because stating facts (which the public assimilates almost by osmosis from radio bulletins or headlines) is not as important a part of the job as interpreting them, the communicator must have a perfect understanding of his subject and often must take sides on issues.

In France, the professional standards of journalists have undergone important changes. Traditionally, newsmen in France and other Latin countries have been more interested in expressing opinions than in presenting facts. It was considered more important in an article to interpret an event than to describe it, leaving a few hints to the reader as to what the facts were. The "I" still appears all too often in the copy of Continental journalists, whereas it has been taboo for journalists in English-speaking countries. *The New York Times,* for example, has strict rules about newsmen keeping their opinions to themselves, limiting the expression of personal opinions to critics and columnists. If this policy were laid down at the *Nouvel Observateur* or *Le Monde* there would be protest demonstrations and several resignations. Even *Le Monde,* which is not a newspaper of opinion, lets most of its reporters air their views in their articles. The articles of its most celebrated writers are not reportage in the usual sense, but interpretations. But this second nature of the French journalist is changing, in part because professional schools have been in existence for some time now, a few of which have begun to grant degrees in journalism. These schools are inculcating in young journalists a respect for facts and objectivity.

More important perhaps are the changing economic conditions of the French press. The decline of the once-vigorous opinion press has led newsmen to the conclusion that personalized and polemic journalism is perhaps behind the times. Concurrently, the concentration of ownership has created newspaper monopolies in many cities, which has put to an end incessant partisan quarrels between competing papers. In this circumstance, the small local newspaper has adopted an accommodating neutrality, both in style and in opinion. The government television monopoly, accused for years of broadcasting propaganda, made under former Prime Minister Chaban-Delmas a timid, perhaps only tentative, effort at impartiality. Objectivity has become the word of the day. Consequently, the French journalist of the 1970s displays a more professional attitude toward his job of informing the public.

THE AMERICAN PRESS ON THE ATTACK

It is a curious irony that, at the same time that Europe moves toward objectivity in reporting, advocacy and subjective journalism are becoming the vogue in the United States.

Prestigious American journalists like Henry Luce had for years attacked the myth of objectivity, one of the sacred cows of the American press. Even the most objective reporter, the critics claim, for reasons of space chooses among the facts at his disposal. Next he arranges them in order of importance. After that an editor decides whether the story will appear prominently in the newspaper or will be consigned to oblivion in the back pages or perhaps the wastebasket. Each decision involves an arbitrary judgment by human beings, hence subjectivity.

Dissident journalists and colleagues sympathetic to their viewpoint insist that the hypocrisy of "objectivity" works in favor of powerful institutions—government, universities, and companies, which are well equipped to present their own versions of the truth. Thus a number of publications and individual journalists, to set themselves apart from bland television reportage, have adopted an aggressive attitude, devoting themselves to unveiling political scandals. The muckraking tradition of early twentieth-century American journalism had fallen into disuse when *Life* and *Look* (before they folded) began sending their reporters out on the scent of scandal to dig up corrupt mayors or paid-off athletes. One of the better-known muckrakers is Jack Anderson, who specializes in printing secret documents which the powers-that-be like to hide from the public. Anderson checks out his material as best he can, even going so far as to show it to his source to see how he reacts, then prints damaging extracts in his column, which is syndicated in some hundred dailies. At the beginning of 1972, he delivered to his readers the minutes of Henry Kissinger's secret meetings during the war between India and Pakistan, as we noted earlier, and the famous memo detailing the collusion between the Republican party and ITT. It was he who in July 1972 rushed into print with the false information about drunken driving of Senator Eagleton, but this was one of the very few times he did not score true.

With a narrower readership and a limited impact, the underground press, which consists of hundreds of small anti-establishment, sloppily printed publications with a circulation of a few thousand each, considers itself an anti-press. Its self-appointed role is to uncover anything that the Big Media will not touch. As part of the fallout of the underground papers, the American press is beginning to stir. Even the stuffed-shirt *New Yorker,* long a favorite magazine of the upper middle class, has become, as *Time* Magazine noted in May 1972, one of the most socially activist of its kind, specializing in violent anti-government polemics. Even though practically all the dailies and television channels are still content to present the news in the traditionally "objective" manner, the most modern-minded of them are learning how to fight tooth and nail all over again.

THE NEW JOURNALISM

What is called the New Journalism in New York today refers to a few exceptional journalists with a gift for writing: Tom Wolfe (who has assumed the role of the movement's theoretician), Jimmy Breslin, Gay Talese, Dick Schaap, Charles Portis, Gloria Steinem, and the renowned Norman Mailer. The concept took a giant step forward with the publication of Truman Capote's book *In Cold Blood,* which showed that a journalist can write like a novelist providing he pins down reality in its most minute detail. Nevertheless, the New Journalism remains controversial in that its principles clash with every tradition of American reporting: the author's own "voice" is heard in no uncertain terms; the first person is used; the investigation is reconstructed in narrative form; and, if need be, part of the story is invented in order to make it appear more "real." For the New Journalists, the question of reality goes beyond a strict respect for facts and objectivity; their personalities are allowed to intrude, often heightening the ring of truth since they are not hiding behind the mask of so-called neutrality. The aim is to convey a sense of concretness to their material.

Though Europeans may be amused be the American discovery of the first person singular at a time when Europeans are beginning to understand its limits, the New Journalism is more than a passing egotistical fad. It is a form of saturation reporting which transcends subjective impressions. After accumulating details on the unfolding of an event and probing the personalities of the people involved, the genuine New Journalist is capable of thinking and talking like the people he has interviewed. This way he feels justified in putting his own words in someone else's mouth or describing an event he has not witnessed. Take a run-of-the-mill press conference, for example. The New Journalist will arrive before his fellow newsmen, so as to record the physical aspects and atmosphere of the surroundings, thereby giving a fuller and truer rendition of the situation to his readers. It goes without saying that he has to work harder; more important, he has to write well.

SHIFTING ROLES

At the heart of all the changes in the journalistic profession is the shift in the relative roles of the mass media. Radio and television devote a good portion of their time to pure entertainment, but they are also the prime source of "raw news" (what could be more raw than the image?) and the "instant" news. In order to survive, daily newspapers, which cannot compete with the speed by which the electronic media can cover a late-breaking news story, are moving in on the traditional reserve of the weekly publication: to explain the meaning of news items the gist of which the reader has probably already heard on the radio or seen on TV. This in turn is forcing the weeklies into territory traditionally reserved to the monthlies—in-depth analysis and examination of important issues from a particular angle. But what is left for the monthlies? To become specialized in certain areas, probing deeply into fields that interest only a limited number of readers.

By definition, a newspaper used to be a vehicle for reporting the news. That is no longer sufficient. It must be an instant reference tool, a mirror reflecting the lives of its readers, an outlet for forceful current news, a defender of small or big causes, a directory of public services, useful information, and entertainment. While this new situation represents a wealth of opportunities for the journalist as communicator, it also poses a challenge to the profession, for the modern journalist must be able to shift from one specialization to another with ease, and to do so several times in the course of a career.

Chapter 4

From Our Correspondent in Harry's Bar

In a Europe where trade barriers no longer exist thanks to the Common Market, the closest, most powerful, and therefore most important country for France is Germany. Yet just about anything a Frenchman has ever learned of Germany when he was at school is useless information today. If he lives in Paris and does not speak German, how does he come by vital information about this new "cousin-country"? There are articles in *Le Monde* or *Le Figaro* twice or three times a week and in the weeklies; major elections, political crises, spectacular crimes are reported on television. That is about all there is, and it is really not very much.

If you are interested in India, the most populous democracy in the world, whose economic situation could spell hope or danger to our planet, how can you get a good picture of what is taking place there if you are sitting in New York? If India goes to war with Pakistan, there is an unending stream of information via all the media at the same time and in massive doses. Eight days after the end of the conflict, the flood of information dries up to its normal trickle of an article a month on the average in *The New York Times,* a newspaper that takes foreign coverage seriously. Considering that we are talking about half a billion fellow human beings, the normal coverage of India is quite inadequate.

On the other hand, you might argue that neither your profession nor your personal taste forces you to become deeply involved in what is happening abroad. Whatever you think, put yourself for a minute in the place of your congressman to whom you delegate the task of representing you in important discussions on foreign policy. You expect him to be well informed about events in Germany and India. How does he learn about what is going on in other countries? In just the same way that you do—through the media. He is not routinely provided with

151

intelligence agency reports. The only person to have at his disposal a world undercover network is the President of the United States: he has the CIA. And, in view of a few recent mishaps, Mr. Nixon probably has adopted the very healthy habit of not believing every bit of news he hears. So, just like you—or just about like you—Richard Nixon, Henry Kissinger, Georges Pompidou—all those people who decide what is going to happen in the world every day—depend for a substantial part of their information on what they read in the press or see on television. As the Watergate cover-up began to unravel, everybody in the White House had to read *The Washington Post.* But where does the press get its information? From its own correspondents abroad, if the publication or the network is wealthy enough, or from the big wire services of the world press. Actually, the information that is the background for public opinion that will affect major global decisions depends on a few thousand men—the foreign correspondents. This is an incredible responsibility. Are there enough of them, are they well equipped and talented enough to do the job? It is a question that comes up surprisingly rarely.

BARELY A HANDFUL

It is not easy to assess the significance of the network of foreign correspondents in the world, because there are so few analytic statistics on the extent to which the number of foreign correspondents affects the transmission and accuracy of the news. There are, for instance, only a handful of French foreign correspondents abroad: if we discount the Agence France Presse (AFP), only *Le Monde, Le Figaro, France-Soir,* a few weeklies, and the ORTF have special correspondents. Each of the three dailies has between five and ten, practically all of them based in Washington, New York, London, Bonn, and Moscow. Agence France Presse and the fourth largest news service, the British Reuters, each employ a few hundred journalists.

The only country where the press has enough resources to maintain a vast foreign network is the United States, with its two major wire services—Associated Press and United Press International.[1]

Generally speaking, foreign correspondents still remain in a

[1]UPI's annual budget is more than $50 million.

152

class by themselves. Of 1,700 American dailies, only seventeen (1 percent) have foreign correspondents on their regular staffs. The only paper with a real "network" is *The New York Times,* with about 40 full-time correspondents and 75 stringers.

Time (forty-seven correspondents), *Newsweek* (twenty), and McGraw-Hill, Inc. (twenty correspondents for *Business Week* and a few technical publications) control the only other "private" networks in the American press. The other publications that can afford it have foreign bureaus in four or five major capitals.

The only quantitative study made of the American correspondents resulted from the personal curiosity of Russell F. Anderson who, in 1951, directed the McGraw-Hill World News network. He asked his correspondents to take a head count in their respective countries. The tally was updated in 1963, 1966, 1969, and 1971 by Anderson's successors.

According to that report, from 1950 to 1971 the total number of American correspondents rose from 500 to 1,339. (The three major TV networks have a combined total of approximately fifty foreign correspondents.) The significance of this number lies in the fact that these journalists alone provide just about every bit of news that the United States receives about the rest of the planet. In addition, their services extend to numerous other countries, because AP and UPI dispatches are used throughout the world by hundreds of influential dailies.

The Americans have the lead by far. France and Great Britain, thanks to their wire services, have a few hundred each; Japan, whose thriving press has an intense curiosity about foreign matters, has several hundred. (Figures are unavailable on the Soviet Union, but Tass must have an adequate network.) The remaining countries are content to look out on the world through the eyes of from ten to a hundred of their native-born. This adds up to a world total of several thousand correspondents, not half the total of foreign diplomats. But the influence exercised by the correspondents, with their direct access to public opinion, is much more powerful than that of diplomats.

BIRDS OF A FEATHER . . .

The actual numbers of correspondents are only part of the story: the geographical distribution of this small group of key men is a further modification of their access to the news of the world. Thus of the 1,399 American foreign correspondents in 1971 nearly half of them—669—were working in Europe. Out of the 300 covering Asia, about a third were in Vietnam. The Middle East, a fertile source of headlines, had eighty-eight journalists. That left for the rest of the world, including the whole of Latin America and Africa, no more than 250 correspondents.

In the framework of continually tight budgets, the coverage of each region at a given time varies according to what is happening there. When President Kennedy inaugurated the Alliance for Progress at the beginning of his term of office, the media believed an interesting era for Latin America was about to begin and increased their personnel stationed there. A few years later, when the Alliance had produced only a few minor results, the correspondents went elsewhere, leaving on that enormous continent (historically considered as belonging within the sphere of influence of the United States) only 150 journalists—as many as in Great Britain alone.

The fact that the Third World receives less news coverage than the rest of the world is both an injustice and a mistake. One immediate effect of this negligence is that the problems of these countries receive less attention from the people of the industrialized nations than the opening night of the London theatrical season. Which weighs more heavily on the future of the world?

John Wilhelm, Dean of the School of Journalism at Ohio University, notes that in February 1962 UPI did not have a single dispatch from Chile. In the Chilean press in the same period, the following was reported: A Chilean had become the youngest cardinal in history; the Inter-American Development Bank had granted a loan of $2.8 million to Chile; inflation had reached such a point in that country that banking transactions were practically suspended; the President of Chile had finally agreed to back the Alliance for Progress.

In this roulette game of news coverage, Europe necessarily wins more often than it should. Paris, London, and Rome have as many correspondents in Washington and New York as the latter have in Europe, because there are more newsworthy events taking place in these areas. Any editor-in-chief in a developed country knows his readers couldn't care less what is going on in Africa or South America, except, say, when a diplomat is kidnapped, which makes better copy than a *coup d'état* on those continents, nowadays considered old hat. Thus, editors devote only an occasional column to these areas. Limited sources of information and few articles on these subjects keep the readers from becoming interested in them.

News coverage of a country seems to be proportional to the country's wealth. A 1958 study of the press of eleven countries revealed that, as a general rule, news from the United States and the U.S.S.R., then Great Britain and France, was given much more newspaper space than news from other countries, including neighboring ones. For instance, the Brazilian papers devoted three times more space to Great Britain than to nearby Argentina; the Indian press gave more space to France than to neighboring Pakistan. Even the French press prints more lines about the Soviet Union than about Belgium, Luxembourg, Switzerland, and Spain put together.

LONDON, CAPITAL OF AFRICA

The arrival of a foreign correspondent in a country he is not too familiar with was well described by Harry Schwartz, writing in *Foreign Affairs* in 1970:

> A correspondent turns for help wherever he thinks he can get some. He visits the American and other friendly embassies for such briefings as they are willing to give, paying the price of being influenced by the diplomats' personal or national orientation toward the local situation. He hires an interpreter, a native who immediately becomes an encyclopedic source of information and misinformation about the local scene as well as a provider of translations. He haunts the bars frequented by other correspondents in hopes of picking up information—or at least exciting rumors that he can attribute to "informed sources"—from his more knowledgeable colleagues.

A well-known British journalist has described the foreign correspondent jetting from trouble-spot to trouble-spot, equipped with little more than "a portable typewriter and a serviceable turn of phrase; his principal sources are taxi-drivers, barmen and other foreign correspondents."

First among the problems of a permanently stationed correspondent in a foreign country is the amount of territory he has to cover, which hampers his work. The correspondent for *Le Figaro* in Brazil in 1961 was based in Rio, where the official language is Portuguese. His territory consisted of the whole of South America, where the language is Spanish. He naturally spent a great deal of time flying from one place to another. An American correspondent, who had the modest assignment of covering all of Africa, settled in Lagos, Nigeria. He soon realized that in order to get from one African country to another he often had to go via Algiers or Paris for lack of local flights. Not only that, incredible red tape required by the different African republics made him wait so long to get the proper visas that he often arrived in a place too late to get the facts which occasioned his traveling there in the first place. He ended up basing himself in London, where the telephones really work and from where direct flights could get him to major African capitals quicker than if he lived in the middle of the continent.

Paradoxical as it may seem, many correspondents hate to travel. Generally speaking, they constitute a one-man office in the capital city where they are stationed and cannot leave without the risk of missing an important event. At least this is the excuse of those who prefer city life and the routine work of getting news by telephone contacts.

FOUR KEY QUESTIONS

Anyone can get a pretty good idea of the worth of a correspondent by asking him four questions:

1. *How long have you been here and how long do you expect to stay?* It takes a newcomer from one to two years to familiarize himself with a country and to build up a network of contacts. But it often happens that, just when this has been accomplished, he is assigned to a new post. A survey taken among 1,500 American correspondents between 1966 and 1969 showed that in three years 62 percent of them had been reassigned. This turnover amounted to only 57 percent in Western Europe, but reached 94 percent in Vietnam. There are some notable exceptions, like Robert Farrell, who spent twelve years at the McGraw-Hill Paris bureau and developed for himself better access to sources of information there than many French reporters. But the general rule usually is the opposite. The correspondents have too little time to get to know the country or to be able to use what they have learned. Jean-Jacques Faust, before

becoming a managing editor of *L'Express,* had first been correspondent for the Agence France Presse in Teheran, where he learned Persian, then in Cairo, where he made a brave attempt to learn Arabic. But these accomplishments were of little use to him when he was transferred to Rio de Janeiro.

2. *Do you speak or read the language?* As a general rule, when a correspondent arrives in a country, he does not know the language (unless, perhaps, he happens to be going to an English-speaking country). This is not only the case with languages most Westerners might not hear frequently or be expected to know, such as Finnish or Japanese. Only a minority of fifty American correspondents in Paris speak French well enough to carry on a telephone conversation. If correspondents do not know the language, they are cut off from 90 percent of the sources of information, particularly the most important and most available of them all—the local press. They have to turn to nationals who speak their own language, translators, and interpreters. Even if they do try to learn the local language, it takes time to master the idioms and subtleties of a language and in the interim their understanding will suffer.

3. *What are your main sources of information?* If a correspondent can read it, the local press provides him with most of the news he needs. But this has its drawbacks. In the Communist bloc and in the majority of the Third World nations, the local press is under absolute government control. Not only does the correspondent not have the means to check out the statements made in the controlled press: he also must be careful about his relations with the powers-that-be. If his dispatches are too free or too skeptical of the official line, he risks, at the least, cutting off the few sources he has; at the most, being told to leave the country. In Moscow, foreign correspondents are restricted to the capital and often are not allowed to have offices outside their small apartments. They find they can get through to important officials only if they are considered "reasonable" or "cooperative." Otherwise, they must be content with reading *Pravda* or with information from their own embassy or consulate. If they are expelled from the country, their employers often are equally blamed. *Time,* after the Soviets expelled one of its correspondents, was not allowed to reopen its Moscow bureau for several years.

One way for newspapers to get around many of the problems above is to employ correspondents who are citizens of the country they work in, which costs the newspaper less than keeping an "expatríate" there, which, with secretarial and cable fees, can cost them $50,000 to $100,000 a year. But the situation of correspondent-nationals can be very touchy in authoritarian regimes. They do not benefit from the quasi-immunity which a government bestows on foreign journalists for reasons of international public opinion. Irénée Guimaraes, a Brazilian national who is *Le Monde*'s correspondent in Rio de Janeiro, has been arrested and questioned by the police several times because the dictatorship feels he reveals too much in his articles. It took much more courage for him to practice his profession than it would for a Frenchman in the job.

In industrial countries with a varied press, a correspondent's job is a hundred times easier, in some cases too easy. The United States, for example, is a paradise of information; a foreign correspondent can spend all of his waking hours following the news provided by the important media. That is the most some correspondents do. More than once I have read an article in *France-Soir* from its Washington bureau which sums up in its entirety the contents of a *Time* or *Newsweek* piece that appeared two days earlier. It would be more economical for the Paris office to do the same work of digesting, since these weeklies appear on the newsstands on the same day as they do in New York.

The correspondents who work almost exclusively from published material may have an excuse in that paradoxically—even in the United States—they do not have easy access to political figures. The United States Information Agency was created to provide foreign correspondents with a great deal of background material; this is very helpful but is not the same as direct interviews. Important politicians have their hands full with their own press and prefer to give their time to representatives of media that reach their constituents at home. As a result, generally speaking, the majority of the contacts foreign correspondents have are with other correspondents, and this intellectual incest can give rise to some strangely distorted news.

DOES IT EVEN GET PRINTED?

Another question rests on the relations between the foreign correspondent and his employer. Do the correspondent's articles get published, and, if so, how much are they modified? Not only do a limited number of correspondents cover world events but not everything they write gets printed. Agence France Presse and the large American news agencies have correspondents in Lima, Peru, for example. To do their job and to justify their assignment the correspondents cable in daily dispatches dealing with such matters as the decisions of General Velasco's government, the discovery of mineral deposits in Amazonas, or a fatal aircrash in the Andes. At the main desk in Paris, editors sift through all the foreign dispatches to find articles of interest to their subscribers. Around 20 percent of what the Lima correspondent filed that day will be sent out over the teletypes. But even this 20 percent contains much more information about Peru than the average paper wants to print. Thus twelve pages of copy written in Lima appear in the *St. Louis Dispatch* or the *Sud-Ouest* of Bordeaux as a ten-line filler.[2]

I tried to measure the "productivity" of the Paris bureaus of some big American publications. Paris, unlike Lima, usually interests readers, and the American media have a firm foothold there. *The New York Times, Time, Newsweek,* and *Business Week* all have offices there with three or four journalists each and their full-time secretaries. Depending on the size of the office, each publication spends between $100,000 and $200,000 per year, or $2,000 to $4,000 a week. From November 1 to December 15, 1971, I counted the amount of space these publications devoted to Paris. I found that during this period, *The New York Times* printed a column a day on the average, *Time* two-thirds of a page per week, *Newsweek* a quarter of a page, and *Business Week* an eighth of a page. Thus, during normal periods of time in which no world-shaking event takes place, it is understandable that the correspondents consider themselves underused; yet they are not underemployed, for in those periods they have written from four to eight times more than the space that will be allotted to them.

The correspondents best known to the public work for dailies, radio, and television. They are known either as a result of signed newspaper articles which are sometimes cut but rarely rewritten or their appearances on the electronic media. The correspondents of wire services and magazines like *Time* used to

---

[2]A 1954 study by *Journalism Quarterly* revealed that the average reader reads about 20 to 25 percent of what is printed in a paper. By applying this figure to 283 topics sent out on a given day by AP, the authors of the study concluded that after the newspaper itself has made its choice and the reader has made his, the reader has seen about nine of the items.

be content with anonymity. Their copy was not even considered as an article and only served as background material for a writer sitting in the home office. Two reform measures in recent years have placated some of their growing unrest. Nowadays, somewhere in the article, which is still not signed, the correspondent's name is dropped ("As Pierre Messmer declared to Charles E. Eisendrath of *Time* . . ."), and, when the deadline allows, a semifinal version of the article is cabled to the correspondent for his corrections and remarks. Technical difficulties, the high cost of cables, and tight deadlines have prevented the full implementation of this system.

NEWS IMPERIALISM

In the field of world news, as in other fields, the big powers so dominate the news-gathering process that the Egyptians, the Argentinians, or the Swedes are forced—without even realizing it—to see the world through the eyes of the Americans, the English, or the French. Even though just about every country has a national press agency, very few of them have the means to finance a veritable world network, as do the larger wire services from the leading world powers.

Moreover, the politically slanted information offered by various national press services—for example, the Communist-bloc agencies—means that only part of their dispatches are usable. Therefore only the news networks of the four biggest agencies—AP, UPI, Reuters, and AFP—have worldwide clients. Since the four agencies supply most of the newspapers in the world with foreign news, they have been denounced in some quarters for exercising imperialism of information.

The same factors apply to filmed television reports. Few countries have the means to send costly mobile camera units out immediately to any part of the world where a significant or interesting event has taken place. Television stations throughout the world have signed contracts with the American networks, the BBC, and the ORTF, to rerun their coverage, which is often broadcast by the American satellite network. This does not mean that occasionally Swiss, Russian, or Japanese crews do not film little-known aspects of the war in Indochina, but generally speaking the reports sent out nightly to the rest of the world about that area have for years and years been the work of Americans.

Without diplomatic pressure or spending a penny extra, the big powers manage in this way to influence the opinion of the rest of the world. A handful of publications are used as a source of ideas for other publications around the world: *The New York Times, The Economist* of London, and *Le Monde* of Paris. These three publications are consulted regularly by columnists or editors who, before they begin their own commentary on an issue, prefer to know what the "masters of the art" think about it. Thus, they tend to incorporate in their own articles the prejudices and even the errors of the journalists in New York, London, or Paris, who after all are only human and liable to make mistakes themselves. John Chancellor of NBC has noted the disproportionate amount of influence the British press exercises in Washington—partly because it is written in the same language.

NOT ENOUGH—NO MATTER WHAT

Regardless of the extent to which foreign news is manipulated, distorted, or delayed—factors that apply almost equally to national and local news as well—the main problem is still that national presses devote too little space to news from abroad. In 1971, in the American dailies, the order of importance of subjects covered, based on the number of lines allotted, was: 1. the environment, 2. urban problems, 3. finance, 4. racial conflicts, 5. foreign news. Yet, as we have seen, the United States is the country best equipped for foreign news reporting. The fact is that the American people are mainly interested in themselves, their homes, their neighborhoods, and their schools and are less interested in the problems of the Third World and international politics. This is equally true of the British and the French. With only few exceptions, the daily newspapers do not regularly report foreign news outside of the major events in the major countries.

Because the solution to such key world problems as disarmament, overpopulation, pollution, and free trade can come about only through international agreements, it is vital that public opinion become less provincial and less oriented to a narrow view of national interest. Perhaps the only way to achieve this end is for the public to become better informed about the rest of the world. Only the media can meet this challenge. The decision to devote more space to foreign news obviously cannot be made by the correspondents themselves. It is up to the publishers and editors-in-chief. All it requires is the courage to stop catering so overwhelmingly to popular preference, which is all too appealing from the commerical point of view. Would that be too much of an effort?

Part 3
Overinformation

Chapter 1
Beyond Gutenberg

Writing as a form of communication has evolved very slowly over the centuries. Thus, like sequences in a slow-motion film, it is easy to assess its components.

Words have been transcribed in written form in two ways. One method consists of representing sounds by means of a code: the alphabet is an example. The other reproduces words, ideas or images directly, through a system of ideograms. Historically the ideogram came first. There is a logical development from the drawing of an animal on a wall to the simplified, then symbolic, representation of the hunter's quarry. For two of the world's greatest civilizations, ideograms were the only written language. These were Ancient Egypt and China, which still uses them (though Mao Tse-tung has initiated studies for the development of a system of phonetic writing). The ideogram was a major step in human progress—it enabled man to preserve facts and ideas. In civilizations deprived of some form of writing, the sum total of available knowledge could never exceed what man's memory could retain. A sociologist has observed that, when an African tribesman dies, a library is buried with him. With the "invention" of the ideogram, man could set ideas down and pass them on to his descendants. It is noteworthy that the first usage of the ideogram was for the transcribing of laws. Of necessity, written inscriptions were initially simple and precise, devoid of stylistic niceties.

The limitations of ideogramatic writing are obvious, for a different sign is required for every idea or image, which makes learning to read a life-time occupation. Until this century, the ruling mandarin class of China was made up largely of those who could read the 10,000 to 15,000 characters that composed the written language. The Japanese have succeeded in reducing the number of characters they use to 2,000, but this is still too much of a strain on the memory of most people. The disadvantages of committing such a large number of ideograms to print are obvious. As a result, there is much less business correspondence in Japan than in Occidental countries. Even very important contracts are concluded by telephone and are rarely put into writing.

The advantage of the alphabet over ideograms is that, with the fewer than thirty different letters in most languages that have developed an alphabet system, any idea or image can be conveyed. The development of the alphabet, much simpler to master than ideograms, did not mean an automatic expansion of the literate class. An obstacle to widespread literacy up until the twentieth century was the reluctance of the elite to share information, its main source of power. Another was the lag in development of technology to reproduce the written word and make it available to a large number of people. It took time to copy letters by hand, and the materials suitable for writing on, like parchment, were rare and expensive commodities. A great step forward was a Chinese invention called paper, but it took ten centuries for it to reach Europe: Italy introduced paper to the Western world as late as 1276; in France, it was not available until 1348. Initially paper was as expensive as parchment; only around the year 1400 did the price begin to fall. From that time on, the reproduction of ideas and stories became commonplace. Writing was no longer restricted to essential religious, historical, and legal texts. Poetry, that "extraneous" individual expression, began to flourish. If writing remained unquestionably a technical skill, it was no longer in the luxury class of the goldsmith's art.

Printing was not invented by Gutenberg; it existed well before his time. During the reign of Charlemagne, the Chinese were already making a form of woodcut which, pressed onto paper, enabled them to reproduce prayers or decrees. Since the Roman era, Western nobles had the ability to stamp their personal seals onto documents, which constituted a form of printing. The appearance of plate engraving made it possible to produce a number of copies of a given text, but the process was too complicated and slow to make its use adaptable to wide dissemination of long texts.

Gutenberg's fame rests on the mistaken notion that he invented movable type. Actually, the idea first dawned in the East in the eleventh century; a Chinese named Pi Ching is credited with it. Well before the birth of Gutenberg, the Chinese and Koreans were casting characters in lead, which is still the basis of the system used in printing *The New York Times* and *Pravda*.

Gutenberg's essential contribution was to develop the idea into an integrated system by a series of improvements in detail. He perfected an antimony lead alloy of the right density, neither too hard nor too soft. By making it practical to produce matrices and finding the correct formula for inks, he opened the way to centuries of unchanging practice. Gutenberg's own fate has a familiar ring. Having sunk too much money into research he was forced out by his financial partners, far more concerned with balancing their books than changing the course of civilization.

But whether they intended it or not the capital investment of Gutenberg's successors did change the history of the world. From the sixteenth century on, it was possible to distribute thousands of copies of books and pamphlets. All the ideas of the day, no matter how pernicious they were to the powers-that-be,[1] could be quickly written, quickly printed, quickly read, and quickly forgotten.

"ELECTRIFYING" THE PRESS

For five hundred years after Gutenberg there was no technological revolution in the means of reproducing the written word. Even in the age of the telephone, radio, and television, the only improvements in printing consisted of cutting costs and production time by means of mechanical composition (linotype) and the rotary press. The printing process still involved the use of lead on paper. But in the last twenty-odd years, revolutionary new techniques have come onto the scene—photographic and computer typesetting.

Photographic processes make composition cheaper and more versatile. A computer corrects errors infinitely faster than a proofreader. And it can be done at a distance: copy is punched on a keyboard in *Time*'s New York office and the type is automatically set in Chicago, via telephone line. Page make-up also has

---

[1] In 1671 Sir William Berkeley, governor of colonial Virginia, offered thanks to God that the printing machine—harbinger of heresy and revolt—had not yet reached the colony. He prayed that it should never enter.

been automated and requires fewer workers. The daily *Le Provençal* of Marseilles, for example, found that stories sent in by local correspondents (covering fairs, exhibitions, award presentations, etc.) could for the most part be planned for in advance, even in terms of length. Therefore, space allotments could be programmed to allow for, say, twenty-three lines and a two-column photo four inches high for the annual dance of the Nice Bowling Club. As a result, the corrrespondent has to tailor his report to the exact line count, but, since he can file later than he could under the old system, his deadline is less stringent.

In 1970, *Life* experimented with a new layout screen. Instead of trusting to his intuition to envision a photo enlarged or reduced for the requirements of the page, the art director could put the photo into a two-and-a-half ton machine, which showed the photo in color in the desired size and in the precise page position. By twisting buttons, he could vary the combinations until he arranged the layout exactly as it suited him.

The advent of offset printing, cheaper and cleaner than traditional letterpress, means buyers of large-circulation magazines can read without getting their fingers dirty. The process will probably be adopted by the daily papers, making it possible for them to reproduce color photos or advertising of quality similar to that of magazines.

Some newspapers have already gone beyond Gutenberg with integrated photographic composition and offset printing. A number of them are going even further. The Florida paper *Today* (circulation 50,000) is setting up a system whereby writing, corrections, typesetting, and layout can be done without using a single piece of paper. The writer types his article on a keyboard which throws the lines on a cathode tube set in front of him and simultaneously stores them in a computer. To go over his copy the writer reruns the lines on the screen and makes his changes and corrections. The editor screens the copy by the same process. When the copy has been corrected and approved, a simple push of a button enables the computer to compose the story photographically on sensitive film from which the offset plates are made. No more secretaries, no more typographers. The whole installation will cost *Today* $150,000—cheap if it works out.

The Japanese have gone so far as to develop a plastic film

which could replace paper when the ecological imperative brings deforestation to a halt. At present, this plastic paper costs twice as much as newsprint and absorbs ink too slowly for most applications, but it is already being used for maps and art reproductions.

MICROFICHES AND TELEDELIVERY

The main technical revolution in written transmission is in storage and duplication of material. Tens of thousands of new book titles are published each year, without counting the mass of written data produced within governments and businesses by secretaries, typewriters, and photocopying machines. If only a small percentage of this output is to be preserved, some less space-consuming method than rows of bookshelves had to be found. I have on my desk an approximately one-inch transparent plastic square on which National Cash Register has printed the 1,245 pages of the Old and New Testaments. Microfiches like this one can be projected onto a screen where the material can be read or photocopied; using microfiches, the great classics can be stored in a single matchbox. It means that schools and libraries can have access to vast stores of culture and technical literature at little cost.

The Encyclopedia Britannica sells a "microbook," a box with a screen that the reader can set on a table or on his knees which enables him to read page by page a whole volume recorded on microfilm. Bell and Howell has a portable model, weighing less than three pounds, into which ninety-eight-page microfilms are inserted and read.

The most spectacular changes of the last few years have been in duplication. The company where I was employed in 1964 did not have a photocopier. Everything worked more or less smoothly without one, but a fascination with progress and gadgets prompted us to introduce the magic box. Within two months it was producing 5,000 copies a month. Since then, of course, it has become a way of life.

What ten years ago was a method to save secretaries the trouble of using carbon paper has mushroomed into a giant paper-consumer that competes with printing, publishing, the post office, and the press. Lightning-fast photocopiers that reproduce both sides of a typed sheet as well as color make it possible for any well-equipped office to turn out hundreds of copies of long reports or other business documents. Any secretarial pool has now the same printing capacity as Gutenberg's workshop.

The copier has shaken the publishing industry because copyright laws cannot prevent company or university libraries from copying whole sections of books or reports. How do you sell several subscriptions of a newsletter to a large firm with a good duplicator? One American publisher tried to foil the copiers by finding a paper for his "confidential letter" that could not go through the machines. Two years later a new machine appeared that was capable of handling this paper as easily as other paper.

Another development is long-distance duplication via telephone. For example, a portable machine set up in any hotel room can send insurance contracts to the home office on the very day the agent in the field has secured them. COMSAT is able to transmit a full newspaper page by satellite in less than eight minutes. The "electronic mailman" is a device that opens the envelopes dropped into an ordinary mailbox, photographs their contents—even if handwritten—and transmits them instantly to the post office at the place of destination, where copies are automatically sealed and delivered the same day by the regular mailman to the proper addresses, all without being seen by human eyes. This will cut delivery time to virtually zero, whether from New York to Washington or London to Tokyo. The Japanese envisage using long-distance photocopying for the transmission of news; at Osaka in 1970 they exhibited an experimental system which would eliminate such intermediaries as printers, mail trains, and newsboys. In each house an apparatus the size of a large television set could print out on paper tape articles, photos, and advertising, exactly like a newspaper in everything but appearance. Conceivably there could be several channels for each set, producing dailies, magazines, and books. Oddly enough, the main snag holding up the process seems relatively trifling: how to restock the paper. But one day, when the costs of such sets can be reduced to the point of making the device marketable, we will begin to bury Gutenberg. Happily for the traditional newspapers, the technical possibilities are far more advanced than their profitability.

THE VOICE CATCHES UP

While writing was making its impact on cultural life and widespread communication, the voice was marking time in the Paleolithic age, in technological terms—a sound emitted by the mouth and picked up by the ear. By shouting, you could make yourself heard within a radius of yards. Limited though it was, speech remained the only method of issuing commands and spreading information in an illiterate world. St. Bernard preaching in the open air, without benefit of microphones, was able to generate a movement as far-reaching as the Crusades.

From Demosthenes and Cicero to the present day, it was not enough just to have an idea to convince an audience, one needed a very strong voice as well. For thousands of years, the only technological advance was the rudimentary development of the science of acoustics in medieval cathedrals—the echo chamber—which was reserved for religious oratory.

Then, less than a century ago, all this was transformed in a matter of a few years by the sequential discoveries of methods of transmitting the voice over a distance (the telephone), of preserving it (the phonograph), and of broadcasting it (the radio).

The telephone, far more than the telegraph, changed the rhythm of modern life as a result of instant communication. The telephone, by carrying the human voice to the far corners of the earth, has cut delays in communications. You can buy, sell, react, attack, and check something in the time it takes to pronounce the words. Whatever its advantages, the telephone has drastically reduced pauses for reflection and has ushered in the age of overhasty decision-making.

The effect on those wielding power was dramatic: instant instructions could be sent and reports received from ambassadors, military commanders, industrial managers, and regional administrators. These representatives were stripped of the autonomy that distance had bestowed on them, resulting in a degree of centralization that Napoleon could only have dreamt of. Later, in the twentieth century, the advantages of delegating and decentralizing authority were rediscovered, but things could never be the same.

Improvements in electronic communication came quickly and were variations on the two basic discoveries, the transmission and the recording of sound, designed to make them more accessible, cheaper, and more flexible. Fundamentally, it makes little difference whether my voice reaches my New York "correspondent" by the original transatlantic phone cable or the latest satellite—the innovation is in being able to talk to him directly. With radio, too, modification has meant improvement of the basic apparatus. With the transistor came miniaturization and a drop in prices. The set, usually smaller than a book, is now an everyday object which can be used in every room in the house or in the car or carried in your pocket. The place where it is used has changed, but the capacity of the wavelengths and the number of available stations has been the same for more than a generation.

The invention of the tape recorder has vastly improved the quality and facility of sound recording, but the basic process is the same. The cheap cassette may yet give birth to a new form of communication: the spoken letter. After all, people have lost the habit of letter writing. With the cassette it is possible to record and dispatch a long business or personal report with musical accompaniment and sound effects, if desired, for much less than the cost of a long- distance telephone call. The talking letter was tested on the American market, but either because of some mental block on the part of potential users or because the telephone habit is too deeply rooted, it was a commercial failure.

One minor but happy development for the consumer could be the Ampex process, whereby a cassette is recorded to order by the retailer. Instead of stocking and selling records and tapes as we now know them, the dealer would use a recording apparatus linked up with a central studio. The client could order on either side of a record or tape Bach or rock music, both recorded on the spot from studio originals.

THE ALL-PURPOSE TELEPHONE

The telephone today is in a twofold crisis. On one hand, service is deteriorating because subscribers are increasing faster than the investment needed to serve them; on the other, a number of promised improvements are tardy in making their appearance because they are still too expensive.

When my father established the first telephone subscribers association in Paris, after World War I, he was fifty years ahead of Ralph Nader in thinking that a consumers' lobby could force improvements in what was considered an intolerable situation—waiting for the operator, for the connection, frequent circuit breaks, and long waiting periods for phone installations. He would not have believed that a half-century later the complaints in France would be the same, and much worse in most of the other countries of the world. The system in Rio de Janeiro is so decrepit that one has to wait an eternity for the dial tone after picking up the receiver. Companies employ young boys whose sole task is to wait on the line and pass the word on when one can dial a number. The situation is even worrisome in the United States, the telephone Eden, where service has been going downhill fast in the past few years. Still, as Jean-François Revel has pointed out, what the Americans consider poor telephone service can be a miracle of efficiency to any Frenchman.

Like the automobile, the telephone's malaise derives from its success. It has become a veritable extension of the body of contemporary man and requires social as well as technical investment. The crisis is endemic and will remain so.

Many improvements that are already technically possible are likely to take considerably longer to implement than presently predicted; when they do come, they will first be of service to wealthier clients—namely, business corporations. This certainly will be true of the Picturephone or the telephone-television which enables both parties to see each other while speaking. A call by Picturephone will cost ten times as much as an ordinary communication because dozens of telephonic circuits are needed to transmit the image. A trial setup between Chicago, Pittsburgh, and Washington yielded unsatisfactory results, and predictions are that not even 1 percent of American telephones could be equipped with the service by 1980. RCA is working on developing an intermediary device, the Videovoice, which uses fewer telephones lines because it transmits only still pictures, which would be useful for the exchange of documents during business calls.

What about improvements for the general public? The automatic world system will place every country within range of the phone dial. There are two ways to view such "progress." It will be a heady feeling the first time you call a friend in San Francisco by direct dialing from Paris, unless of course you wake him up in the middle of the night. The second time you do it, you'll notice that the international automatic switchboard is busy. If you manage to get to that point, you'll find the circuits of the country you're trying to reach are overloaded. By the time you are finally able to dial the person you want to reach, you may think very seriously about going back to putting pen to paper. In the pre-automatic era,[2] the operator would have made all the repeated efforts to get the call through for the caller. But repeated dialing by oneself does bring home the fact that the systems have to be improved to adapt to the self-service, direct-dialing age. There is the amplifier which allows you to get on with other work while waiting (which could eventually put all those Brazilian youngsters out of work); there is also push-button dialing, which is much faster than the circular system. The memory incorporated into the set retains and repeats frequently used numbers. There is a system for transferring calls received in your absence to wherever you are; for offices, a telephone conference device provides for multiple participation in a conversation among callers across the country and around the world.

Some of these services are available in the United States, only a few in Europe. They do not alter the basic principle of telephonic exchanges, but make them more flexible and practical. If it takes decades for these improvements to be made on a large scale, it is simply because society can only effect this huge capital-intensive modernization at a snail's pace.

THE LANGUAGE OF THE IMAGE

The discoveries which made it possible to capture and reproduce mobile images (cinema) and to transmit them across distances (television) seem to have been the most pleasurable gifts of the twentieth century to the masses. It was with some skepticism that the public went to the showings of the first "movies" at the end of the last century, but the image was so captivating that ever since man has been unable to turn his eyes away from the succession of silent, talking, and widescreen movies, and television.

The telephone provided transmission of a form of expression as old as the spoken word. The cinema, like writing before it,

---

[2]Automatic dialing can contribute to the freedom of expression. Since the Greek colonels installed their ultramodern telephone system, Mikis Theodorakis' friends can call him in Paris—cheaply—from a café without fear of the line being tapped.

called for the invention of a new means of expression, a fresh language. The cinema did for imagination and aesthetics what writing had done for logic and intellectual precision.

When television burst upon civilization the language of the image had already been created, but television offered possibilities of distribution analogous to those the telephone had provided for the spoken word.

We cannot attribute the invention of television to a single man in the way the telephone is credited to Alexander Graham Bell. Many people made their contributions, Bell himself among them. In 1880 the press reported Bell's research had been entirely successful and described the "visual telephone." But it was one of many false starts. France's contribution was the invention around 1900 of the word "television" by a man named Perskyi. The term prevailed over many other alternatives —diaphote, telectroscope, photophone, telephotograph, phototelegraph, radiovisor, and telephonoscope.

While the public at large discovered television after World War II, the BBC had established regular service as early as 1936 and 40,000 sets were in operation on the eve of the Second World War.

After 1950, there was a worldwide upsurge in the purchase of television sets. Twenty years later there were 225 million TV sets (a third of these in the United States) lighting up each day in relays as the sun went down. Thus the world was ready for the first planetary spectacle worthy of the name: the conquest of the moon.

Existing or projected improvements like color, large wall screens, and even the third dimension may not change television-watching habits much, but they will certainly serve to further blur the line between the audio-visual and real life.

THE TRANSMISSION EXPLOSION

In the next twenty years, two already discernible modifications will alter our audio-visual society. One will revolutionize transmission; the other, television.

The first will multiply the worldwide possibilities of message transmission, by satellite or cable. The telephone, the computer, television, and a host of other devices demand it for their quantitative expansion and the more powerful circuits coming into use.

In fact, the entire world transmission network is being re-structured. By modifying existing telephone connections it will be possible to develop a "digital" system providing for the transmission of 100 times more messages than at present.[3] We are speaking now of geometric progression. The first satellite, *Early Bird,* went into orbit in 1965 and provided 240 communications circuits for a period of eighteen months—an investment on the order of $26,000 per circuit per year. In January 1971, *Intelsat 4* was launched with 5,000 circuits for seven years, cutting the investment per circuit per year to something over $1,000.

Cable technology, spurred on by competition from the satellites, is making giant strides as well. The British are experimenting with a megacable which could transmit either 300,000 simultaneous telephone conversations (the most powerful now in service transmits 90,000 simultaneous conversations) or 200 television circuits.[4] These developments have revived planning for a new transatlantic cable, which the launching of Early Bird had seemed to doom.

A genuine world transmission network will exist the day the price of communication between any points on the globe is the same, no matter how close or distant. The main cost is, in fact, ground connections, which satellites will make irrelevant. It will cost the same for a Parisian to telephone someone in Paris or Sidney, Australia. Considering that by 1980 75 percent of the capitalist world's production will be controlled by 200 multinational companies, it seems reasonable that each one would have its own private communications satellite or share in one. That way it would cost the same for an executive to talk to a colleague on the floor below or on the other side of the world. Since satellites can also transmit images and so reproduce documents, most of the time executives now spend in jet planes could be saved through teleconferences. It could even revive the custom of going home for lunch.

The most impressive factor in this vast effort to multiply and modify circuits is the size of the investment involved. The only

[3]Sound waves will be broken down into numerical signals, which means far more can be sent simultaneously down the line. At the receiving end, a computer will reconstitute the signals into sounds.

[4]The Bell Laboratories expect by 1990 to have glass fiber cables transmitting laser beams, theoretically capable of sending 100 million conversations simultaneously.

calculations made have been for the United States, which is way ahead in this field. A.T.&T., by far the biggest company in the field with its more than   million employees, absorbed a quarter of the available capital o the U.S. financial markets in 1970.

Predictions are that, from 1980 on, $40 billion annually will be invested in communications (television, telephone, and satellite)—that is, the value of all the present installations in the United States. In the intervening decade, capital expenditure on communications will amount to 280 billion dollars, or a quarter more than the G.N.P. of France in 1972. For the first time, these figures will outstrip the outlays for transportation.

In the long run, we are heading toward a single, unified system of electronic communications for all kinds of messages. Separate systems for telephones, telegraph, and television will disappear. All kinds of information will flow through the network in the form of on–off signals, appearing as pictures, sound, or print, according to the sender or receiver.

To reach that stage every existing system will have to be replaced. Here again the difficulty in reaching agreements between nations could mean either considerable delay or the creation of troublesome situations by private and multinational companies with both the capital and the will to invest in the place of the poorer governments.

Chapter 2

The Television of Abundance

Fortunately there is no truth to the legend that the average American spends six hours a day in front of the television set. The world's largest Gross National Product simply could not stand the strain. Nevertheless, a glance at the statistics provided by the Nielsen organization, which keeps score in the endless battle of the networks for viewer attention, shows that in the average home the tube is turned on an average of six hours a day, one more hour per day than it was ten years ago. But this does not mean that entire families spend all this time with their eyes glued to the set.

The housewife may tune in in the morning while doing her housework, hardly glancing at the screen. During this time, the TV set serves her more like a radio, except that she may glance at it from time to time when she passes in front of it. The children get home from school at 3 or 4 P.M. and flock to the set for an hour or two to see latest episodes of adventure serials. But it is about 6 P.M. that the whole family gets together, perhaps to watch the news and the evening's entertainment. The average time per person before the set is between two and four hours, a period within limits compatible with physical if not mental health. Looking at TV does take a larger slice of the individual's time than any other activity after sleep and work—certainly more than the time spent at the table. And now two new developments promise to make the average time spent in front of the screen even longer. The optimist sees in this prospect an explosion of popular culture; the pessimist an eclipse of what remains of collective lucidity. These innovations of the "television of abundance" are videocassettes and the cable.

RECORDS THAT PLAY PICTURES

Videocassettes are to the image what microgroove records were to sound. They will be available in shops and by mail. The user simply slips a cassette, the size of a small book, into an apparatus something like a tape recorder, which is plugged in to the television set, and enjoys the program of his choice for an hour or two. The Marx Brothers fan can watch his heroes whenever he likes, and the medical student can make use of a series of color films on biology. The physical fitness buff can follow his fifteen-minute exercise in the privacy of his own room, while the family will be able to choose next year's vacation by comparing a series of travelogues. At the office, a cassette can be used to explain the company's pension scheme to new employees, to train salesmen in the latest technique of selling the improved toaster, to demonstrate the advantages of a coffee percolator for the automobile, or to show the employees a film of the board chairman's yacht.

All this of course can be done today with movie projectors, but the videocassette is infinitely more convenient. Any system that a child of twelve can't learn to operate in half an hour is not suitable for mass distribution—and this is the case with movie reels, threading mechanisms, and so on. Theoretically the videocassette will be as easy to handle as the tape recorder cassette—and that will be the decisive factor in its large-scale use.

And there will be other advantages: the ability to stop the film at a particular point to permit concentration on a specific image, effortless rewind and playback, and recording off the air. The educational advantages increase considerably when the moving image can be frozen at the press of a button. If for instance the cassette is demonstrating how to make a chocolate soufflé, the cook can interrupt the program as often as desired to have instructions repeated. Similarly, a teacher whose class's attention is wandering can go back and repeat a sequence or stop at a particular image to add his own comments. And being able to stop a thriller when the telephone rings and not miss any vital action surely adds to the evening's entertainment.

The videocassette has the same advantage as audiotape over the microgroove record—versatility. The videocassette offers instantly processed home movies, the chance to let the children film and see the results immediately afterwards, to study one's tennis serve right on the court. In theory the videotape recorders that have been on the market for some years fulfill this function, but they are expensive, cumbersome, and cannot be replayed on the household television set.

Finally, the device plugged into your set can record the pro-

179

gram that an outside dinner date makes you miss, the newsreel you have difficulty following from the dining room, or the late movie classic broadcast when you are falling asleep.

Hugh Hefner, the publisher of *Playboy,* has already adapted the standard videocassette to his personal use. A television room in his luxurious Chicago mansion is set up to record five programs simultaneously. Every week Hefner checks off from the local TV guide some fifteen television films to add to his collection of several thousand movies available for viewing at any hour of the day or night. It is a highly exacting system, requiring specialized personnel, but videocassettes will one day make this luxury available to any family.

The possibilities for expanding the use of the television set are so numerous that one wonders why videocassette equipment is not already on the market. Three obstacles remain to be overcome: the high cost of the apparatus, the choice of one system among the different available ones and the kinds of programs to sell.

WHY THE DELAY?

According to the electrical-appliance marketing experts, in order to sell, the videocassette apparatus should not retail for more than $600. Unlike color television, the outlay for the videocassette recorder is only the beginning. There are the cassettes to buy or rent. At this point, the asking price for a videocassette player is around $1,500 to $2,000, and an individual cassette costs $30 to $40.

With prices in this range, even the U.S. market is not ready to absorb millions of videocassette recorders. Manufacturers are consequently condemned to heavy initial losses. Time, Inc., which produces cassette programs, is confident enough of America's obsession with gadgets to predict that in five to eight years one in twelve American families—5 million households—will have a set. But Time, Inc., is hesitant to produce a large number of programs before the uncertainty over the recording process is resolved.

At the moment, there are three systems to choose from: magnetic tape (Sony, Philips), miniaturized photographic film (CBS, Kodak), and record disk (Telefunken, Philips). RCA was working on an ambitious project involving laser and holographic relief techniques but retreated to regular tape. Not only does each system have different drawbacks—one does not provide for home recording, another cannot backtrack, some have no color, others can play no longer than half an hour—but also they are mutually incompatible. If one system captures the market to the extent that most recordings are tailored to it, the other manufacturers will have to scrap their systems. Manufacturers still recall with shudders the fifteen-year battle of the sound tape recorder which pitted metallic, magnetic, and plastic systems against one another. The magnetic tape soundcassette system won, and it is that system which is now used all over the world.

The managers of the large electronic companies have huge investments tied up in these projects, which they could well lose along with their own jobs, so they are hesitant. As a result the films destined for videocassettes are not going to be made until the appropriate player has already been widely marketed. But there is little rush to invest in or buy equipment. There are, of course, a number of old films already available, but who beside Hugh Hefner is going to lay out the price of a Volkswagen just to be able to see *Gone with the Wind* in bed? Fresh material is required, specially designed for the new medium—material that educates, informs, or diverts. Until the industry decides to take the plunge and market the players, there is no incentive to produce programs at great expense when the results are likely just to gather dust on the shelf.

There will be a videocassette revolution, but it is difficult to predict when. The date has already been set back several times. While it seems certain that cassettes will be a big seller in the 1980s, the manufacturers are waiting for somebody else to make the first move and to step in when the first victim fails.

THE UMBILICAL CABLE

If the videocassette people are worried these days, there are smiles on the faces of the men who are orchestrating yet another revolution—CATV, Community Antenna Television, more simply cable TV. The principle is simple, and CATV is to broadcast television what the telephone is to radio: the image is carried on a wire rather than on waves. Not limited to a few channels, the receiver equipped for CATV can pick up programs from a large variety of sources. Radio was invented after the telephone and had the advantage of carrying a voice without a wire. With cable television progress was made in reverse, by considerably enlarging the number of stations and for the first time creating the possibility of a two-way contact between the viewer and the station.

CATV is neither an invention nor a discovery, it is simply the adaptation of an existing system. Since television waves travel in a straight line there are blind spots where reception is poor or nonexistent. This is why, in the United States as well as in France, residents of a town cut off by hills from the transmitter connect by cable to a collective antenna on an appropriate high point. It is very useful in Manhattan, where the concentration of high-rise buildings makes reception particularly distorted. It quickly became clear that these installations designed originally to improve picture quality could be used for a number of other things, like the transmission of programs distinct from those picked up on the collective antenna. It is exactly the same idea as closed-circuit television systems used by business firms or educational institutions to make participation possible for people outside lecture halls or boardrooms too small to accommodate them.

CATV seems to be a far less hazardous undertaking than the videocassette venture, since more than 5 million American households are already equipped for cable. An official commission, in its report "The Television of Abundance," published at the end of 1971, predicted that from 40 to 60 percent of Americans will have cable TV by 1980. Various firms, civic groups, consumer organizations and universities are already scrambling for licenses to transmit in a particular city or neighborhood.

At present cables normally have about ten circuits, but in the future will have no fewer than twenty and as many as forty, of which several will be two-way, allowing for an exchange of signals between the viewer and the transmitter.

The uses of the cable can be divided into two distinct categories: individual television and services. It has been projected that every community will have its own station catering to its own needs. It will cover such things as the Municipal Council meeting, the wedding of the corner garage owner, news of a forthcoming cattle vaccination program, and previews o films that will be shown in the local movie house (if there still is one). These subjects may not be of overwhelming interest, but they are the bread and butter of the local newspaper. In larger towns there will probably be several channels to satisfy the most varied tastes.

It will also be possible to watch first-run films or theatrical performances at home. This will require some means of payment—probably an electronic credit card—to activate and pick up transmission. The idea is hardly new: one only has to think of Paris at the turn of the century, when the telephone network was being built; it was possible to subscribe to the "theatrephone" and hear through the telephone receiver performances at the Comédie Française. In one of his letters to Reynaldo Hahn, Marcel Proust mentions having heard a complete production of *Pelléas et Mélisande* on the phone. In the future, specialized TV channels will compete for the dissemination of news with specialized magazines, which at the moment feel, with some justification, that they have been immune to the inroads of television. But it is quite possible to conceive of an economic and financial channel with direct stock market coverage, or medical, scientific, or literary channels.

One of America's greatest social concerns today is minority group expression. And here CATV really has new possibilities to offer. Black Americans and Chicanos are increasingly clamoring for greater access to the television channels. They want to express their demands, explore their own history and culture, speak to one another—using this powerful instrument to create stronger racial and social bonds. But mass television provides little opportunity for presenting a large number of such programs, whereas CATV would make such continuous specialized programming possible. In a city like New York, the Blacks, the Jews, the Irish, the Italians, the Puerto Ricans would welcome their own "ethnic" channel so as to offer some alternative to standard homogenized American culture.

One of the most colorful traditions of British democracy is that in Hyde Park anyone with a willingness to mount a soapbox can speak his mind to crowds that vary in density according to the interest the harangue generates. He can do this without being bothered by the authorities. Cable television will provide an electronic version of this forum. In New York there is an experimental "open channel" which will soon be a regular feature in every American town on the cable system. On this channel, any group, however small in number, can present its speakers, discussions, or entertainment to 90,000 subscribers in Manhattan. The service has been in existence since a government regulation began requiring each cable network operator to place at least one channel at the public's disposal. As Theodora Sklover, who manages Manhattan's "open channel," explains it, even the American Nazi Party could express its point of view. That's what free access is all about.

Whether it serves to further democratic expression or simply as a catharsis for a particular group, all potential users will have to master the technology of image production. The Alternate Media Center has taken over an old Greenwich Village movie house and provides courses in handling video cameras and recorders; equipment is lent to groups that want to make their own programs. The first experiment along these lines in France has a more commercial than social character. In a housing development at Port-Sud, outside Paris, residents prepare their own programs. Instead of staging debates in public meeting halls, they go to the studio, and the spectators do not have to leave their own living rooms.

TV SERVICING THE HOME

A society must keep its citizens informed if it is to survive. In a village, notices outside public buildings announce weddings, repairs of the electrical network, or an opening for the job of assistant highway surveyor. There was a time when urgent news was distributed by a town crier, armed with bell or drum and a loud voice, who stopped at virtually every street corner to shout his message. When the community grows and spreads, a local newspaper becomes a necessity. Now with a television network confined to as few as a hundred houses, information can come straight into the living room.

In modern urban complexes, CATV is in direct competition with the press. For the first time, the local paper is up against an electronic medium capable of providing most of a newspaper's services, even to the point of carrying classified ads.

There is no reason why an average-sized city should not have a channel entirely devoted to sports and horse racing. This possibility has moved Otis Chandler, publisher of the world's thickest newspaper, *The Los Angeles Times,* to predict that its frequent 200-page editions may be cut in bulk by four-fifths within fifteen years. He foresees CATV gradually taking over services the paper is now obliged to provide, but he does not regard this as a threat to *The Los Angeles Times,* for with lower paper and production costs the profits should be even higher. Moreover, the paper will own several of the CATV channels. CATV offers local tradesmen the ideal advertising service. In Montgomery, Alabama, advertisers can buy a thirty-second spot flashed to 8,000 homes for about $5.

Whereas broadcast TV merely provides the passive viewer with a program, CATV eventually will enable people to reply, ask questions, make purchases, even have their homes protected through the two-way cable. It can be plugged into an alarm circuit at the police station. Through a "yes–no" button mechanism in each household, an electronic opinion-polling process could be mounted, with the possibility of gauging preferences in everything ranging from television programs to general elections. With a simple coding and dialing system, an individual may be able to ask a linked-up library to flash on the screen the pages of a book or document he needs. It will even be possible to "read a newspaper" on a TV screen. In just ten seconds a 300-page newspaper in a special screen-adapted format can be projected. One page at a time can be kept on the screen while being read. After he has read the page, the viewer can dial another, which will appear within ten seconds. Rather than turning the pages of his favorite paper, the reader can select the pages he wants to see on the paper's own CATV channel. As news breaks, articles can be modified or replaced in this constantly changing newspaper, which can be consulted at any given moment.

Televised shopping will revolutionize consumption. Using a series of dials linked to a supermarket's own circuit, the customer will inspect the items that interest him, then punch out reference numbers and quantities to place his order. Payment will be by electronic credit card, a coded tape replacing the signature. This kind of ordering can be done at any hour of the day or night, seven days a week, because the shop's computer needs no rest.

MORE EXPENSIVE THAN AIRCRAFT

Considering the fact that a hundred years after the invention of the telephone less than a quarter of French homes are equipped with one, there is reason to wonder whether by the year 2000 France will be blanketed by the more complex CATV cable. On the other hand, television sets are far more numerous than telephones. It may well be that for political reasons cable equipment in affluent societies will command the kind of priority in social investment that super highways now have. In any case, enormous capital will be needed. According to the Stanford Research Institute, in the United States investments for cable could exceed $30 billion dollars in the next twenty years. In comparison, all the aircraft owned by the U.S. airlines at present represent a $9 billion investment. But investors seem disposed to put money into a promising growth sector: unlike standard television, the cable system will not be free but will cost each subscriber directly from $60 to $180 a year for programs and services.

By 1980, when half the households in the United States could conceivably have cable, income from the systems should be some $4 billion a year, more than all present TV advertising billings. In fact, the essential question about CATV is how it is to be financed. The Sloan Commission has reported that the frequently abysmal standard of American television is due to its dependence on advertising, hence a mass audience. It is hoped that CATV does not fall into the same trap and throw away a real opportunity to improve the cultural level of the programming. But the temptation to turn for funds to advertisers rather than viewers is very strong in a society where commercial practices are deeply entrenched. In the French experiment at Port-Sud, the mini-network is financed exclusively through advertising. The financing of cable TV does pose a dilemma: if subscribers pay the bulk of the costs (allowing some advertising, of a local nature and in measured quantities, which provides a very real service), CATV may develop slowly, but the programs will be tailored to a variety of viewing tastes. If the advertisers pick up the tab, cable television will grow rapidly, but the programs will be adapted to the advertisers' needs, and television will have missed its second chance to escape commercialism.

NOT ENOUGH JUST TO INVENT

Several times a year, the press announces some new system of electronic communication or expansion of the possibilities afforded by discoveries of the previous years. The reader gets the general impression that he is well into the era of instant communications. Then the next day when he tries direct dialing from Los Angeles to San Francisco, his call is delayed by a busy-circuit signal. The fact is that the press, the public, and the inventor tend to overlook the gap between development of a process and its adaptation to general use. Not only is this gap quite real, but it is frequently widened by faulty economic calculations or, particularly in the case of communications, political considerations.

Among the projected developments based on risky economic calculations is the computerized data bank which would service many countries or even the whole world via computer terminals. If communication costs drop regularly, as is hoped, why go to the trouble of filing and grading the same reference information in different places? Archives of medical, scientific, or legal material accessible to the whole world are conceivable, and should be centralized to avoid costly duplication. The principle has been discussed for years, but bringing it about is another matter. *The New York Times,* which probably has the most comprehensive archives of any daily newspaper in the world, set out to put its whole library on microfilm a few years ago, then into a computer with a television screen console. It promised to be the dream system for any enterprise whose business is information.

But after a few years the project had to be scaled down. The goal is no longer coding the entire content of the archives—press cuttings, documents, and books—but only the complete editions of *The New York Times* and a few dozen other key publications. This would be no small achievement in itself. For electronic documentation to be efficient, each key entry must be accompanied by a list of available articles and a brief summary of their contents. It is a huge undertaking to provide a brief précis of scores of years of editions of dozens of papers, and it involves many years of work. The system was to have gone into service in 1970, but its inauguration was postponed by at least two years—and has now made a slow start.

It is possible to use the screen and control panel system only in *The New York Times* offices. Outside clients have to be content with a Telex message giving them the résumés attached to the key words in their queries. If they want the clipping itself, they have to wait for a photocopy by mail—hardly a convenient system for daily newspaper publishers. Furthermore, the service is offered during working hours only, and its availability to foreign clients has not yet been scheduled. Despite the limita-

187

tions, the system represents a monumental effort, so costly that it will be very difficult to operate in the black. The technology is relatively conventional—computer and microfilm—but vastly complicated programming is needed. As usual, the bottleneck can be traced to the human brain, which has the task of condensing and classifying the material.

On occasion, the miscalculation of one company trying to initiate a technological advance results in retreat by all others. On August 28, 1967, CBS announced the launching in 1970 of EVR, a videocassette system developed in its laboratories. With the early announcement, they hoped to cut the ground out from under competitors known to be working actively on similar projects. CBS representatives visited manufacturers of electronic equipment and publishing houses in all the industrial countries. To the electronic manufacturers, they proposed associate manufacturing contracts for the EVR equipment, and to publishers they offered exclusive contracts for sale of their programs on cassettes. CBS retained exclusive recording rights, and set up a European operation with headquarters in Britain. Establishing links with Hachette of France, Mondadori of Italy, and the Swiss Editions Rencontre, CBS believed it had brought under one umbrella the most powerful enterprises in those countries and could insure EVR's success from the outset. The problems began when the EVR partners were incapable of establishing a firm, fixed price for the cassettes. By the 1970 target date, not even the demonstration material was available, although prospective customers were assured that it did exist. In the meantime, CBS's competitors announced the imminent introduction of their own systems, and EVR's partners were no longer sure of having backed the right horse. Their doubts went deeper with each postponement of the launch date, Then, in December 1971, more than four years after the announcement of EVR, CBS said it would not manufacture the cassettes; it would only prepare the programs. CBS thus acknowledged a pre-natal videocassette crisis and thereby aggravated it severely. Who then would be willing to undertake the kind of risk involved after the American giant's retreat from a failure that had cost a cool $10 million?

Chapter 3

Knowing It All, Instantly, Anywhere

Night had already fallen on June 19, 1815, in Ostend, Belgium, when a weary rider, who had ridden his horse into the ground, leapt from the saddle to the deck of a waiting ship that was already weighing anchor. The following day the same man spurred a fresh horse mercilessly from Folkestone, England, to the London stock exchange. There he found Nathan Rothschild leaning against a pillar and whispered briefly into his ear. The other brokers watched this out of the corners of their eyes, for Rothschild was a powerful man known to have reliable sources of information. Rothschild, on receipt of his news, began to sell stock; the entire exchange followed suit. Everybody thought Rothschild was unloading because he had the first news of a Napoleonic victory at Waterloo. If the Corsican was once more to hold sway over Europe it would be a grave threat to British prosperity. Stock values plummeted, but then Rothschild began buying everything up low. Some hours later, the news of Wellington's victory reached the British capital and the market took wings. Rothschild had made another fortune.

By sending a personal observer to the battle and organizing a precisely scheduled, traditional communications technique—the horse and the wind-driven ship—Rothschild received a key piece of information at the critical moment. The financial flair that made him sell initially rather than buy heavily allowed his plan to yield even greater profit. This legendary market coup shows that information is valuable raw material. It has to be detected, extracted, and above all carefully utilized, because errors in handling it can mean disaster. Apart from the massive increase in available information and new transmission techniques, the great change since Waterloo is that the importance of the news has become generally recognized and it has become an intimate part of daily life. Plastic and transistorized gadgets still exercise their fascination, but what really counts is the information they divulge and the impact that it has on society.

BEFORE THE DELUGE

From Marathon to Waterloo, the most pressing thing after a battle was to make the victory or defeat known. It took a few hours for the Greek runner to reach Athens after the battle of Marathon (the runner became one of information's first heroes, though legend has it that he fell dead at the end of the race). Rothschild's messenger made it in a day. But more often it took several days or weeks to bear the tidings of battle, as was true of Caesar's Gallic wars, Napoleon's successful campaign in Egypt, or Custer's battles in the West. When the news finally did come through, it might understandably be greeted with disbelief, particularly if the news was bad: error was such an everyday matter in communication. Until this century, the news in general could be characterized as scarce, late, expensive, and usually wrong. To risk a fortune or coup on such a questionable commodity was a dubious venture indeed.

The press was virtually nonexistent before the eighteenth century, when gazettes with circulations in the hundreds began to appear. A provincial French village would learn of the King of France's death some weeks after his burial. That same village was unlikely to hear anything at all of the demise of an English monarch. There were no statisticians to proclaim to the world that carriage production was on the increase, no journalists to question the chancellor after his audience with the king. The court at Versailles, to the frustration of those barred from it, was a giant rumor mill, the major vantage point to study changes in government and policies. There could be no popular protest at the imprisonment of an intellectual like the Marquis de Sade because hardly anyone knew he was an intellectual, much less that he had been imprisoned.

The withholding of information was a classic practice of governments. There was little reason to fear a revolt spreading when downtrodden peasants set a few châteaux on fire, for the news hardly got beyond the adjoining parishes. In France, Germany, or Russia, few people strayed far from their own land; in fact, to do so without authorization was illegal. The French

Revolution could not have taken place without an information revolution. Though there had been no technological innovations to speak of, posters, pamphlets, and travelers were disseminating unheard-of ideas in a matter of months. This new custom of spreading information and disseminating new ideas in itself had a greater impact on the nineteenth century than Samuel Morse's invention of the telegraph.

It was in the still-recent past that an almost instinctive suspicion of news developed, since for thousands of years information that was distorted or simply wrong arrived too late to make any real difference. Thus, not only was the vehicle less important than the content, but the role of the news itself was determined by its credibility. The same is true today. One can just as easily be wrong in refusing to believe a piece of correct information as in placing too much trust in inaccurate news.

For example, there could have been nothing more crucial to Hitler than getting his hands on the plans for the Allied invasion of Normandy. And in fact he had them, thanks to the master spy "Cicero," a valet of the British Ambassador in Turkey. Even though the Nazi general staff had verified the accuracy of Cicero's earlier information on Allied movements, neither the generals nor Hitler believed plans for "Overlord" were authentic. And so a piece of priceless information became worthless.

More recently, a survey of Moroccan villages showed that, although 88 percent of the inhabitants had heard of the American lunar flights, 63 percent did not believe the news. It is not enough to spread news; cultural gaps must be hurdled to insure its credibility.

It is equally dangerous to base a policy on inadequate information. In the depression year of 1936, when statistics indicated unemployment was rife, the Popular Front government of Léon Blum in France decided to reduce the work week to forty hours. The idea was to force industrialists to take on more workers and thus reduce unemployment. Unfortunately, the statisticians had not yet developed techniques for averaging out seasonal fluctuations, and the figures available to the French government disguised the fact that production was already picking up again and unemployment was in fact falling. The abrupt establishment of the forty-hour week had too sudden an impact on industry's productive capacity, stifled the recovery-in-progress, and plunged the country into a new round of economic difficulties which brought down the Blum government several months later. Even today, it is not unusual for a business to be approaching bankruptcy without the firm's awareness, because of faulty accounting or want of adequate information.

THE NEWS FAUCET

In the century between the invention of the telegraph in 1840 and the outbreak of World War II, all the foundations of modern mass information were laid: the rotary press (1847), the telephone (1870), radio (1922), and television (1930). The fall of kingdoms and disintegration of empires ushered in the idea of freedom of expression. New political and material conditions meant the destruction of centuries-old patterns of thought and behavior. Once scarce, slow in arriving, costly, and inaccurate, the news became abundant, instantaneous, cheap, and precise.

Previously, the informed man was a privileged being; now he is a mere consumer who is quite prepared to squander his news resources. He may still hesitate before throwing out food or leaving a book he has purchased unopened, but he does not bat an eyelid when his market-bought fish is wrapped in a newspaper whose purchaser merely scanned the headlines. Periodicals pile up on the tables of subscribers who have no time to read them. Radios and television sets are idle much of the time while the torrent of information they offer is picked up by a succession of small minorities of available listeners.

The price of news has become absurdly low. For the cost of a week's supply of meat, the reader can buy an annual subscription to a daily paper providing him with dozens of pages crammed with articles. As for the news on radio and television, it is either free, as in the U.S., or the set owner is subject to a "subscription" fee, as in Europe and Japan, rarely more than $30 a year.

In fact, the news is a by-product of advertising, and because access to news is within range of virtually everyone's budget, news in democratic societies is one of the most available social products. Perhaps because of this, the quality of news is the area where the most progress has yet to be made. Examination of the quantity of news gathered in a single day is not assurance of its quality. The growth of the news professions has been accompanied by increasing reliability and a more demanding public. Nevertheless, exaggeration, generalization, oversimplification, omission, misinterpretation, to say nothing of basic factual error, still mar the disseminated message. Inaccuracies and untruths are all the more dangerous in that the prestige of the various media leads to the belief that the content is worthy of the package, and error is sown in the minds of people who, unlike their forebears, have not been alerted to lending a skeptical ear to everything they are told. Of course, the major portion of information is generally correct, whereas a century ago the reverse was true. But this fact makes the little that is wrong still more dangerous, because trusting readers, even the most attentive, have no way of distinguishing the few errors from the largely accurate news.

THE WORLD AT YOUR FINGERTIPS

If the inventions that are the base of modern communications date from before 1940, the multiplicity of refinements made since World War II, particularly since 1960, have given them almost total flexibility. Transistors, satellites, computers, and photocopying devices have put the world at man's fingertips—theoretically at least. News is received from anywhere in the world virtually as it happens, regardless of the subject or where the information is stored.

Wherever it happens: Every community on the planet has telephones or at least a radio transmitter. Journalists are widespread. If none are at the local scene, there are people capable of reporting what happened. Portable movie and television cameras make it possible to transmit pictures from the most inaccessible areas, whether under the sea or in outer space. The only limits, which are far from negligible, are political. It can be more dangerous to take a photo of an unauthorized site in the USSR than to go down into a volcano with a movie camera.

Whenever it happens: Radio made direct reporting possible, bringing to millions of listeners political speeches and sports events. The latest development is Mondovision, by which satellites can transmit an event to the entire planet as it happens. Thus, at 3 A.M. French families in Normandy watched the first step taken on the moon, and the Japanese saw the finals of the soccer World Cup as they had breakfast. The fascination lies in the sensation that "this is going on right now before my very own eyes."

Direct coverage is most controversial when it influences and changes events themselves. Students manning the barricades in Paris in May 1968 heard radio descriptions of the movements of police units and could take measures to evade them. Perhaps it is true that, as was mentioned earlier, an event has not taken place unless the media have been there to record it and bring it to the attention of the public. On occasion, leaders of student demonstrations in the United States seemed to be awaiting the arrival of anticipated TV camera crews before going into action.

Wherever you are: Although the written press is not the front runner in the technological speed race, the reader looking for sifted and digested information is happy to know that he can find in any of the world's large cities a copy of *Time* or *Newsweek,* which print simultaneous editions in several continents. Here again, whatever difficulties these publications encounter are political rather than technical. In any event, man is never too far from some source of information, even if it is only the radio. I remember being in a jet airliner over Venezuela at the same time the crew of Apollo 8 was splashing down in the Pacific. Our French pilot realized that most of the passengers were extremely interested in the moon flight and provided us with a loudspeaker account of what happened during and after splashdown. Winging along at over 500 miles an hour, we were able to follow second by second the end of a space flight taking place on the far side of the planet. Cultural and political differences today are the sole obstacle to the presentation of an objective supply of information, and such differences can undo what electronics creates. The information is available, but if you happen to be traveling in Kabul or Jakarta you can be left in total ignorance through lack of knowledge of the local language.

To retain our links with the world wherever we may be, all means of communication will have to become genuinely portable. This is now technologically, if not yet economically, possible. For years the Japanese and others have been able to visit temples on Sunday with a transistor pocket radio and an ear plug. In this way they can attempt to synthesize Buddhist serenity and the excitement of a baseball game. But miniaturization has other compensations. In the United States a gadget-minded company president can avail himself of a Portable Executive Phone, an attaché case–type appliance containing a telephone which works almost adequately.

The automobile seems heaven-sent for the accumulation of communication gadgets. The automobile telephone already exists. For the present, however, in France it can be as expensive as the car it is fitted to, and it works only within a radius of twenty miles of Paris. Connections will inevitably extend throughout France, and when the price is low enough many families will take off for the weekend with a telephone in the car, since it will probably still be difficult to get a regular phone installed in a country cottage outside Paris. Those two or three hours Sunday evening spent in traffic returning to the city can be used for chats with friends also caught in traffic jams. Telex for the car has also been developed commercially and will someday transform the lives of doctors and other professionals who have to be on call for emergencies. While the doctor is with one patient, the equipment in his car will be typing out the names and symptoms of other patients who have left messages. It is also conceivable that videocassettes can be used in the car, but cable television in a vehicle will, by definition, remain impossible.

Whenever you want: American radio stations that provide news twenty-four hours a day (interspersed with commercials) can, with accuracy, be termed "news faucets." A turn of the knob and you can ascertain that no one of note has been assassinated since breakfast time. There are not enough stations in Europe for this degree of specialization, but the stations do manage to broadcast news bulletins every hour, and often in the morning every quarter of an hour. You need never wait more than fifty-five minutes for news of the world. But the big step forward in the availability of news will be automatic recording off the television set—with a clock preset to start and shut off the device in your absence.

The major inconvenience of television has been that the viewer must adapt his schedule to the hour of the program or else miss it until reruns. When French television ran a series of quite exceptional quality on André Malraux every Saturday night for two months, few people could be absolutely certain that they would not have to miss two or three of the programs because of business trips or social engagements. The same problem arose in Britain and the United States with the serialization of *The Forsyte Saga.* Soon, however, television will be able to be used much as the newspaper is now, taking up as much or as little time as one wants. The difficulty, of course, is scaling down a television screen to pocket size, though some people predict this will be possible before the end of the century.

Whatever the subject: At present, most of what is broadcast is mass entertainment. All the electronic media seek to make money by catering to the largest possible audience, trying to offer something for all tastes and to please everybody. The result is necessarily superficial. Only books and magazines are currently adapted to satisfy demanding appetites, to cover a particular problem in depth, or to provide specialized areas of knowledge. Another electronic revolution will be needed if specialized knowledge is not to remain exclusively in the domain of libraries, which themselves (except for the addition of photocopiers and microfilms) have hardly changed since the nineteenth century. But greater change is predictable as a result of computers, from which vast stores of facts can be retrieved for those who know how to feed them the proper questions. As we have seen with *The New York Times* project, the main obstacle is the enormous codification chore involved in documentation. As long as it is a matter of numbers and scientific data, coding and questioning systems are relatively easy. But when it comes to abstracting ideas and concepts into the system, it is difficult to know where to begin to attack the problem. Nonetheless, the storage capacity of computers grows tenfold every three years, and it is clear that manufacturers will devote increasing effort to studying ways and means of cramming data, concepts, ideas, quotations, documents, references, and whatever else into this colossus of the memory so voracious for items to retain. We can thus see the day when a student or a professional will be able to consult, via a direct control board or CATV, local libraries, universities, or archival centers catering to specialized areas of interest. One will be able to call up on the screen a verse from the Koran, the Secretary of the Treasury's latest speech, an obscure legal judgment, the annual report of Coca-Cola, the recipe for eel pâté, or a street map of Singapore. By then, or even earlier, the proliferation of CATV circuits and the efficiency of cassettes will make available specialized indepth news bulletins, commodity market quotations, or a profile of the used car business—all at the turn of a dial. The people in the trade call this "narrow casting," and there have already been experiments. Thanks to sound cassettes, the doctor who only has time to "read" when he is in his car can assimilate the latest developments in the profession without taking his eyes off the road.

Thus, we will be able to know all, at any given time, immediately, and everywhere in the world. Technologically, this is already possible. Yet these myriad services will remain only in the realm of the possible without an enormous outlay of capital to place them at the disposal of a wide range of people. Since the investment of capital must be spread out, the new services will make their way into everyday life little by little over the next twenty years. However, as we are all too aware, twenty years is a very short time.

INFOPOLLUTION

We do not have to wait twenty years to observe the triumph of the electronic media in modern civilization and the omnipresence of image and sound. It is clear today that information dissemination—like industrialization, the vastly increased use of the automobile, and urbanization—is one of those great progressive steps that create headaches for future generations. The problems connected with information are already apparent—on both qualitative and quantitative levels.

On the quantitative level, the overwhelming amounts of available information are having a polluting effect on humans similar to the effect of industry on the environment. Ecologists have defined pollution as the production of a substance in such quantities that it cannot be used again or absorbed by nature. Detergents clog the rivers, throwing up foam which kills the fish; DDT saturates the soil, the plants that grow in it, and the flesh of the cattle that feed on the plants. Nor is that all. Even before the advent of "the television of abundance," as we have described it, the quantity of information showered on the human mind has reached alarming levels.

How many pages are really read, radio and television programs genuinely listened to or watched, in the average American home where the TV is on six hours a day, the radio two or three, and at least one daily paper is delivered, to say nothing of

197

specialized publications for parents and children? American publishers bewail the fact that 60 percent of their countrymen never read a book. (In France the figure is "only" 50 percent.) Considering the amount of time taken up by the other media, it is something of a miracle that as many as 40 percent of Americans do read books. Information is at flood proportions in professional life too—reviews, reports, memos, and computer printouts—masses of facts which executives must soak up or risk being left behind.

Not only is there too much information, it is transmitted too frequently. A four- to eight-page weekly bulletin would fill the basic needs for most professional men to stay on top of their jobs. But neither the frequency of issue nor the number of pages of a publication is determined by the amount or the importance of the news, but by the amount of advertising that can be sold. This explains why the American fashion industry, hardly indispensable to the survival of the species, can support a newspaper published five times a week, *Women's Wear Daily,* while general news of modern science, which both serves and afflicts all of mankind, is jeopardized by the scarcity of advertising revenues to keep the monthly *Scientific American* afloat. Journalists paid by the line for padding stories to fill the space between the ads are pumping more calories than protein into their readers' brains. The audience may be learning "more about penguins than I want to know." How much of the deluge of information really interests the average reader-listener-viewer? Obviously very little. Lacking the resolve to turn off the radio or to get on the train without a newspaper he is saturated by repetitive advertisements, empty opinions, and endless details of inconsequential events. Little of what is read or heard in these circumstances is absorbed in any coherent fashion or retained in the mind for reference in a moment of reflection or during a discussion. So much time is spent in actually acquiring information that little is left over to evaluate it and formulate original or new ideas. Our channels are so plugged up that soon we may no longer have the initiative to think for ourselves. Mass information, potentially an invaluable aid to knowledge and culture, has become a form of forced feeding for whole peoples.

The kind of person who is capable of dying of thirst beside a faucet marked "non-potable water" would probably never ask himself whether some of the information he is getting might be unreliable. Not that journalists are dishonest or perverse or are out to deceive the reader. There are, of course, rogues and incompetents in the profession, but they are quickly enough spotted by their colleagues, whose sense of professional ethics is usually quite high, and the rogues and incompetents rarely get very far. But we have already seen how the conditions under which journalists work justify considerable skepticism about what the media are producing.

In a normal day's work, newspapers print the official lies of governments, business firms, political parties, and labor unions without sufficiently screening for the truth. When the public learns that it has been duped, the press shares the blame. Furthermore, even with the best journalistic intentions in the world, the speed with which a paper goes to press in order to beat out the competition does not always leave time for serious checking of facts. These two sources of error—among the many that exist—were spelled out by Pope Paul VI in "Communion and Progress," his 1971 message dealing with information.

It is the very nature of journalism to be superficial. The journalist is by definition slightly informed on a multitude of subjects; the brief time in which he has to absorb information means that, although the public might regard him as a specialist, he is more often a moron in the eyes of experts. One only has to read a newspaper article on a subject one knows well to pick out errors and omissions. How could it be otherwise when the writer has just a few hours to acquire information one expert has been storing up for years?

Even with the financial and material resources available, some information gathering is disappointing. During the India-Pakistan war, American camera teams were sent to transmit color filmed reports directly by satellite. The problem was that the Indian authorities placed most of the combat zones off limits to the press. All the viewers saw was a reporter standing in a landscape that might as well have been Texas, telling them what the press officers had told him—information they could as easily have gotten from the morning paper. Without content, an orgy of technology cannot provide an interesting program. But since the television networks spent a fortune on the operation, they decided to show their correspondents standing in anonymous fields.

Even the best of television commentators sent at vast expense to Peking to cover the Nixon visit—an historic event that had to be given blanket coverage—were reduced to reading the menu twice at the endless banquet where they had to fill time with words.

This mixture of technological marvels, of constant hammering at the mind, of disappointing content will be instrumental in shaping the media in the next decades. Even without the intention of making political propaganda or serving as Orwellian techniques for manipulating the masses, it is inevitable that these elements will profoundly transform the society in which we live.

Chapter 4

Electronic Politics and Business

Two explorers once found themselves face to face with a dinosaur. One turned tail in flight, but his partner told him: "Don't worry, they're vegetarians." "I know it," his companion said as he ran, "but does he know it?"

Shared information is the basis of all good intelligence. Wars have often broken out through errors in interpretation. Each side suspects the other of aggressive intent, and, when in doubt, the wisest move often seems to be to deal the first strike. The Kremlin and the Pentagon call this concept "preventive warfare." Only the advent of the nuclear ICBM, almost as dangerous for the attacker as the attacked, has made the prehistoric "first strike" concept obsolete. The Hot Line is a product of this realization. It has become so dangerous to misread the intention of an adversary that it simply cannot be allowed to happen. Full discussion must be possible at all times to eliminate the slightest hazard of a false move being made on the basis of a false impression. Whereas secrecy once was considered the key to success, the ready exchange of explanations today has become the absolute condition of security. The quality, the accuracy, and the speed of information have, in the strategic diplomatic world political area, come under acute scrutiny, and the importance of military information has been recognized. Less delicate developments in everyday life are slower to exchange hands and less care is taken. Consequently, it is more difficult to gauge the impact of the information explosion on national politics and business or social life in general and on the personal existence of each and every one of us.

REALITY AND PUBLIC OPINION

A society obsessed by information has a tendency to stress the short term, if not the immediate. American sociologists attributed most of the racial and social strife that has swept their country in the 1960s to what they termed "the revolution of rising expectations." Thus, they explained the contradiction of discontent intensifying at the very moment that actual progress had been made in the living conditions of groups and individuals. Spurred on by the image of what is still to be gained, particularly as shown on TV, hopes constantly outstrip results, and the dissatisfaction produced by the gap between the real and the desired becomes psychologically intolerable.

The determining factor in social evolution is no longer what in fact happens, but what the citizen believes is happening and what he thinks about it. For the first ten days of a 1963 miners' strike in Northern France, the government took little notice. But when opinion polls indicated that the movement had aroused considerable public sympathy, General de Gaulle took the matter personally in hand. Conversely, labor union leaders have learned that in a society where 80 percent of workingmen own refrigerators, their wives will no longer tolerate for more than two hours power cuts induced by labor union strikes. For most democratic European countries, a major political event is not a government decision or a parliamentary vote, but the monthly popularity rating of the party and leaders in power. Because 1970 polls in Great Britain showed that the Labour Party's popularity exceeded the Conservative's for the first time in three years, Labour Prime Minister Harold Wilson decided to advance the date for general elections. Unfortunately for him, the opinion poll is still far from being an exact science: the move cost him the election and the premiership.

The lion's share of arbitrarily determined priorities is created by the media because of the human tendency to take notice of events that monopolize the news columns. Baby seals with their large, dark eyes are particularly photogenic; because the campaign to save them included a host of stories with photographs showing their white fur stained with blood, a campaign was successfully mounted to persuade women not to wear sealskin coats. At the same time, slaughter of delightful Astrakhan sheep at birth continues and people wear their pelts without anguish because nobody has yet photographed and called attention to this equally brutal scene.

More worrisome are the inequities regarding human beings. When French peasants block the roads, students throw up barricades, or shopkeepers set off firecrackers during a minister's meeting, the press has a field day. With a little reportorial exaggeration, public opinion is deeply moved and government concessions are just around the corner. But people without access to the headlines—old people, the handicapped, or immigrant workers—invariably get the short end of the stick because the media do not stir public opinion in their favor.

MAINTAINING INSTABILITY

One of the most easily confirmed consequences of media activity is the instability that can be created through the media's ability to exacerbate certain trends. This happened during the world monetary crisis that took shape in the 1960s. As soon as dollars started to move *en masse* into Germany, the press described it as a flood. The movement did in fact take on vast proportions because even modest speculators wanted to benefit from the situation. The press in turn wrote in terms of a veritable panic. Then all holders of capital got the news and reacted accordingly, and the dam burst under a pressure that had been generated solely by the media. The same kind of psychic battering ram brought about the devaluations of the dollar in 1971 and 1973.

Any spectacular event is immediately flashed to the whole world and can set off tragic chain reactions. The form of protest of the first Vietnamese bonze who set himself on fire and burned to death was imitated not only in Vietnam but in the United States, Czechoslovakia, and France. We can go for weeks on end without a case of air piracy, but when one successful hijacking hits the headlines, half-a-dozen more attempts follow. When an ingenious skyjacker introduced the parachute-jump escape early in 1972, it was inevitable that there would be many imitators in the following weeks. Dr. Edward Teller, father of the H-bomb, is not insensitive to the problems of the media. In speaking of his love for America, he remarked there were two institutions he would suppress—the Mafia and TV. If it were a case of only doing away with one, he would choose TV. Innovative ideas, good and bad, travel around the world in a matter of hours and set off "epidemics" which, happily, are often short lived.

At one time, it was thought that the national press, radio, and then television would become the great unifiers by disseminating a common culture and language throughout a given country. And so they were in the first years. There was a noticeable falling away of regional accents as people heard standardized pronunciation on the airwaves. But when ethnic minorities in the United States and regional groups in Europe began to rebel against this very assimilation, the media became their spokesmen with equal efficiency. An inspired and eloquent leader given five minutes of air time by a television network more interested in his originality than in what he has to say can launch a political movement. In this way, the grievances of the Quebeçois, the Belgian Walloons, the Bretons in France, and the Jura autonomists of Switzerland have surfaced and crystalized protest movements over the past ten years with aggressive demands, even armed rebellion. Thanks to fast-moving and widespread information, such minority outbursts are increasing rather than fading.

The audio-visual media transform the politics of any country, whatever its political system. In putting the people and the government face to face, so to speak, television transcends the intermediary mechanisms for communication between the elected and the electors. The President of the United States, for example, can pre-empt prime time at will to bring his version of an issue to the public; whereas members of Congress claim this violates the broadcasting "fairness" doctrine since Congress can air its views only during news or public affairs programs or when special circumstances result in broadcast coverage of Congressional or Senate hearings. Nevertheless, opposing views do receive wider and more immediate coverage than was ever possible prior to the advent of radio and television, and opinion polls reflect their impact on the public, which in turn often affects governmental decisions on a given issue. Soon cable television will virtually serve as a "referendum" on the local level. The first experiments of this nature have already been implemented in small towns and villages of the provinces of Quebec and Ontario, where anyone who has anything to say to the community—whether doctor, school principal, parent, mayor, or councilman—appears on TV. Whichever spokesman goes over well on television has a definite advantage—since the TV camera relentlessly exposes the speaker's weaknesses unless he has mastered TV "style." Live coverage of municipal council meetings provokes a barrage of telephoned questions and public reactions, transforming the meeting into a public forum. The members of the council will see their power contract when the public has an immediate way of expressing its views. In this situation we can readily discern the advantages ("participatory" democracy) and the disadvantages (demagogy) of the technological revolution on politics.

POLITICIANS IN SEARCH OF CAMERAS

Right or wrong, everybody is convinced that today television is *the* political medium. Politicians are unhappy at having to speak before an audience of a few hundred or several thousand, when a television broadcast can bring them hundreds of thousands or millions of viewers. But a highly diversified system is needed if televised debate is to be measured and lively. In France, television is in much the same situation as a nuclear deterrent—it's either total war or nothing at all. Speaking on the ORTF, a political figure reaches 15 million French homes. The only alternative is the local banquet hall. The French politician waits for "his" annual or biannual appearance—if he is one of the select few whose talents or stature can open the doors of the studios—and spends the rest of his time in the wings.

The advantage of an abundance of politics on television is in restoring a certain balance by removing the novelty. In the early days of TV, any politician with the right looks and verbal delivery could score an easy triumph. During the 1960s, after the famous Kennedy-Nixon debates, political experts were convinced that a blue shirt and a sufficient television budget were enough for a candidate to beat his opponent. This dogma was shaken by the failures in the 1972 presidential primaries of John Lindsay, considered by many to be America's most telegenic politician. When all the contestants appear on television, traditional factors come into play: originality means more than charm or eloquence, and any lack of sincerity in expression is a disaster in close-up. Yet the fact remains that you cannot win political victory without using television. Since the assassination attempt against George Wallace, proposals have been advanced to make TV appearances virtually the only form of campaigning.[1] This will mean additional problems for candidates: getting onto the screen as often as possible and having something interesting to say each time.

There is another side to the central and quasi-exclusive place the media occupy in politics. Their freedom is coming under increasingly close surveillance by the authorities. In a country like France, where the monopoly situation has enabled the government to exercise a scandalous degree of control over television, the political views of the news anchorman are a matter of concern at the highest levels of government. In the United States, where First Amendment guarantees of freedom of the press have been a reassured part of the national heritage, there is increasing concern that government licensing practices for TV and radio stations can have a covert and undermining effect on news coverage.

TELEVISED BOARD MEETINGS

Business has been as affected as politics by the communications explosion. Big companies have the means to pay for gadgets long before the price drops low enough for the general consumer's use. A middle-management employee, according to the American businessman Simon Ramo, spends sixty hours a week away from home to perform forty hours work, because of transportation. As a result his output is further reduced to thirty hours efficient work, because of fatigue. Businessmen are highly receptive to the prospect of being able to work part time or several days a week at home—not because the company wants to make their lives any more agreeable, but simply because the traffic jams in every major city in the world incur intolerable social costs in hours lost, vehicles used, pollution, and fatigue. President Nixon once observed that America can send three astronauts nearly 300,000 miles right on schedule, but it can't send 300,000 men three miles away without huge delays. Let us imagine the executive of tomorrow in his suburban home where he has installed his office. He has a direct line to his company's switchboard. It can be hooked into an ordinary

[1]George Wallace may well himself have been a victim of media-obsession. Arthur H. Bremer, who shot him, wanted to achieve world renown by assassinating President Nixon, but could not manage it. That he fell back reluctantly on Wallace is shown in his diary: "The reporters will see that Wallace is dead and say 'who cares?' All I'll get will be three minutes on the evening television news."

set-up which permits his secretary to dial his number and transmit incoming calls, just as if he were at the midtown office. At hand is a long-distance photocopying machine which reproduces the documents he needs to read. A telephone speaker enables him to participate in conferences. If he is a top executive, he has a Picturephone. Using the direct line to the company computer, he types his calculations on a keyboard and gets back the figures he needs. Aside from personal contacts, he can do most of his work at home. Except for the Picturephone, these appliances are not very expensive. It awaits an increase in the capacity of communications cables and the economic feasibility of installing such resources—which could be pooled by neighboring businessmen who live in the same suburb—before such systems become commonplace.

Some companies are anticipating a great increase in world telephonic capacity and are planning their reorganization on that basis. Schlumberger, Inc., the archetype of the multinational company, is incorporated in the Netherlands West Indies but has its headquarters in New York, and its French president spends most of his time in Paris because French shareholders have a controlling interest. Schlumberger has oil exploration rigs all over the world, including many at sea. The company's present organization is regionalized, with plants in France dependent on French management, for example. But, with its increasing diversification of activities, the firm is gradually being reorganized along lines that reflect these activities: oil exploration, electronics, precision instruments. This means that an executive in Paris takes orders from his line superior in Texas, whereas the boss of a man in the same Texas building may be located in Paris. This organizational principle contrasts with American multinational companies which center their chains of command in the United States. With what Schlumberger will spend on Telex and telephone costs, the company could doubtless operate a small airline (as they already do now), but they would not be able to achieve the same degree of efficiency and flexibility.

The regearing of communications takes place at a time when the big cities have become uninhabitable and will certainly have a gradual influence on where big companies decide to establish their registered offices. Fifteen years ago the apex of an American executive's career was to be assigned to New York, where the headquarters of many firms were located. Today, despite substantial financial incentives, companies have difficulty in persuading their executives to bring their families to the city's traffic bottlenecks, filth, high crime rate and disintegrating schools. Since an organization's success depends on the quality of its employees, more and more companies are considering relocation to the residential suburbs, providing there can be a faultless telecommunications set-up. When the automatic telephone system between Paris and Nice is not jammed during office hours, the Côte d'Azur will hold out more appeal than the Place de la Bourse. Real decentralization in France depends more on the telephone system than on increased air service or more superhighways.

Eventually, company board meetings will be held before a closed-circuit television camera with the whole staff as spectators. As yet only a few American firms are dabbling with electronic media for company information. Smith, Kline, and French, the Philadelphia pharmaceutical manufacturer, has set up a screen outside the entrance of its cafeteria to insure that every employee coming in has the chance to see the firm's four-minute news program. It is changed twice a week and is a veritable newsreel of the firm's activities. Management retains control of content and is not yet ready to air panel discussions between management and union representatives, although this possibility is not ruled out in the long run. Concurrent with the development of internal circuits is the tendency on the part of the government to force corporations to disclose more and more about themselves (such as the profits from each product line rather than just the overall figure in the annual report). It is difficult to see in such circumstances how a company can deny its own employees information that is open to the government, the company's shareholders, and even to the general public that knows how to find the facts. What is to prevent live coverage of a board meeting, with personnel asking questions by internal telephone in the manner of the small Canadian communities?

BOSSES AS COMMUNICATORS

Clearly, a new type of business leader will be needed who can hold his own during public debates in areas hitherto shrouded in secret and security. The new managing director will have the qualities of a public figure who knows how to get his point of view across; he will be a professional communicator, like a journalist or a politician. When Ralph Nader attacked General Motors, the chief executive at the time, James Roche, was forced to go on television, but forty years in business had not prepared this reputable executive for such a television confrontation, and he lacked the necessary verve and presence. On the other hand, when at its general meeting in 1972 I.T.T. had to explain the company's involvement in a political scandal, the oratorical skill of President Harold Geneen averted a stockholders' uprising. Before World War II, managing directors in industry were for the most part engineers: then, with the ascendancy of marketing, top executives tended to be drawn from the sales staff. In the recent past, with costs a matter of primary importance, the way to the top was through financial management. But the increasing phenomenon of consumer-advocate stockholders challenging management policies in stockholders' meetings, quite public in nature, points the way to the top chair being occupied by the skilled negotiator or debater.

If television offers undreamed-of opportunities to persuasive talkers in an era that otherwise seemed destined to be dominated by mathematicians and scientists, the plethora of information is also likely to restore the intuitive "thinker" to some sort of eminence.

In the 1960s, the concept of Management Information Systems was very much the vogue, presupposing that future executives would be decision-making machines hooked up to computers. MIS involved putting a company's information resources and data requirements (quantitative, scientific, financial) into a computer which would arrange these elements into models of all possible future configurations. Each managerial office would be equipped with a terminal through which each executive, after an exhaustive course at IBM, would be able to conduct a "dialogue" with the computer. At any time of the day he could get the production figures of the Caracas plant or the weekly budget forecast for the leasing center in Dublin. He could introduce theoretical variants of any factor in the firm's operation (for example, what would be the overall effect for five years if executives traveled tourist rather than first class?) and have the answer in no time at all. In this way every variation under consideration would be converted into figures, allowing decisions to be made with all the vital factors at hand.

The literature on MIS reached flood proportions before doubts began to set in. Already strained to keep abreast of the stock market and retain actual business figures and personnel data, the computers would be called on to simulate programs of a cost and scope that would have given NASA pause. Given the burgeoning growth of firms via diversification and mergers, the program could only chase after reality without ever catching up. Nowadays, MIS seems like a dream solution for a society better organized economically and more stable than capitalism can offer. To be sure, computers do provide considerable amounts of information that would otherwise be unavailable. Balance sheets and descriptions dozens of yards long are spewed out by the computer departments of large companies. The sad part for the programmers who put in long hours preparing these highly refined systems is the limited use to which management puts them. Not many executives will admit it, but they hardly glance at the material.

Few places are so overflowing with information as upper-echelon management offices. The fashion for market research studies, analytical budgetary studies, midterm forecasts and socio-demographic sales statistics means so many fat volumes for the chief executive to take home over the weekend, the only chance he has to sit quietly and study them. What is to be done with such a deluge? If he can read fast enough to examine all these reports, he will have no time left to reflect on their contents, which necessarily means that he will be forced to make hasty, even if highly documented, decisions. If he only reads the summaries, it could mean that considerable consulting fees and expenditures for internal computer teams are yielding very little.

Considerable effort has been expended over the past fifteen years to provide greater information about products and their successful marketing. In the future the stress will be on better use of data, based on individual or team interpretation and insight. Only human imagination and intuition—the ability to see the large picture—enable the dry facts and figures to yield the best results.

THE CONSUMER

It is in marketing, the commercialization of products, that we can best put our finger on the consequences of the overdevelopment of communications. Technical refinements will increasingly force business firms to adapt their products to the highly personalized tastes of the customer. Computers already can compile a dossier on each citizen, drawn from lists that grow daily longer. When a single list combines the owners of cars (with make and age of the vehicle), telephone subscribers, homes with television, electricity consumption levels, complete with geographic locations, there will be a far more complete consumer profile for each household than any now available. With this instrument at its disposal, advertising will turn more to individual contact with the consumer (computerized personal letters, telephone contacts, and house visits) than general and haphazard forms of promotion whose effectiveness no one can gauge with precision. By the year 2000 when a substantial number of homes are equipped with Videophones, the carpet salesman who now more often than not telephones in the middle of the meal will finally be able to show you the irresistible colors of his Shiraz without your having to leave the table.

Paradoxically, the consumer will have greater difficulty in choosing because, like the company director, he too will suffer from a surplus of information—too many products, too many available possibilities, too much information about each of them. Furthermore, for lack of time to choose according to his best interests, he will decide on makes, names, and labels he is familiar with. He will pick Nestlé, a name he knows, over Supermilk, in the firm belief he is buying a better product. Right or wrong, such impulsive behavior will encourage the concentration of consumer products under a few hundred worldwide brand names, about the number the average buyer is capable of remembering.

The experience of recent years demonstrates that it always takes longer to establish new technologies than anticipated. Toward the end of the 1960s, American bankers were predicting the imminent cashless society. The buyer would pay for his merchandise by inserting his credit card into the electronic cash register of the local grocer, service station, or telephone booth. Four years later, faced with the depressing prospect of the colossal investment this would require, some bankers speak in terms of no change at all. But that will not be possible either, since the American government has predicted that the 24 billion checks that went through the banking system in 1971 will double by 1980; like it or not, something will have to be done to throw up some electronic-transaction dam against this flood. If we won't quite have a "cashless society" certainly it will be one in which less cash is used and fewer checks have to be processed.

Chapter 5

How Not to Be Driven Nuts

What will the earth be like when it is crammed with 20 billion human beings? There are 3.8 billion of us today, and the unending refrain of the ecologists is that we are headed for serious trouble if we more that double that figure. There seems little doubt that we will reach 7 billion at the end of the century, and population growth will not stop there. Will it stabilize at 11 or 15 billion? The current debate on how many people the earth will be able to feed is based only on estimates.

The futurologists of the Hudson Institute in New York, in order to describe what a world with 20 billion people could very well look like to our descendants a century from now, have drawn up hypotheses which they call the "a fortiori" world, which could be the world of the year 2100.

Out of 200 million Frenchmen (today there are only 50 million), 75 million would be concentrated in the northern Lille–Paris–Strasbourg triangle. They might have to live in high-rise buildings resembling silos. Among these skyscrapers, "vertical ranches" would go up—buildings devoted to raising cattle under artificial light with ersatz feed. Storing the consumers side by side with the producers is seen as a possible solution to the problems of food supply. For the whole of their lives people living literally piled on top of one another (cemeteries will be located in the high rises too) should try to refrain as much as possible from moving out; otherwise, the sheer number could seriously short-circuit the system. This is why—thanks to TV, which will have become the center of life—children will learn at home, parents will work and shop and the family will even be able to get medical check-ups in its own apartment. (Individuals can be checked for fever, blood pressure, even have cardiograms administered all through a relay connected with the hospital computer.) Television will also be

212

the basis of all leisure activity. To insure that society remains stable, everyone might have to spend at least ten hours a day quietly in front of the TV, undergoing a transfusion of images to the brain.

Does this kind of world make your flesh creep? You may tell yourself this won't happen in your own lifetime, but you can't count on that too much, because the medical profession and biological research are determined to keep you alive longer. Perhaps it is not worth having children if they are to lead such a life. On the other hand, how can you be sure that the world we live in today has not virtually reached that point? The information and communications explosion is already exposing your mind to a fantastic internal invasion of words, sounds, and images.

What a paradoxical situation. After millions of years of reflecting to a ridiculous degree on limited, unchanging knowledge, we have suddenly become caught up in a torrential downpour of knowledge and know-how which is likely to drown out thought and reflection.

TWENTY-FIVE YEARS OF FORCED MEDIA

The average American listens to his record player 60 hours a year, his radio 800 hours, and watches TV for 1,300 hours. According to these figures, compiled by the CBS marketing department, this person is exposed to the equivalent of ninety days and ninety nights—three full months—of media stimulation per year. While it is possible to eat and watch TV at the same time, a singular degree of numbness of the mind would be necessary in order to listen simultaneously to two or more of those three sources of sound. Since sleep and work each take up 120 days a year, there are only thirty-five days a year or two-and-a-half hours a day that this average person is not sleeping, working, or being subjected to noise. If this is so, then how much time is left in this life for reading, reflecting, or silent pleasures of existence? No need to wait for life in a silo to see that the life we are leading today has changed more in the last twenty years under the influence of electronics than it has since the time of the Pharaohs.

To the ninety days a year eaten up by electronic media we must add another ten devoted to reading, even if only a newspaper. The average American, provided he does not read very much, is therefore influenced by some form of the media 100 days a year—about one-third or a full twenty-five years of his life. Yet no one forces him into it. Nature demands a minimum number of hours of sleep. Society demands practically as many hours of work. In both cases it is simply a matter of keeping alive. However, nobody is forced to spend twenty-five years of his life watching TV or listening to the radio or reading newspapers. And this is only the beginning, because videocassettes and the cable are going to mean more TV programs than ever to watch. When you come right down to it, it is not terribly important that forty years of a person's life is consumed by the media rather than twenty-five. A major crisis confronts us already, perhaps just as threatening in its way as a nuclear holocaust, which somehow is still unthinkable. During the twenty-five full years of his life span taken up by the media, the reader–listener more often than not is exposed to mediocre material, sounds, and images which can in no way improve the mind. When by some fluke there are exceptions—programs of quality on television for example—they often conflict for viewer attention as a result of careless or competitive broadcasting which causes them to be run at the same hour on different channels. This is especially the case in the United States and Canada where the competing TV channels not only do not coordinate their programs but, on the contrary, try to pull in the same audience at the same hours. In France, where the two TV channels are owned by the same government body, it would be an easy matter to balance serious and light programming each night. Yet this is not done. Whenever quality programs replace variety shows and light comedy, they are likely to be shown on the two channels at the same time.

Experiments showing that the media, especially television, have effects on people similar to drug addiction are just beginning to come to light. Early in 1972, a military chaplain remarked that the lack of television programs in English had an unfortunate effect on the American troops stationed in Germany. The typical soldier and his wife were being forced to talk to each other at night and were discovering that they really didn't understand each other. Later in 1972, the results of a more systematic experiment were published by several Munich psychologists. They had asked 184 families to refrain from watching TV for a year. At the beginning, the people being studied went to the movies three times more often than before, spent twice as much time visiting friends, reading, and playing games. But it did not take long for the urge to watch the tube to return, and one after another the subjects went back to the habit. Even though they were paid for each day they did not watch TV, none of the subjects could refrain more than five months.

The reasons given for the lapse: tensions rose in the family; arguments, even hitting the children, increased; the frequency of sexual intercourse between husband and wife diminished (but infidelities did not). These disturbing symptoms declined after the return to the long, silent, hypnotic evenings. Television, suggested one of the psychologists, masks certain conflicts and acts like a drug. Many more experiments obviously will be needed in order to draw proper conclusions on this withdrawal syndrome, but taking into account the portion of people's lives given over to watching television, it would not be surprising to find out that the habit has become practically irreversible—if not for any given individual, at least for society as a whole.

SUBMERSION AND ISOLATION

Exposed to heavy bombardments of sound and light, many laboratory animals and some prisoners of totalitarian regimes are pushed to the edge of madness. The TV viewer has not quite rached this point, but under the constant crossfire of messages he undergoes daily, whether they are electronic, printed, or posted on a wall, he has the constant feeling of being submerged. He is being told more things than he has the capacity to absorb, much less to understand. Eight percent of French TV viewers questioned were found incapable of expressing an opinion about a program they had just finished watching. Fifty percent of a group of Americans could not remember a single item of a thirty-minute CBS evening news broadcast they had watched two hours earlier. People in the advertising business estimate that the American individual is exposed to something like 500,000 advertising messages per year. But, according to George A. Miller, a psychologist at Harvard, the average person has trouble keeping track of more than seven elements at a time. Questioned about available brands of a single product there are very few people who can name more than seven. We can gather the extent of the waste of advertising when we know, for example, that twenty-two brand names of soft drinks are advertised on American television.

We can also understand that, assaulted and flooded in this way, the human mind rejects most of what is thrown at it—which is after all a healthy reaction. Nevertheless, there are people who have guilt feelings about this. They feel guilty when they have watched a mediocre program right through to the end, seen a bad film, or read a worthless article. They feel guilty when they go into a bookstore and see thousands of books of interest to them, but which they know they will never be able to read. They feel guilty for not keeping abreast, even superficially, of everything that is worth knowing about.

For most others, the reaction is the opposite—apathy. They sit down in front of the TV set or turn on the radio whether or not there is something interesting on. The only difference is, when the program is really bad, they grumble about it, but go on watching or listening just the same. In many cases, the memory weakens because it is never put to use. The capability and the desire to think fade out. As soon as an empty moment occurs during the day, people turn a knob, as they would light a cigarette, and music, news, or images emerge to take over their brain activity.[1]

The discussions held in French cafés—talk that can be as meaningless as it is endless—have been ridiculed in France for a long time. But the great leveler, television, has been able to do away with this ingrained habit. True, the level of discussion was superficial, but at least it helped keep alive two habits: expressing oneself and communicating with others. Now the former gossips have switched from sitting together over a glass of wine to sitting alone in front of their TV sets. Families hardly talk among themselves any more except for basic necessities: "Pass the sugar." "We have to pay the plumber." "Nancy got back home at midnight again." "I got a raise." "No. Not tonight." Even if the art of conversation was never a favorite pastime of the masses the need to fill in the long silences led to some human exchanges. When every head is turned toward the screen, nothing else is seen, nothing is said. This is why, as the American

[1]More than 50 percent of Frenchmen questioned in 1972 considered television above all a way of relaxing; 19 percent only considered it a vehicle for information.

chaplain remarked, when an extended stay abroad deprives couples of television and two people find themselves face to face, they may discover they have nothing to say to each other. The children, glued to the TV set before they can even talk, do get some training in how to speak at school, but they may not have their first real conversation with their parents until much later, during adolescence, say, when generational conflict suddenly makes the family realize that they do not understand one another. As for what remains of friendships and social relations, it could well be on the way to dying out—victim of the videocassette. The mediocrity of TV today still allows those who have preserved a bit of intellectual curiosity and the taste for reading to escape without too much difficulty from the post—8 P.M. spell. In some circles it is still chic to let it be known that one never watches mind-numbing television. As a woman said to her husband before entering another couple's house, "Just because they don't have television doesn't necessarily mean they're intellectuals." People still do visit with friends from time to time. But when excellent programs are available, suited perfectly to your interests, no matter how intellectual, won't you say—perhaps rightly—that, by spending the evening watching them in your own home, you will learn more interesting things than going out to dinner with people whose every word you already know by heart?

AUTUMN LIVE AND IN COLOR

A cartoon shows a man in his bedroom, surrounded by his TV and radio, cassettes, hi fi set, and he says: "I really have a full life." If Pascal in the seventeenth century worried that man did not know how to remain in his bedroom, he would have just the opposite concern today. Another cartoon shows a TV viewer watching the image of a tree losing its leaves and saying, "Hey, it's fall!" The more the media develop, the more the rupture with physical life and nature widens. In industrialized countries, the automobile took the consumer out of his home. Audio-visual entertainment brought him back inside, perhaps once and for all. True, vacations in other parts of the world and weekend traffic jams are sufficient proof that the habit of traveling has not disappeared. But how many adults are happy to find the magic box in their country place or their hotel room? How many

217

hours of walking in the forest, sports, or simply working around the house are sacrificed to Eurovision soccer or to a subaverage Sunday afternoon film? There is no doubt that television gives us an opportunity to explore the entire world with a facility that satisfies even the most curious. But it prevents you from experiencing through your own senses the lights, smells, sounds, sensations of nature that every animal needs to feel alive physically. A health magazine gives this advice on how to relax: "Close your eyes, stretch out and listen to the birds sing. It's easy—excellent recordings are available at stores." In advanced countries, tens of thousands of nature lovers are rebelling against these synthetic sensations, which young Americans call "plastic." But they represent a very small minority. Every year life by proxy creates a growing number of adepts who do not even realize that they have made this choice.

Lastly, the cultural heritage of a country or language group wilts rather quickly when the financial necessities of programming force practically every television network in the world to imitate American TV. The fabulous commercial success of *The Untouchables* (the series wherein Eliot Ness shows himself to be even more tireless than incorruptible, since he hunts down gangsters throughout 120 installments) is a nonpolitical example of the cultural steamrolling of ninety countries. If ever they meet one day, Icelandic and Iraqi children, kids from Thailand, Uruguay, France, and Cameroons, will have common memories: the 1930s in Chicago. Only the Americans produce series long enough and cheap enough to fill up the empty hours of other nations' television networks, which lack financial means to produce enough programs of their own. Has a culture without the means of expressing itself on television today a chance of surviving other than in museums and "typical" nightclubs for tourists? We take great care to give young people balanced diets, but we inflict upon them more and more, all over the world, run-of-the-mill TV shows completely out of touch with the linguistic, cultural, and geographical environment in which they will spend their lives.

THE GREATEST EDUCATOR

Children are the major concern of those who wonder about the social consequences of television. Statistics show the extent of the problem. Before going to kindergarten, the young American

218

has already absorbed 3,000 to 4,000 hours of television. By the time he finishes college, he has spent more hours in front of a TV set than in class. As usual, the situation had become irreversible before people got up in arms about it. Anne-Marie de Vilaine summed it up in *Le Monde:*

> Televison makes (children) passive, gives them a false image of the world and the taste for the easy way out. It numbs their sensitivity, makes them aggressive or scares them by confronting them incessantly with violence; it deprives them of sleep and harms their vision. It turns them away from reading and sports; it has an adverse influence on their schoolwork; it gives them fragmentary information, a haphazard knowledge, makes them confuse the real and the imaginary, and makes them adults too quickly. Such are, according to some people, the major drawbacks of the influence of television on children.
>
> Others, and their numbers are growing these days, concede that television has a certain number of beneficial powers. It instructs, it informs, opens up the mind, it makes (children) happier and more sociable, it gets the family together, and some even say that they get rid of their aggression by watching scenes of violence on the TV screen.

These remarks summarize a whole range of favorable and unfavorable criticism which, as Miss de Vilaine admits, remains to be proved one way or the other. Twenty years after the introduction of TV into the home, not enough systematic studies have been made—not even in the United States—about its influences on the minds of children. The U.S. government funded a $2 million official study carried out over eighteen months by the Surgeon General, in order to get the answer to one single question: "Does violence on television have harmful effects on children?"

At the end of 1971 there was an uproar from educators when they learned simultaneously that the Surgeon General's investigation had come to no definite conclusions and that the TV networks had been consulted in the choice of the members of the committee supervising the research. Precious time and a good deal of money had been wasted despite the need to know more about a problem which could be more urgent than the arms race. An increasing number of vehement spokesmen are warning the world of the dangers of overpopulation, but they seem strangely complacent about the pollution of the minds of entire generations.

219

Yet hope is as justified as alarm when one measures the advantages for education in the use of audio-visual means. These advantages are untapped because the number of TV sets in classrooms, the quality of educational television programs, the development of a means of expression specially suited for classes on TV, remain insufficient for a real revolution in teaching. The only experiment that has gained notice is *Sesame Street,* a program conceived by the Public Broadcasting Service, the only noncommercial TV network in the United States. *Sesame Street* was the first attempt to use animation techniques, color, and music to bring preschoolers into closer contact with words and numbers. It is conceivable that someday videocassettes will make the teaching of modern mathematics available to as many countries as now see *The Untouchables.* In view of such a large market, high-quality teaching, with the remarkable methods of inducement and demonstration inherent in the medium, could be prepared by teams of the best teachers in the world and easily financed. If the lessons given by the best teachers in each specialty could be recorded and put at the disposal of each center of learning, it would be a contribution to the fight against the inequality of opportunity.

WHAT THE BRIGHTEST LIKE BEST

Luckily, the pessimists are not always completely right. Having survived the plague and Nazism, mankind might avoid being plunged into numbness by advertising and the media. The higher the general level of education, the better the chances are for healthy reactions. One way to look into the future may be to examine the attitude of the best minds of today and their reaction to the media. It might give a clue to the tastes of the masses a few decades from now. Some American researchers questioned several thousand people from all walks of life—mothers, policemen, dentists, cowboys, secretaries, civil servants—on this subject. The only thing all of them had in common was an IQ placing them in the top 2 percentile of intelligence in the nation. IQ tests, of course, only measure a form of logical intelligence, but they have the advantage of providing a sampling of people that at least use their brains.

The subjects first listed their favorite television programs in this order of preference: news specials, movies, news programs, nature shows, and sports. Comedies, detective stories, variety shows, and westerns came last. The majority of subjects watched TV less than the average person. Instead of four hours per day per person, nearly 37 percent of the participants in the test watched TV less than one hour a day, and 35 percent between one and two hours. The higher the level of education, the less they watched television. While nearly 60 percent of Americans in general consider television their major source of news, half of the subjects of this investigation cited newspapers as their primary source, followed by radio (18 percent), television (17 percent), and magazines (14.5 percent). At the same time, 48 percent of them stated that they watched the evening TV newscasts regularly.

Asked what they prefer to do when they had a free evening, 45 percent named watching TV, 42 percent their favorite hobby, 38 percent listening to records, and 18 percent listening to the radio (the total goes considerably over 100 percent because they could choose several categories). More significant is the fact that nearly 75 percent said that they never or hardly ever took into consideration any TV program when they made plans on how to spend an evening. It is clear from these results that television does not have the same hold on high IQ people as it does on the population as a whole. But, even for those who have the means to free themselves from the tyranny of television, it still plays a very substantial role. The important question for the future is whether better, more diversified and specialized programs will pull these people away from reading, or a certain balance will be maintained.

HYGIENE FOR THE MEDIA

In order not to be driven nuts, we must learn to practice a code of conduct regarding the media that will be more useful to inculcate in children than old-fashioned table manners. By getting organized, one can still take advantage of the great flow of information without being drowned. The main thing is to break old habits. Nothing encroaches more than these daily routines that accumulate like sediment: Everyone of us reads more newspapers and publications than we really need to read. It would be hygienic to stop reading each for one month, once a year (for example, when any of your subscriptions runs out), and refrain from taking up the habit again unless one finds that after four weeks life is just not as pleasant without reading the associated grocers newsletter. Similarly, it will be increasingly necessary to break with radio and television in order to preserve one's own identity. There are a million and one ways to do this, from choosing a "silent" record on a juke box (and then watching the scowls or the bewilderment of the other people in the bar whose mental lifeline you have just severed) to the religious vows of the Amish who reject any artifact invented after the plow. The Club Méditerranée, the largest French vacation organization, has already gotten the point and banned transistors, television, and newspapers in their leisure villages. An American journalist, Jesse Birnbaum, was in the Club's Tahitian village during Nixon's visit to China. He could not stand the isolation and tried to find some way to get news—just like someone looking for whiskey during Prohibition. It took him three days to discover the head of the village huddled in his thatched hut, listening to a shortwave on the sly—just as Europeans listened to the BBC in secret during the German occupation.

More and more, vacation places will make a point of being cut off from the media. This is already true of some hotels in American national parks. The day is coming when newsless cruises will be marketed; when one will have to pay a small extra fee if he wants no TV in his hotel room. At home it is as hard to refrain from turning on the radio for the hourly news bulletin, as it is easy to break this routine in an unfamiliar environment. One of the advantages of vacationing in a foreign country is that, even if a radio or a TV set is at your disposal, it is impossible to understand what is being said. The important thing is after the vacation to try to resist taking up audio-visual habits again, to try to watch or listen only to what presents a real interest. One may completely succumb to the old habits again after two months, but adding this to the month of vacation, we come up with one-fourth of the year during which the yoke will have been thrown off.

To avoid becoming an idiot, it is essential to develop the healthy reflex of the will to interrupt instantaneously an unsatisfactory experience. You realize that the book you are reading is average or mediocre. Don't waste your time—which for you is much more precious than those pages. Put the book down or even throw it in the wastebasket (yes, a sacrilege). Why pretend that you will come back to it one day if you find it boring? By throwing it away you prove to yourself that you have the courage of your convictions. Similarly, do not stay one minute too long in a movie theater if you find the film is bad. Switch off the TV program whose content is not living up to the promise of its title or *TV Guide* description. Respect your time above all, your hours of reflection and life; keep your time in hand and don't abandon to the media what you consider useful or frankly agreeable. When you can shut off your TV set at will, you will no longer have any guilt complexes about looking at fifteen minutes of a film about which you know nothing beforehand. If you are afraid of spending one unforeseen hour alone with yourself, reflecting, or talking with someone close to you, always keep a book near at hand. It too will enable you to escape from yourself, but at least you will be using your mind.

Part 4
Reinventing
Freedom

Chapter 1

A Useful Myth: Freedom of the Press

The owners of French newspapers can rest easy. Their profits may be on the wane, but they can count on the support of public opinion According to a poll published in early 1972 by SOFRES, the leading French opinion research organization, 71 percent of the French people considered suppression of the freedom of the press a very serious matter, whereas only 55 percent were worried about the disappearance of unions and the right to strike. The only issue that alarmed the French more was the possible loss of social security (82 percent)—perhaps because income rather than freedom is involved. In addition, successive reforms of the ORTF reflect the government's concern with the public's appreciation for freedom of expression. But, following faithfully in the footsteps of General de Gaulle (who once asked President Kennedy how he could govern without controlling television), the Pompidou government will not relinquish control of the airwaves at any price. At the same time, grasping that public opinion is highly sensitive to the issue, the government wants to make people believe that the ORTF is independent. An almost impossible task, of course. Our Ministers of Information could benefit greatly from putting up on their office walls a remark made by John Adams 150 years ago, when even the large newspapers sold only 5,000 copies: "If there is ever to be an amelioration of the condition of mankind, philosophers, theologians, legislators, politicians, and moralists will find that the regulation of the press is the most difficult, dangerous, and important problem they have to resolve. Mankind cannot now be governed without it, nor at present with it."

In the last century and a half this important problem has only become even more difficult and more dangerous. The United States is one of the few countries—if not the only one—to have on the whole respected the principle of freedom of the press.

The dilemma Adams pointed out remains essentially the same: even in countries where the law theoretically gives the press a broad latitude of expression, it can never be wholly exercised in practice. Yet, although it has been curtailed, the freedom of the media to use their infinite means of expression carries with it a power which poses a growing problem not only for governments but for society as a whole.

Of the 101 ways to stifle or restrict freedom of the press, governments have obviously invented most of them. The last century has seen the development of an arsenal of run-of-the-mill, violent, or subtle measures, the worldwide effects of which are now evaluated in annual reports of the International Press Institute.

Government control: Since the emergence of broadcasting, governments have taken complete or partial control of radio and television almost everywhere. Inasmuch as television has by far the greatest impact on society, in every country of the world the government controls the major medium, either directly or indirectly. This fact alone brings the myth of freedom of the press down to more modest dimensions. Just as the hare is no match for the hounds, the written press cannot prevail over television in influencing public opinion. Of course the situation varies widely according to the degree of state control. In most democracies (France, Italy, Germany, Sweden, Great Britain) the written press belongs to the private sector, but audio-visual media are owned by the state or public enterprises over which the state exercises a direct influence. This does not necessarily mean—as the French often gripe—that journalists receive instructions directly from bureaucrats. But in times of crisis the government always finds a point at which it can no longer resist the temptation of asserting its stewardship. In France, the "private" radio networks—Radio-Luxembourg and Europe No. 1—constitute the sole exceptions to the monopoly of the airwaves by the state, which directly or indirectly holds a minority share. During the mock revolution of May 1968, for example, the government complained that the private radio newscasts were aiding the demonstrators; it hinted to the stations that the cable linking the stations' Paris studios with their transmitters outside the country—a cable belonging to the Post and Telecommunications (PTT) Ministry—could very easily be cut off. Even in Great Britain, where the BBC, a public institution, considers itself above all interference, an undisguised pressure was applied in January 1972 when a two-hour television program devoted to the Northern Ireland crisis was scheduled to include the terrorists' point of view. The Heath government tried several times to have the program suppressed, and journalists complained about the obstacles thrown in the way of their investigations by the producer, who did not want to anger the Prime Minister.

In the United States, television and radio stations are private, but the airwaves are not. Every three years the federal government reassigns frequencies to each station, and theoretically can refuse to grant a broadcasting license to any station. This threat has been used only a few times, against radio stations refusing to respect the code—which is very liberal, incidentally—of the Federal Communications Commission. However, these conditions make stations careful to avoid free-floating criticism of the government, especially when their license is about to run out.

Physical violence: It is not rare to read about journalists and newspaper publishers being thrown in jail, as in Greece, or tortured, as in Brazil. Yannis Horn, publisher of the *Athens News,* an English-language daily, spent several months in prison for having allowed the following headline to run during Vice-President Agnew's visit to Greece in November 1971: "BOMBS AND SCHOOLCHILDREN WELCOME AGNEW." Released because of heart trouble, Horn was not afraid to write (July 1972) a detailed and violent editorial on the lack of democracy in Greece. He explained his views by citing Luther's reply when accused of subversion: "Here I stand; I cannot do otherwise. May God help me." Even in cautiously democratic postwar Germany, in 1962, when *Der Spiegel* printed an account of the military concepts of Minister Franz-Josef Strauss, the first reaction of the government was to jail some journalists and hold a few of them there for several months. On August 9, 1972, Willy Brandt's Social Democratic government did not hesitate to search the weekly *Quick's* offices in Bonn and Munich, under the pretext of investigating tax violations. *Quick* had just published the secret letter of resignation of Minister Karl Schiller.

Journalists also face violence from sources other than the police and the government. Many have received death threats—which sometimes have been carried out—when investigating the Mafia in the United States and Italy. Disgruntled demonstrators—leftist students and rightist protestors, for example—have also been known to turn on reporters and rough them up on the slightest pretext. Hoodlums, demonstrators, policemen—all try in their own way to interfere physically with the freedom of the press.

Legal action: Proceedings brought against newspapers by European governments are commonplace. During the Algerian war, any French journalist who expressed his opposition to the official line risked being indicted for "attacking the morale of the Armed Forces." This happened several times to Jean-Jacques Servan-Schreiber. In Italy, the editor-in-chief of the liberal weekly *L'Espresso* was prosecuted for publishing political articles, forcing him as the "guilty party" to run for election in order to come under parliamentary immunity. In May 1972, charges were brought against the largest Italian daily, *Corriere della Sera,* after it printed revelations about the murder of a police commissioner in Milan. The International Press Institute immediately protested this attack on freedom of information, just as it had done in Germany for *Quick.* Since the Institute's only weapon is indignation, its effectiveness is usually limited.

The legal action that has drawn the most recent attention was the one the Nixon Administration brought against the most prestigious American dailies in 1971 to stop their publication of the Pentagon Papers. For the first time in American history legal action was directly aimed against the right to publish. The government's unprecedented attempt at prior restraint was the major issue for the American press; however the press throughout the rest of the world was struck harder by the fact that in the United States the President demonstrably cannot halt newspaper publication in advance without a court order. When the Supreme Court—by a six to three vote—decided in favor of *The New York Times* and *The Washington Post* against the government, *Newsweek* (which belongs to *The Washington Post*) printed a triumphal cover showing an American eagle in the background and the headline "VICTORY FOR THE PRESS."

If the United States enjoys greater freedom of the press than European countries, it is not in this respect the ideal place. In October, 1972, the Interamerican Press Society classified the degree of freedom of expression in all North and South American countries. Freedom of expression was unrestricted only in Canada, Salvador, Honduras, Costa Rica, Columbia, Puerto Rico, and Venezuela. In the United States, it was found to exist with "certain difficulties," as is also true in Argentina, Bolivia, and Mexico. Cuba, Brazil, Paraguay, Haiti, and Panama were cited as having no free media.

Expropriations: In developing countries, where the right to property is not sacred and is even looked down upon, the expropriation of newspapers is an inexpensive and expedient way for governments to silence the opposition. In Tunisia, the newspapers belonging to French industrialist Henry Smadja were confiscated one after the other, and their elderly owner spent several weeks in prison. The same thing happened in Greece to Helen Vlachos. In Morocco the *Vigie* and the *Petit Morocain* were closed by King Hassan in November 1971. After expropriating *L'Expresso,* the Peruvian military junta forced Pedro Beltran, a former Prime Minister, to sell his interest in *La Prensa,* the paper he founded, to the workers. *La Prensa* had printed only mild criticism of the military regime. Dailies in Argentina, Columbia, Mexico, and even in the United States all protested, but to no avail, as usual. In South Vietnam, President Thieu discovered a radical way to eliminate the opposition press. He had a new law passed requiring each paper to post a large cash bond to guarantee the payment of fines it might incur for publishing articles dangerous to the "national interest." In September 1972, after the deadline for raising the cash, fourteen insolvent dailies and fifteen periodicals were forced to fold—leaving only one opposition paper in Saigon.

Censorship: When we speak of attacks on freedom of the press, the public immediately thinks of censorship, which as we have seen, is only one of many weapons in an extensive arsenal. Most countries have used censorship during wartime. In France, from the outset of both world wars, officers—often drafted journalists—were sent to all editorial offices in order to "caviar"[1] any news the enemy could use. History shows this to be a prudent measure. During the war in the Pacific, the Americans accidentally got hold of the Japanese naval code and were able to decipher the enemy's messages. A *Chicago Tribune* journalist visiting the front learned of this and, delighted with his scoop, published it. The Japanese of course changed their code immediately. Charges were brought against the unwitting

---

[1]The operation consists of inking out lines to be killed, making the paragraph look vaguely like black caviar.

newspaper, but later dropped for fear other secrets would be revealed in the process.

Generally speaking, newspapers willingly censor themselves in wartime, but precensorship of a more political nature is difficult to carry out in practice. Portugal of course has been living with censorship since Salazar's time. In the spring of 1972 a new, more "liberal" press law came into force, and pre-censorship was replaced by "self-censorship," under which "the publication of tendentious material manifestly opposed to national interests" could be punished by penalties ranging from the closing of the paper to two years in prison for those committing the offense.

For a long time the Greek Colonels had newspaper articles read each night before publication by officers sent to the printing plant for that purpose. But, perhaps because there were more dailies in Athens than captains who could read, prepublication censorship was finally replaced by control after the fact and, in fact, self-censorship.

Intimidation and threats: In most democracies the confrontation between the state and the press is as soft pedaled as it is continuous. The executive power deems the Fourth Estate indispensable as a conveyor belt between itself and public opinion. But the right of investigation and interrogation, which the media consider their own, embarrasses and irritates all governments without exception. Therefore, all governments try to keep a hold on the press without letting it be too obvious. In order to apply their pressure, governments do not consider it beneath them to use invective and police inquiries. When Spiro Agnew launched his verbal crusade against the media, he had no legal means to make them change their coverage, but newspapers and TV stations felt uneasy none the less. This uneasiness gave way to fear when it was learned at the end of 1971 that the FBI was investigating Daniel Schorr, the CBS Washington correspondent, who was on the outs with the White House at the time. The federal agents (on the pretext of considering Schorr for a government job) probably hoped to discover some compromising detail in the journalist's life which would discredit him. Just the contrary took place, for Schorr immediately told his side of the story on national television, revealing to the country how the government was using underhanded methods against the press. Men in power are particularly embarrassed when their devious dealings are made public.

It is difficult for a democratic government to act against the foreign press when it publishes something offensive. About the only pressure a government can exert is on the foreign correspondents stationed within its borders, who, however, have almost diplomatic status. On the other hand, authoritarian countries are rarely concerned about scruples and will expel foreign journalists in a twinkling, as the Soviet Union does all the time.

Financial pressures: It is in the interest of governments to give the press certain financial advantages, so that it will then fear that these may be taken away. In this respect, the French press is just as vulnerable as it is favored, since government aid represents from 10 to 15 percent of its gross. Journalists benefit from personal tax deductions for "professional expenses" which can be 30 percent higher than those allowed for the average citizen (exempting from taxes up to $10,000 of income). From time to time, for obvious reasons, the government circulates the rumor that in the next fiscal reform these exemptions may be done away with. The subsidies to newsprint—which favors paper manufacturers rather than publishers—can be revoked at any moment. Bulk mailing postal rates are minimal, but here, too, it is hinted every once in a while that efficient postal service could require a considerable increase. While these and other fiscal advantages do not allow for real intimidation of the press, they do function to hinder the press' freedom of action.

In the last ten years in France, advertising rates, as well as most industrial prices, have been frozen most of the time. In order to raise rates, a publication had to obtain an authorization from the Ministry of Finance, which was not required to give reasons for a refusal. This obviously made it touchy for a publication to attack the government freely (especially a Minister of Finance), when in a few months a favor might be needed. Finance Ministry officials regretted the unfreezing of advertising rates, for the sight of unusually amiable leaders of the press pacing up and down outside their offices had pleased the bureaucrats no end.

Seizures: Although there is no censorship in France, the police read the first copies of each issue of a publication. If the issue contains, for example, a call to armed rebellion, the plans for the nuclear submarine *Le Redoutable,* or a report on an abortion trial, it can be legally seized. The central police station gets in touch with the Ministry of the Interior, which, on its own authority and subject to future proceedings, gives the order to its agents to seize the publication. At this point, of course, all or most of the edition has been printed and part of it is en route to other parts of the country. Police stations throughout the country are alerted to intercept the publication before it reaches news distributors. The financial consequences for the paper in question can be disastrous. because the advertising printed in the edition will not be paid for, whereas all the manufacturing costs have to be met. For a large circulation magazine like *L'Express,* at its peak periods—May or October—an issue can contain $400,000 to $600,000 worth of advertising. Before 1964, when *L'Express* was a tabloid printed on a rotary press, it was able after several seizures to "caviar" the offending article and go ahead with a new printing and appear on newsstands only twenty-four hours late. At that time, taking into consideration the type of printing, the production costs were modest. Today, a tripled circulation and four-color pages demand several days in the plant, making any publication delay quite expensive. But since it changed format, *L'Express* has never been harassed—the heyday of seizures in France ended along with the Algerian war.

The only case of seizure during the Pompidou regime seemed ridiculous—a satirical weekly *Hara Kiri Hebdo,* which elects to call itself "stupid and nasty," was seized in 1971. As has been true in general of all the newspapers seized in France, *Hara Kiri Hebdo* came out on top, because the free publicity the government gave the magazine by seizing it more than compensated for its financial losses, just as *L'Express* registered an increase in circulation after every seizure. In West Germany, too, the great success of *Der Spiegel* dates from the charges brought against it in 1962 by Franz-Josef Strauss, Minister of Defense. No doubt this boomerang effect has taken the punch out of this form of policing.

Dining out: On a day-to-day basis, no coercion, threat, or ban is more effective for limiting freedom of expression than good intentions. Ever since the Phoenicians invented currency and until not so long ago, a generous gift in a sealed envelope was the surest and quickest way of keeping journalists in line. Many pen-pushers used to live a good life by getting hard news and not printing it. This form of blackmail, never very extensive, is responsible in large measure for the belief among some businessmen that any journalist can be bought for a price. As a matter of fact, a part of the French financial press can be bought today. Contracts are made with companies registered on the Paris Bourse for modest annual retainers. In exchange, the newspaper prints the company's press releases and, when the paper does an article on the firm, it submits the material for a reading beforehand, then modifies it if need be or kills it for a further small consideration. Such practices still exist in France despite the fact that since the war the fashion of writing more freely about business has cut down on them.

In recent years, simultaneous growth in professional ethics and salaries has meant that real journalists are no longer for sale—at least they cannot be bought with money. But dining out is another matter altogether. To rub elbows with the powerful, to have a meal with a minister or an important company president—these factors create ties. Politicians and businessmen know very well that by showing journalists a bit of consideration (and not only when they have something to ask from them) they may be repaid in kind. When a newspaper is seized or a fellow newsman jailed, the entire profession stands as one man against the offense, but at the end of a lunch at Maxim's the cabinet minister no longer seems so condescending or dishonest. When the next scandal breaks and his name is mentioned, he will be asked by telephone for his version of the story before being vilified.

But freedom of information is not held in check uniquely by political power, as many newspaper publishers would have people believe. The financial system with which the media interact daily exerts a much stronger influence than those who govern.

The coercion of profits: Real freedom of expression would mean being able to publish anything of interest to as few as several thousand people. Unfortunately, in practice, publications that cannot count on a minimum number of advertisers do not have much chance of surviving. Thus, because furniture, decoration, and home appliances feed a thriving industry whose expensive products are of interest to just about every consumer, there are myriad magazines of the *Better Homes and Gardens* type, with limited news content and repetitive photos of furniture and gadgets. Conversely, since book publishers cannot provide advertising budgets worthy of the name for most books, not one literary magazine intended for a wide readership has been successful in France.

The influence of advertisers: In a 1972 film, *Tout le monde il est beau,* Jean Yanne played the role of an Honest John of the airwaves who decided one day to try out the products of his advertisers and report his findings live on the air; every conceivable institution, from management to unions, panicked, the former out of fear for their profits, the latter for their jobs. The madman is therefore fired and replaced by someone ready to play the game according to the rules. The lesson here is that the independence of journalists in the "consumer society" means that they are not explicitly required to sing the praises of the companies whose advertising budgets directly or indirectly pay journalists' salaries. But if a sport writer specializing in automobiles announces the results of comparative tests on different cars over radio stations Europe No. 1 or Radio-Luxembourg, he is begging to be fired. Because of advertising, the golden rule about news concerning any products of private industry is to observe the highest degree of discretion—to treat them with an "objectivity" that borders on respect. France has, of yet, been hardly touched by the tide of consumer reaction and consumer protection.

McCall's magazine, nodding to the trend toward consumer advocacy, hired Betty Furness to write a regular column. When the April 1972 issue appeared without her column, it was learned that the publisher, Ray Eyes, had scrapped the article because it revealed that Kool Aid is a completely synthetic product. It so happens that Kool Aid is a General Foods product and General Foods is one of the major advertisers in *McCall's,* which was financially fighting for its life.

Privileged treatment can be accorded industrial concerns in more subtle ways. For twenty years the American Cigar institute offered prizes for the best press photos of people smoking cigars. Even photographers of the very sober *New York Times* won $50 prizes, which meant very cheap publicity for the cigar industry, compared to paying for the photo's space at standard advertising rates.

Monopolies and concentrations: In industrialized countries, the formation of small monopolies through an uninterrupted succession of mergers and concentrations is the most characteristic phenomenon of the postwar press. In virtually every city, there is only one newspaper, and 63 percent of American distribution is now controlled by groups or chains of newspapers. In practically every country (except the United States), there are only one or two national television networks. Before the war, France had dozens of private regional radio stations. They have been replaced by three nationwide networks (France Inter, Radio-Luxembourg, and Europe No. 1). Monopolies necessarily bring on laxity. Why make costly efforts toward quality journalism when you are the only paper in town? Why defend an opinion when it will offend part of the readership? As for journalists, when they find themselves faced with an extremely limited number of potential employers, they need an extraordinary capacity for self-sacrifice to risk displeasing someone. Amazingly, gutsy, independent journalists are still to be found here and there.

Low pay: Only a quality press can use its freedom effectively. Before the truth can be printed, it must be tracked down. Editorial quality depends entirely on the caliber of the men who write and edit the paper. Now, with rare exceptions, the journalistic profession is underpaid in every country in the world. A monthly staffed by two or three full-time personnel or a weekly with a half dozen needs a lot of luck to produce high-quality material. Usually enough money is available, but the owners are not interested in investing it in their editorial staffs. Only the big media remunerate fairly the few talented people who insure their reputation. In Paris, for example, a few of the more powerful editors and writers will receive from 10,000 to 25,000 francs a month ($2,000–$5,000), while the more numerous lesser lights have to make do with subsistence wages, even though the work of the latter guarantees the basis of the quality of the information making up the articles. It is no surprise that the best of them often give in to the temptation of careers in advertising which pay twice as well.

Owners and employees: Even those who live off the press contribute in their way to stifling its freedom of expression. Some owners have a very special idea of the freedom of the press, because their major concern is to use their newspapers as a springboard for their other careers. For the mayor of Marseilles, for instance, it is convenient to own the city's daily: it gives him a formidable power base. But the readers of the Marseilles *Provençal* should not expect their favorite newspaper to scrutinize Mayor Gaston Defferre's administration too closely.

Journalists who are quick to criticize their employers and the system may devote to internal rivalries the time and energy that could be used to track down facts. Suddenly, when they attain their goals, as they did at *Le Monde,* they no longer have any desire to welcome new talent which would reinforce the paper's quality, because it would mean interesting competition for high-level positions.

Last, the demands of the craft unions have caused the disappearance of many newspapers, either through bankruptcy or mergers to save labor costs, thus reducing the diversity of expression essential to freedom. Through their rigidity and their corporatist spirit, they have played a large part in preventing the launching of new independent newspapers, of new vehicles for ideas.

ILLUSORY OBJECTIVITY

The tacit agreement between the public and the press would seem to require that in exchange for their freedom the newspapers supply objective news. This concept is, in reality, a delusion. Just as the freedom of the press is curtailed through a multitude of restraints, so objectivity can only be theoretical. It is certainly desirable for journalists to make an effort to be objective and to take into consideration varying opinions or contradictory versions of the facts. But their milieu and working methods inevitably affect the content of what they write and make absolute objectivity impossible to achieve.

The readership is for the newsman a silent majority to which he is accountable. The opinions and prejudices of the readers leave him a narrow operating margin. Abortion is not upheld in the tradition-minded *Femmes D'Aujourd'hui;* neither are speed limits in the motorist's *Auto-Journal,* nor taxes on capital gains in the businessman's *Les Echos.* If only by omission, readers are often served nothing but a menu fashioned to their tastes which therefore rules out objectivity.

Too much news, not enough journalists—that is the basic formula of the newspaper business. Since the newspapers do not have enough time both to examine all the facts and to print them, it is probable that frequently they unconsciously opt for the easy way out. Numerous organizations and individuals are aware of this and exploit it for their own profit. If the information sent to newspapers is well presented, concise, and suitable to be printed as is, the chances of its standing apart from the monotony of other press releases are greatly increased. For example, for every newspaper that takes book reviewing seriously enough to hire competent writers for this purpose, twenty others are satisfied with reprinting the blurb prepared by the publisher. Some add a few words of their own, but most are content with supplying only a headline. In place of objectivity, the reader is presented with what, in essence, is an advertising squib. Similarly, even a daily as renowned and powerful as *The New York Times* prints on its financial pages information that essentially reflects the point of view of the big corporations. The reason is not that this paper has made itself the systematic defender of big business; rather, these companies are well equipped to distribute news about themselves. This does not mean that *The New York Times* prints their statements word for word. It means that even that newspaper does not have enough specialized writers with enough time to do much more than gather a few additional bits of information over the phone. As for companies that do not send out press releases, the newspaper hardly ever makes reference to them, unless something unusual or particularly newsworthy has occurred.

Another reason for an absence of objectivity is that many journals, even those not considered "opinion sheets," tend to develop a house "line" reflecting the thinking or personality of its founder—e.g., the slightly morose skepticism of *Le Monde* (H. Beuve-Méry), the efficient modernism of *L'Express* (Jean-Jacques Servan-Schreiber), the pro-masculine permissiveness of *Playboy* (Hugh Hefner). Although such a line is never codified in written rules and no direct coercion is exerted on the staff, it does not take long for the dominant point of view to be expressed to the exclusion of all objective opposing opinions. In general, the staffs of any organizations adopt such similar points of view that they cannot detect their own predilections and prejudices. If the head of personnel of an airline company retains his position for a long time, the stewardesses of the airline all tend to resemble one another; similarly, on a journal where the top man has strong opinions or a distinct style, the team and the product end up by having a family air about them.

When journalists from various publications attend a press conference or travel to an international convention, they move in a herd. Reporters of the same specialty from different papers know each other well and frequently talk together, thus reaching a kind of consensus about what they are currently covering. There are always mavericks who go counter to the prevailing viewpoint, but what most readers, viewers, or listeners receive conforms to the overall opinion of the professionals. Dissenting views are rarely presented.

In the case of a local newspaper, any hope of objectivity in the coverage of regional events or personalities is sheer wishful thinking. The editor and the journalists, who know the local personalities inside-out have for the most part a predetermined attitude about them. Small-town papers also know their readership and cater to it. Why should they write favorably about someone they do not like? Why should they get on the wrong side of the public by spreading news people have no desire to know? This tendency is only human, perhaps, but it does not serve the cause of objectivity.

The very conditions of the journalistic profession inevitably distort news content. News has to be written for deadlines, which can affect niceties of accuracy.[2] Space limitations also restrict the advantages of a full acount of an event, with all the shadings that might emerge. Headlines also play a part in coloring the news. When the headline for an article has to be written, nine times out of ten it must be made to fit into a certain number of letters allotted to it. What nuances or reservations can be conveyed when space for only thirty-four letters is available? In addition, in order to attract the reader to the article, it is necessary to emphasize the most original or dramatic element—which is hardly ever the most important. At the same time, the story must be simplified, which means that factors tending to modify snap judgments will be left out.

In the case of television, the more channels there are and the more program hours to fill up, the more the quality and professionalism of a news documentary is likely to deteriorate. Very often, a news crew must produce a one-hour program for the same amount of money an advertiser spends on a thirty-second spot commercial. Therefore, it is not surprising that an advertising jingle for a kitchen deodorizer is occasionally bubbling while an account of working conditions of women puts you to sleep. It is not the subject that makes news boring but rather too tight a budget and too few newsmen available.

[2]In his book *Journalism and Government,* the journalist John Whale points out that fast work is the chief cause of inexactitude, and that a comparison of the first and final editions of a newspaper or of the morning and afternoon wire-service news shows that extra time allows for the correction of errors.

If we add to these factors the inevitable errors in gathering information and in interpreting it, we can well wonder if there ever can be any relationship between what has taken place and what is carried in the media. More often than not, there is barely any.

WHO PROFITS FROM THIS MYTH

These four words, freedom of the press, have no magic for a Russian citizen. But for someone living in the West they are a key political element. Freedom of the press, perhaps because of the obstacles it meets in practice, remains one of our great myths, and the fact that the myth is still very much alive bestows upon it a great power. There are therefore large numbers of people who benefit greatly from this shared belief—and to question it is almost a heresy.

First and foremost, the myth gives to the capitalists who own the media the cachet of those who serve the public interest. Even though newspapers are often very profitable investments, few people regard press tycoons as they would ordinary industrialists. Whenever their profit margins are threatened, newspaper owners do not hesitate to cry out that freedom of the press is endangered. For them, the myth makes money; chocolate manufacturers and the transport industry would love to have such an irrefutable negotiating argument. On December 1, 1971, the United States Congress once again demonstrated the tie that exists between the myth and the wallet. When President Nixon was clamping controls on industrial prices, Congress voted to exempt the press, saying that if the press had to go through Washington to raise its advertising rates, the government would have a tool for intimidating it. When Giscard d'Estaing, the French Finance Minister, imposed price controls on the press along with other industries, he was not embarrassed by such scruples.

In their own way, journalists benefit just as much from the myth. It turns ordinary professionals, who would be educators, business executives, or civil servants if they were not members of the press, into knights in shining armor, defenders of the man in the street, if not sacred cows. Anyone who attacks journalists is likely to be pilloried as a murderer of freedom. It is rewarding for a professional to be able to pass from time to time for a vestal virgin.

The conflicts between journalists and owners over power and money almost always come down to this kind of argument: "Sir, my freedom of the press is purer than yours!" Each camp is vying to see which can better exploit this myth in the future. The journalists would like to monopolize it forever, creating for themselves the advantages of an impregnable bastion of independence. The owners are slightly on the defensive about their profit-making when it comes to crossing swords with the journalists on the issue of independence.

Under normal circumstances, when no major scandal is breaking, men with political power also profit from the myth of freedom of the press, for, as we have seen, they know how to manipulate it to assure good coverage of their activities and they are adept at convincing journalists to defend their point of view. What purpose would favorable headlines or comments serve for a government or a large corporation if the press had the reputation of being their lackey? It is to their obvious advantage for the press to remain free and independent enough for the public to believe that it is completely so.

Despite all that has been said, despite the unattainability of the ideal, the ordinary citizen can benefit from the very principle of this freedom. Even though the press is not really free, what has nonetheless come to be called a free press plays a crucial role in the democratic process, because it does inform the public more freely and more objectively than other sources of information. It does so in an incomplete way, it is often biased and wrong—but, still, it informs. This is why citizens of advanced democracies can hardly argue with the following:

—As with other freedoms, it is only when we are deprived of it that we really understand what freedom of the press means.

—Quibbling over the exact definition of a free press is an indulgence and a wonderful luxury that is denied in most countries of the world.

—In order for a press to be free, it must have, in addition to the right to publish, sufficient financial means and access to information.

—Though freedom of the press can be damaging, prejudicial, and unfair to individuals or institutions, it is far less dangerous than the power to decide the restrictions to be imposed upon it.

—The only way to correct the imperfections of freedom of the press today is to maintain a diversity of the means of expression.

Chapter 2

Only the Rich Are Really Informed

Every country has the media it deserves. Indeed, the media themselves provide only a slightly distorted image of the society they mirror. Everything is reflected in them: the level of economic development (via the number, the wealth, and the variety of newspapers and radio and TV stations); the national temperament (the style and manner of media treatment of people); the political regime (the freedom given to journalists and how they use it); the level of the culture (language style and the quality of the material); and, finally, everyday life, the weather, and mass taste (through advertising). This is the reason why, abundant or meager, free or controlled, the media can vary as much between Niger and Japan today as between eighteenth-century gazettes and modern television in France. If in the developed countries most consumer products look alike, this is not true for the press, which retains the stamp of local traditions and prejudices, petty quarrels, and varying life styles. The information system has become the equivalent of a country's folklore. Like the latter, it is not always cheerful.

COMPARATIVE GEOINFORMATION

In 1970, an American was about 100 times more in touch with the outside world than an inhabitant of India. I came to this conclusion after a nonscientific evaluation of figures provided by UNESCO. The "index" I devised takes into account newsprint consumption, postal traffic, the number of TV sets, radios and telephones. Taking France as base 100, we find the United States in the lead with 320, or almost double the second place country, Sweden, with 175. Then come most of the Northern European countries and Japan with a rating of 135. France at 100 is followed by two industrialized Communist countries,

Czechoslovakia and the USSR, both under 80. Italy and Southern Europe are 75, Israel 58, Mexico 40, and Greece 30. At the bottom are poor countries, such as Egypt 25, Brazil 22, Morocco 10, and India barely 3. A fact that will surprise no one is that this division corresponds to levels of industrial development. Thus we can differentiate among "post-industrial" nations (the United States), advanced industrial nations (Northern Europe and Japan), those which have reached the level of mass consumption (Southern Europe), and the underdeveloped countries. Within this global classification, one should note peculiarities specific to certain countries or blocs. Communist countries use relatively less newsprint, no doubt because advertising is practically nonexistent. The Swedes and the Japanese use the mails relatively less, perhaps because both have excellent telephone networks. In Japan's case, typewriters are scarce because of the ideogram system of writing. The Soviet Union holds an honorable place in the audio-visual field but trails between Portugal and Mexico when it comes to the telephone and mail services. Israel is ahead of France in telephones. Mexico beats out Japan, Holland, and Italy in the number of radios per capita. France holds a middle rank in each sector, except for a slight advantage in mail service. The United States, champion in every field of communications, is followed very closely by Sweden, which nearly equals the American record in the number of telephones per inhabitant and newsprint consumption per person.

LOW-COST PERSUASION

Comparing advertising expenditures by country provides another perspective: it measures the commercialism (in literal and figurative senses of the word) of the different nations. Curiously enough, in 1970 Ireland devoted the highest percentage of its GNP—2.23 percent—to advertising (but Ireland's GNP is smaller than the annual turnover of the twentieth-largest private company in the world), followed by Switzerland (2.18 percent), and the United States (2.11 percent). France, with less than 1 percent, is far behind Argentina, Singapore, Lebanon, Hong Kong, and Costa Rica. But when it comes to advertising expenditure per individual inhabitant, the United States recovers its supremacy with $94 annually. This is quite a modest sum, in view of the fact that every American buys nearly $4,600 worth of goods and services yearly. The above tends to show either that advertising is not the all-powerful dictator of consumption it is made out to be or that, at the rate of less than $100 per year, it does not take very much to persuade an American.

In the same vein, it seems that a mere $20 a year is needed to throw the French into a buying spree, but a German or a Swede will not move unless that figure is doubled, while a Swiss refuses to pull out his wallet unless $68 has been spent to persuade him. We see, then, that for equivalent family budgets the exposure to advertising varies from one to three in different European countries, which should make us wary of any possibility of scientifically measuring the marginal efficiency of this controversial social expenditure. One conclusion can be drawn from these figures: advertising is doubtless a phenomenon of affluent societies, since the United States alone takes up 59 percent of world media advertising. The inclusion of only five other countries—Germany, Japan, Great Britain, Canada, and France—accounts for 83 percent of world advertising expenses. These figures, broken down by country, are conservative, because they measure only expenses inside national borders. In France, Germany, or Canada, such American firms as Colgate and General Motors are among the biggest advertisers. It is therefore safe to assume that the worldwide media owe more than 70 percent of their advertising revenues to the United States alone.

Taking a broader look, since it is fashionable these days to talk macroeconomics, three main types of economic structure can be distinguished in the world written press (the rather limited range of the electronic media makes their comparison less significant):

1. In the most developed regions of the world, the circulation figures of newspapers and publications are at a very high level and advertising is the major source of income (slightly over half for the dailies, more for periodicals). On the other hand, the phenomenon of mergers of publications and press enterprises, which is gaining momentum everywhere, tends to reduce the number of newspapers. Those that survive become economically stronger for it.

2. In the Communist countries, circulation figures are high but not so high as in the West on the basis of population. Sales of

newspapers are almost the only source of revenue, and ownership of the relatively few publications that do exist is concentrated in the hands of the state, directly or through institutions like unions and the army.

3. In underdeveloped countries, circulation is very limited; for lack of advertising, direct sales are the major source of income. In their capital cities, there are many different publications (as in Paris, London, and New York at the beginning of the century), while in the countryside there are practically none. Ownership is private or nationalized, depending on the country.

THE LONDON–TOKYO AXIS

Only in developed countries or in small industrial pockets of poorer countries has a truly flourishing press been able to come into existence through advertising. Depending on the area, geographical and political characteristics have a substantial influence on the structure of the information industry. A nation with a federal type of government usually does not have a national daily that reaches the entire country. This is the case in the United States, Germany, and Switzerland (for the latter, as well as for Belgium, linguistic divisions make the existence of a nationwide publication even more difficult). The two national press systems that differ the most are to be found in the United States on the one hand and in Japan and Great Britain on the other. The individualism of each locality, political decentralization, and great distances have meant for Americans a daily press fractured not only by region but by city as well. The international reputation of *The New York Times* does not automatically assure its presence in the New York area. The combination of the increasing physical weight of each issue, a saturated urban transport system, and the commercial aggressiveness of smaller local competitors has in fact limited to its own backyard the circulation of a paper some people consider the best daily in the world. Not all Americans live in a city prosperous enough to afford a high-quality newspaper. The fact there are no more than a dozen such newspapers (out of a total of 1,700 dailies) is due to the small amount of attention given by owners to editorial investments. Nationwide circulation in the United States is thus the privileged domain of the magazines, which have suffered more than the dailies from television.

Newsstand sales play only a small part in the distribution of most magazines and many newspapers. Publications are delivered directly to the customer: magazines by mail, daily or weekly papers by home delivery.

On the other side of the coin, we have two island nations far apart in both distance and history: Great Britain and Japan. Contrary, for instance, to the United States, both countries are dominated by a few dailies. Rail transport, organized before the end of the nineteenth century, permitted rapid distribution from capital cities whose importance had been established by the prestige of royal dynasties. A marked homogeneity of culture and a definite civic sense allowed a handful of publications to reach dominant positions. Every day in Japan and in the United Kingdom one paper is sold for every two people (compared to one for every four in France). This means enormous circulation figures. In Britain, *The Daily Mirror* leads with 4.4 million copies, followed by the *Daily Express* (3.4 million), *The Sun* (2 million) and the *Daily Telegraph* (1.5 million). In Japan, whose population is twice that of the British Isles, *Asahi* sells 6 million copies in the morning and more than 3 million in the afternoon. Two other big national dailies, *Yomiuri* and *Mainichi,* top 6 million, and the financial daily *Nihon Keisai* sells over one million. It is no surprise that magazines have paled in the shadow of such a powerful and all-encompassing daily press. The few monthlies suffer low circulation in Japan, but the big dailies themselves print supplements which take their place. In Great Britain news weeklies are replaced by the Sunday press, a hoary British tradition which for the last few years has included color magazine supplements. The circulation of the Sunday editions of the dailies is higher than the weekday editions: nearly 5 million for the *Sunday Mirror,* more than 4 million for the *Sunday Express.* Similarly, quality newspapers such as *The Observer* and the *Sunday Times* (independent of, and not to be confused with, the *Daily Times*) published only on Sunday fill the role of both *L'Express* and *Paris-Match.* The entire structure of the British and Japanese press, including the weeklies, is modeled on the rhythm of the dailies. The variety of columns in the daily press, the quality of articles, the number of pages and generations-old habits have prevented the magazines from developing (which proves that they are not indispensable to a nation). In Britain, *Picture Post,* an imitation of *Life,* lasted only a few years, and attempts to introduce a newsmagazine have consistently failed.

However, there are radical differences between London and Tokyo because of the gap in economic growth between the two countries (2 to 3 percent annual rise in GNP in Great Britain as opposed to 8 to 10 percent in Japan). In London the recent history of the press is replete with collapse and stagnation, whereas in Tokyo there is nothing but circulation growth and new technical investments which will allow for even quicker printing. Three British dailies with more than 1 million readers each have disappeared in the last ten years, absorbed by the *Daily Mail*, whose circulation has nonetheless dropped by 500,000. In the same period, British dailies as a whole lost a total of 1.5 million customers. A detailed analysis of this figure indicates that the popular press—with the largest circulation—lost 1.8 million readers whereas the quality press with lower circulations (*The Times,* 350,000; *The Guardian,* 330,000; *The Financial Times,* 170,000) gained 200,000. The latter, however, are not exempt from financial difficulties, for these three quality dailies are still too many for the narrow advertising market on which they depend. In Japan, the distinction between a popular press and a quality press is not relevant, since the largest circulation paper in Japan, *Asahi Shimbun,* is also considered the country's best. A healthy sign for the future of the Japanese press is the fact that a very high advertising revenue does not quite come up to half the total income of the newspapers. Distribution in Japan as well as in Great Britain—unlike the situation in France—is considered as a service rendered to the reader. Even more than in the United States, there is practically universal home delivery for all publications.

FRANCE CHOKED BY A MONOPOLY

Between the two extremes of America, on the one hand, and Japan and Britain, on the other, the German, French, and Italian presses depend upon intermediary structures. Regional dailies coexist with nationwide dailies published in the capital, which (especially in France) are fighting a losing battle. A national magazine press has made its presence felt, and, though stronger than in the two island countries, it is less powerful than that in the United States.

In Germany and Italy, politics and geography dictate the structure. In each there is a strong federal tradition (the political union in both cases being only a century old; in each the communications network does not allow for rapid distribution, and, rather than a dominant city in each, there are several regional capitals). These features aside, the German press is prosperous while the Italian is vegetating. At the end of World War II, there were 265 Italian dailies; now there are eighty. The *Corriere della Sera,* the largest, does not sell more than 600,000 copies. With a slightly larger population than France, less than half as many copies of newspapers are sold in Italy (6 million). Adding to this picture very slight advertising, it is not surprising to discover that there is hardly one Italian daily that makes a profit today. In Germany, on the other hand, 523 dailies sell a total of 22 million copies (for a population only 20 percent higher than Italy's); over a dozen periodicals each have a circulation of more than 1.5 million copies, and forty-eight others more than a million. Advertising in Germany represents more than 70 percent of newspaper income. There are fewer journalists in Germany than in France, but those in Germany are better paid. In short, Germany has a rich, well-managed press which can count on continued prosperity since the German people have faith in their printed press, a confidence which has been building up over the years. In 1963, the German people were asked in a poll which means of information they would choose if they could only have one. Thirty-seven percent chose the press, 25 percent television, and 11 percent radio. Eight years later, in 1971, in answer to the same question, the results were 66 percent for the press, 15 percent for television, and 7 percent for radio. This certainly does not mean that the German public is turning its back on television (they would be the only people in the world to do so), it means they expect entertainment rather than news from it.

In France, the distribution structure and the not very prosperous situation of the press stems for the most part from the outrageous monopoly held by the Nouvelles Messageries de la Presse Parisienne (NMPF) and the newsstand dealers. Theoretically a cooperative, the NMPP is dominated by France's biggest publishing concern, Hachette, whose newspapers traditionally have been badly managed. These powerful lobbies (the NMPP and the vendors) have united to effectively block any innovation which might inconvenience them. In this way, three developments that could have put the French press on a really sound footing and prevented the current "press crisis" were nipped in the bud: subscriptions for magazines, direct delivery of dailies to customers, and large-scale distribution of Sunday papers. The first two are an absolute condition for large circulation. It is obvious that having to go to the newsstand every time you want to buy a publication—as the distribution monopoly forces readers to do in France—is an obstacle to increased circulation. By refusing to distribute papers on Sunday, the monopoly has deprived the French press of a weekly boost, which in the United States as well as Great Britain, insures heavy sales and profits.

PROFITS SWEDISH STYLE

A glance at the press in major industrial countries would not be complete if we left out Sweden, which, despite difficulties in other sectors, remains a privileged spot for newspaper publishers. Sweden conforms to the general model, in terms of merger and concentration. In 1945 it had 177 dailies; today there are no more than 100. Although the Social Democrats have been in power for forty years, they have not been able to prevent most of their newspapers from dying. Since 1963, the government has tried several different kinds of subsidies. In 1971 a 6 percent tax on advertising was created to subsidize the second-rank dailies in a given city or market, which are in the most danger of disappearing (the few remaining Social Democratic papers are in this category). But nothing seems to be able to check the decline of the partisan press in advanced societies. On the other hand, the survivors in Sweden benefit from a three-pronged prosperity: a population of voracious readers with a high level of education (and long, long winter evenings), who buy more newspapers per person than any other country in the world; a level of advertising expenditures per person twice that of Great Britain and Japan; and a government television network which has not yet decided to take advertising and therefore does not pose competition for the press. Thus the major morning daily in Stockholm, the *Dagens Nyheter*, sells as many copies in a country with 8 million people as *Le Figaro* in France (with seven times Sweden's population). It has a yearly gross income double that of *Le Figaro* and until very recently had close to a 25 percent profit margin before taxes. Since the economic crises of 1970–1971, which cut into the advertising revenues, profits have "dropped" to 14 percent before taxes.

In small, compact Europe, with Stockholm, Rome, and Paris in the same time zone, there are considerable disparities in the financial structure of the press, in readers' tastes, and in advertising rates. What does the prosperity of a newspaper—prime condition for independence and quality—depend on? Thankfully, a great deal depends on the drive of the specific management of a given paper. But no one publication can modify on its own such detrimental characteristics as the lack of advertising in Italy, the distribution monopoly in France, or the declining popularity of the partisan press in Sweden.

LENIN'S PRESS

"Why should we condone freedom of the press? Why should a government that does what it deems good allow itself to be criticized?" Richard Nixon, Georges Pompidou, Edward Heath, and so many others would surely endorse this remark of Lenin. But, unlike Leonid Brezhnev and Chou En-lai, they do not have the means to enforce it. For Brezhnev and Chou En-lai the press is not the Fourth Estate, but a means of conveying their policies. This is not the only difference between the press in Communist countries and what we are used to. The economic system and geographical conditions also contribute to its specific physiognomy. Since the press plays a key political and educative role in the USSR, it necessarily has a broad readership. Moreover, since competition is not considered a virtue, the few publications that do exist have huge circulations. The popular monthly for women, *Rabotnica,* sells more than 10 million copies; the one for peasant women, *Krestjanka,* more than 5 million. A monthly health publication sells some 8 million copies, and the satirical weekly *Krokodil* reaches 5,500,000 readers (eleven times more than the French satirical weekly, *Le Canard Enchaîné,* for a population which is only five times larger than that of France). The famous official literary magazine of the Writer's Union, *Literaturnaya Gazeta,* has a circulation of 1.2 million, and *Novy Mir,* running slightly against the grain—it has printed several Solzhenitsyn texts and the works of other dissident writers— has to be satisfied with a mere 140,000 readers. Even with more than 3,000 local papers, the daily press is dominated by two whose task it is to mold public opinion throughout the country—*Pravda*, the Communist Party newspaper, and *Izvestia*, the government organ. *Pravda* illustrates clearly the economic peculiarities of the Soviet press. With more than 9 million copies printed (a 4 percent increase since 1966), it is now the biggest daily in the world, even bigger than the Japanese *Asahi Shimbun* and *Izvestia*, which sells only 7 million. In order to insure unity of information and ideology, the paper is sold throughout a country which is nearly 6,000 miles wide. It is therefore printed simultaneously in forty-two plants across the country. In several of the plants, facsimiles of the pages are received from Moscow by cable or even satellite; other plants are serviced by special Aeroflot flights. To be delivered on time to all the big centers of the USSR, *Pravda* is sometimes sent into the most remote corners of Siberia by helicopter. What permits such a vast and rapid printing is that *Pravda*, unlike Western newspapers, has very few pages—six on the average. Its thinness, the result perhaps of a lack of advertising, makes it one of the most profitable newspapers in the world, despite its newsstand price of less than a nickel. According to its managers, profits are 27 percent of sales. Even if socialist accounting is at least as suspect as capitalist, such figures are phenomenal. Does it mean a profitable press can be run without advertising? It is of course indispensable for the editorial staff to be satisfied with six pages (which are often devoted to printing Party texts in full) and for readers to have no other choice but to buy it. *Pravda*, despite its world record for circulation, has only 140 people on its editorial staff, half the number on *Le Figaro*. The most popular feature of *Pravda* is put together by the fifty staff members assigned to the "Letters to the Editor." This department is a kind of national complaint bureau; 10,000 letters arrive daily at *Pravda*'s offices, reflecting all the gripes of the Soviet people against the red tape of Communist society. This public safety valve has official backing, and sometimes helps to correct wrongs after a *Pravda* journalist goes on the spot to check out facts.

JEN MIN JIH PAO

Jen Min Jih Pao ("The People's Daily"), the major Chinese newspaper, cannot rival *Pravda*'s circulation, even though there are four times as many readers. But since in many

Chinese villages it is a duty to read in groups and to meditate together on articles, the paper's influence is probably much more widespread than the official circulation figure of 2 million indicates. The little we can say about Mao's press always runs the risk of being false or out of date, especially since the havoc of the Cultural Revolution. We do know that all media are under the direct control of the Department of Propaganda of the Chinese Communist Party. All newsmen are appointed by the local hierarchy of the Party, subject to approval by higher-ups. To insure greater security, the printed and electronic media are forbidden to pick up news from sources other than from the New China News Agency, which is the only source of foreign news. Understandably under such conditions, direct censorship is unneeded. *Jen Min Jih Pao* is printed daily in Peking and in five other cities. It is the official Party organ, founded in Yenan in 1948, and has only six pages. Another daily is the *Kuang Ming Jih Pao,* the "private" organ of the nominal non-Communist parties. Specializing in cultural and educational articles, its four pages reflect the views of the Chinese intelligentsia. Lastly, *Chieh Fan Chun Jih Pao* is the daily of the Popular Liberation Army, and in 1966 was the official paper of the Cultural Revolution. Many other publications appeared at that time but did not survive the tumult.

In the Chinese press of today, every article considered for publication must have a political angle. There is no such thing as presenting news in the Western sense of the term, such as government shuffles, plane crashes, or (as yet) moon walks. The internal purges of the Party remain unknown to the reader. Foreign news consists mainly of reports of strikes which are throwing capitalist countries into turmoil and antiwar demonstrations in the United States. In any given issue of *People's Daily,* on the first page are announcements of Party decisions, an editorial, and commentaries, as well as news of meetings and conversations with foreign diplomats and heads of state. Page two is devoted to national news and letters to the editor. Foreign news usually appears on pages three and four, and the last pages carry reports on the achievements of individuals or groups, personal stories, propaganda poems and . . . a bit of advertising. Olaf Lagercrantz, editor-in-chief of Sweden's largest daily, noted during a 1971 trip to China that Chinese journalists were sent in groups of seven or eight to work three months on farms or in factories in order to learn the wisdom of the masses, to contribute labor in exchange for their education, and to recruit correspondents among the workers and peasants. It is difficult to evaluate even now all the consequences of the Cultural Revolution, but as far as we can tell it seems to have resulted in even more uniformity in a press which has never been noted for its diversity.

However, in July 1972 a campaign was launched in *People's Daily* (in the form of a letter printed on the first page) against lengthy and insipid articles, which were called "monotonous, dry and boring." This letter, sent by professors of literature, noted that the new dogmatism was disastrous for readers. Reacting to this in a disciplined way, the editor of the paper suddenly remembered that thirty years earlier, Mao Tse-tung had called some of the Communist cadres' articles "long and stinking." Could this be the beginning of a new look for the Chinese press?

THE UNDERINFORMED COUNTRIES

While a large number of people in the West are fighting a losing battle against obesity, a third of the world's population is suffering from malnutrition. The situation is the same in terms of brain food. For billions of people, the major obstacle to freedom of the press is more a lack of press than a lack of freedom.

In 1961, UNESCO defined a basic goal for the development of information in the poor countries, not only as a good thing in itself, but also because economic progress demands education and a system of circulating ideas and news. UNESCO recommended that these countries move as quickly as possible to a level of ten copies of a daily paper for every 100 people (the rate was twenty-five in France in 1970), five radios (thirty-two in France) and two TV sets (twenty in France). The UNESCO report stated that the hundred nations, composed of Asia, Black Africa, and South America, and representing a combined population of 2 billion people, or 66 percent of the world total, had not reached this bare minimum. Therefore, two-thirds of the world's population lacks the necessary means to keep in touch with what is going on in their country, much less "abroad."[1] Yet, during the last ten years, progress in propagating news and ideas has been slow. Radio involves a minimum of technical problems, therefore seems to have made greater advances than any other medium. But, as far as newspapers go, Wilbur Schramm, a professor at Stanford University who was responsible for the UNESCO report, remarked that at the current rate of advancement UNESCO's goals would not be met in Africa until the year 2035.

Naturally, there are wide disparities. Latin America has quite a number of publications. Rio de Janeiro and Santiago each have a half dozen dailies. One of the best newspapers in the world is São Paulo's *Estado,* owned by the Mesquita family. But outside the great urban centers, the influence and the circulation of such newspapers quickly wane. On the other hand, Africa is a desert as far as the printed press is concerned. There is only one daily in the Cameroons (population 5 million) with a circulation of 12,000; one daily in Guinea (population 3.5 million) with a circulation of 5,000. Of the two dailies in Niger (population 3 million) the most important one, *Le Temps du Niger,* has a circulation of 1,300. Throughout Africa, the governments have complete control of the audio-visual media, but their use of television for propaganda remains limited because they do not have enough means to produce their own programs and therefore have to buy practically all of them from abroad. This has insignificant implications since most African countries can only count one TV set for every fifty to one hundred families, with the exception of Egypt, which has one set for every twenty-five families.

But even if these basic requirements were attained the circulation of necessary information for development might be hampered by censorship and dubious quality of content. In Peru, where television is, for the most part, privately owned, nearly 40 percent of air time is devoted to advertising, which makes commercial American television channels seem like cultural sanctuaries by comparison. In Srihanka (Ceylon), for the pur-

[1] In Morocco, the daily newspaper was at one time considered a luxury product. For a fraction of its price, one could borrow it for a short time from the vendor, who would then pass it on to another reader, and, by the end of the day, return it as unsold. To foil this, the publishers used a bit of glue to stick the pages together to make sure that the ones that had been turned back had not been read.

pose of punishing an unfavorable press, the Bandaranaike government has upped the newsprint import duties from 5 to 80 percent in the last ten years. In addition, the publishers have to pay a 55 percent tax on all imports. Ankara, the capital of Turkey, has twenty-three dailies (as many as Morocco, Algeria, and Tunisia put together), but most of them only sell from 100 to 1,000 copies and can only be called newspapers in an official, statistical sense.

Even in India, where freedom of the press is part of the British legacy, in April 1972, Mrs. Ghandi took the step of restricting the number of pages to ten per day. She argued that the excessive amount of imported newsprint weighed too heavily on the balance of payments, even though the biggest daily of India sells only 300,000 copies. In point of fact, the measure was intended to bully a press too involved with business and too critical of the socialist government. As far as the other media are concerned in India, enormous technical possibilities are hampered by formidable cultural barriers. The English futurologist Arthur Clarke stated in January 1972 that a single orbital satellite could provide India with television broadcasts on family planning, cattle feeding, and other vital education at a cost of $1 a year per viewer. Unfortunately, a lone satellite can not cope with the fact that India has fourteen states—each with a different official language. In addition, there are more than fifty other languages each spoken by more than 100,000 people. The technical dream remains just that, because the cultural situation makes a national network impossible. Only the small local radio stations are able to broadcast information, each in its own tongue.

BORDERS IN SPACE

The example of India points up the gap between solutions suitable for the most developed countries and the means available to the Third World. Professor Schramm, in a statement made at the end of 1971 in Singapore, noted that educational television programs cost on the average five times more than radio programs. But the underdeveloped countries—like the industrialized ones—are fascinated by the possibilities offered by television in the field of public education. Therefore, they neglect thoroughly exploring the possibilities of radio. A nation like Japan, on the other hand, relies for after-school education or training on a combination of radio and correspondence courses, even though—more so than any other country, with the exception of the United States—it has the means to provide educational programs via television. The results have been excellent, which goes to show once more that financial or technical means are no more crucial than a rational approach to the problems to be solved.

Finally, the fact that technology can someday quickly and cheaply solve all of the problems of "underinformation" signifies nothing in view of current political realities. A great deal has been said about satellites which could broadcast directly over national borders to private sets (not relayed by intermediate ground stations, as is the case today). The advocates of a private commercial TV network in France believe that in the long run the eventuality will break the state monopoly. But even if the technical means are at hand, worldwide television will be long in coming. France made an effort in this direction (far from its own borders) with the Socrates project, which was to have sent educational programs to every French-speaking African country. The project failed because the countries concerned could not agree on the programs to be broadcast. In August 1972, Andrei Gromyko asked the United Nations to adopt a resulution which would make illegal any television broadcasting that would interfere with internal affairs of any country without its consent. If such interference were to occur, each nation could take the steps it deemed necessary, not only over its own territory but also in space. The Soviet Union has the means to destroy satellites that are a threat to them. For them, it is an urgent matter to guard against an invasion of ideas—and advertising. We can be sure that many countries (like France, unfortunately) would give a sigh of relief if an international agreement were signed to guarantee noninterference with each one's favorite propaganda tool. The only consolation is that history shows that it has always been impossible to stem the flow of ideas permanently.

Chapter 3

Nothing Is Sacred Any More—Not Even Money

As Alphonse Allais has pointed out, money helps one to withstand poverty, and, since up until this century poverty was the general rule, it is only natural for money to have been uncontestedly popular. Now, however, thanks to economic growth, the people in a handful of industrial countries have emerged from penury and attained relative affluence. But this relative material security has taught them that having money in hand is not in itself totally satisfying. The dawning realization that the accumulation of wealth is not an end in itself but a means to an end has lead many to dream about knocking the golden calf off its pedestal. Without as yet having the means to by-pass money, they do have the means to criticize it. One man saw this eventuality as early as 1930:

> When the accumulation of wealth is no longer of high social importance, there will be great changes in the code of morals. We shall be able to rid ourselves of many of the pseudo-moral principles which have hag-ridden us for two hundred years, by which we have exalted some of the most distasteful of human qualities into the position of the highest virtues. We shall be able to afford to dare to assess the money-motive at its true value. The love of money as a means to the enjoyments and realities of life will be recognized for what it is, a somewhat disgusting morbidity, one of those semi-criminal, semi-pathological propensities which one hands over, with a shudder, to the specialists in mental disease. All kinds of social customs and economic rewards and penalties, which we now maintain at all costs, however distasteful and unjust they may be in themselves, because they are tremendously useful in promoting the accumulation of capital, we shall then be free, at last, to discard.

This Maoist, this visionary, this *naïf*, was John Maynard Keynes, the British author of *The General Theory of Employ-*

ment, Interest and Money, whose theories are credited with having brought the capitalist world out of the Great Depression. Lord Keynes was one of the very few economists who knew how to turn his theories to personal advantage; he became a millionaire by playing the stock market. Who had a better understanding of the principles and practice of money? Keynes had the knowledge and intelligence to assess the underlying relationship between money and the public good—both in its negative and positive aspects. His prediction that capital accumulation would at a certain point be seen as a barrier to the "enjoyments and realities of life," made more than forty years ago, is only now being recognized in a small part of the world, the industrialized West. It is understandable that in areas where the contradictions between money and moral values are the sharpest questions should arise. One of these areas is the information industry. Everything about the relationship of the media and money is being and will continue to be questioned, contested, and, inevitably transformed.

CONCENTRATION AND PROFITS

A. J. Liebling, the late, talented writer and critic of the press, warned that freedom of the press was guaranteed only to those who own the press. Since the war the number of owners has declined at an increasingly high rate in every industrial country. From Social Democratic Sweden to free-enterprise America, the same economic conditions have eliminated small newspapers to the advantage of large ones, which have regrouped to form more powerful and more profitable economic units. These regroupings are systematically attacked by the journalists, who have attempted to alert public opinion to their dangers in France in May 1972 when the Hersant group, owner of seven small dailies, took over *Paris-Normandie* of Rouen; in vain the newsmen countered the take-over by striking, stating: "A newspaper that falls under the sway of a financial group is no longer a free newspaper." There was no professional or political criticism of Robert Hersant, since no one could reproach him for keeping a tight rein over his other newspapers. It was the principle of concentration that the newsmen opposed.

It could be said that demands for independence threaten the normal functioning of the market in the information industry;

259

nevertheless, a vocal minority of newsmen insist upon it. The concern over independence versus mergers is not limited to leftists. The official report of a commitee of the Canadian Senate on the media concluded that an intolerable situation existed if the public interest in such a vital area as information depended on the greed or the good will of a small group of privileged businessmen. The claim that in a capitalistic society bigger industrial units are a necessity for optimum functioning in certain fields has seriously begun to be doubted. Although economic units in the information industry are incomparably smaller than those in manufacturing industries, the advent of mergers and the increasing concentration of the media under one umbrella have given rise to violent controversy, and the condition will be less and less tolerated.

An American professor, Hillier Krieghbaum, in his book *Pressures on the Press,* gives a significant example, focusing on the ubiquitous conglomerate ITT.

> Some of the projected dangers of conglomerate ownership loomed very real when the International Telephone and Telegraph Corporation sought to purchase the American Broadcasting Company with its network facilities and motion picture properties. At FCC hearings, one of the questions asked was whether ITT with vast business interests in the United States and abroad would try to tamper with ABC's news coverage in cases where the parent company's interests might be at stake. ITT executives promised that, if they received FCC permission to control ABC, attempts to influence or bias the news would never take place.
>
> When the FCC was considering whether to reopen the merger proceedings in February 1967, ITT naturally watched what Washington correspondents were writing, but what was far from routine was that they complained to the two press associations, *The New York Times, Wall Street Journal* and *Washington Post* about news coverage. According to one report among Washington newsmen, an ABC representative complained to the Associated Press and United Press International. The concern's public relations men argued that ITT executives were dissatisfied because some of the coverage was "incomplete and unfair." After his editor got an irate telephone call, one reporter was quoted as saying "It is incredible that guys like this want the right to run ABC's news operation." The *Columbia Journalism Review,* watchdog of media performance, said bluntly that "ABC News often sounded as if its stories about the mergers were dictated by management."

When the FCC announcement on a delay in effective date of the merger was released, an ABC official is reported to have called AP in New York to complain about a story on the wire from Washington. As Professor William L. Rivers of Stanford University and a former Washington correspondent told a U.S. Senate subcommittee, "The Washington reporter was in the middle of his sixth paragraph when ABC's request that the first paragraph be changed was relayed to him. He refused to change it." Rivers concluded that the ITT efforts not only showed the corporation was "extremely sensitive about news reports" concerning it but that "it will make unusual efforts to shape the reports to its liking."

In the end, the merger between ITT and ABC was turned down.

Above and beyond media concentration, simple ownership of the media by private interests is being questioned by politicians and journalists. The idea that a public service should belong to the public is making a few inroads, but the obvious drawback is the lack of objectivity of the media when they are in the hands of the state. Television is therefore not entirely harmful to the privately owned press. Lack of independence in regard to the political powers that be offers the most solid argument against the idea of nationalizing newspapers.

If state control of newspapers is not around the corner, there is talk of governments extending financial aid to the "deserving" press, that is, the press that actually carries out its "mission to inform." The distinction is a tricky one. In France, subsidies have up to now been given to all kinds of publications, from opinion sheets to fashion magazines. The question of how to tip the scale of aid in favor of the information press, which is in bad financial straits, has been discussed at length recently. In France, an Opinion Press Association was founded in 1972 by two dailies in financial difficulty—*Combat,* run by Henry Smadja, and *La Croix,* run by a Catholic press group headed by Jean Gelamur. The association demanded that priority be given to subsidies for opinion and information newspapers or for those papers in which less than a certain percentage of space is given over to advertising.

This is precisely what was envisioned in a government report on the press prepared in 1972 by Jean Serisé. For the first time it was recommended that government financial help should not be given uniformly, but should vary according to the type of newspaper. For example, dailies with small amounts of advertising would receive a subsidy for their newsprint, which would be proportionately twice that for those whose advertising revenue represents more than 30 percent of their gross. Legislation in the Netherlands similarly takes into account the particular situation of each publication in determining subsidies.

In the United States, when the postal rates were about to be increased considerably, Nixon's friend Billy Graham, editor of the magazine *Decision,* appeared before a Congressional committee and demanded that the bulk mailing rates be scaled "according to an evaluation based on the respective social merits of the publications." In Sweden, a tax on advertising was designed to redistribute a portion of overall press profits to opinion newspapers in difficulty. Whatever method is adopted, there will be a gradually decreasing tolerance of papers like *France-Dimanche* (a sort of *National Enquirer*) receiving the same official subsidies as *Le Monde. If Le Monde* continues to print a lot of advertising, it could receive proportionally less in subsidies than *La Croix,* which gets only 10 percent of its receipts from advertising (not because of its virtuous policies on advertising but simply because *La Croix* does not have enough readers to attract more advertisers).

SEDUCING THE JOURNALISTS

Journalists are hardly immune to the power of money. True, practically all of them would indignantly decline a handout of $2,000 from a particularly tactless businessman who wanted an article written about his company. But if this same industrialist offers a group of journalists a small business-cum-pleasure trip to his plant, he will get what he wants and at a much cheaper price—only $200 to $300 per journalist. The public relations invitation is accepted practice because it saves face. It is immoral to accept cash, but it is bad manners not to write an article (which can even be spiced with a few critical comments) after accepting such an invitation—which is, after all, a payment in kind, though less than the cash payment would have been. Newspapers do not have large budgets for travel expenses, and these little trips—payed for by a company or a foreign country—provide moments of healthy relaxation in the hectic life of a journalist. I have often witnessed scenes like the following: a letter arrives on the desk of the editor-in-chief asking him to come along on a five-day junket organized by the Rumanian government to inspect its new tourist facilities. He does not have time to go, because he has just come back from a convention in Marbella, Spain, organized by the Supermarket Association on the theme of "Distribution and Social Progress." It is out of the question to send his assistant, who has just returned from Colombia where he was the guest of the coffee exporters. But good old Paul has not yet traveled this year. Even though his field is legal reporting, he will represent the paper on the beaches of the Black Sea. When he gets back and submits his brief article, the editor-in-chief, out of sheer decency, will not have the courage to turn it down. The Rumanians will therefore get some coverage in several newspapers, which, if they had paid the standard advertising rates, would have cost them ten times more and would have had less impact on the readers. The way to avoid this subtle corruption is not automatically to refuse all such invitations, because a great deal of useful information can be gathered during these trips in addition to what the host wants you to swallow. It would be better for the paper to have enough money to be able to pay for every trip, every meal, every hotel room. This is a highly costly policy that only a few American newspapers—for instance, *The Wall Street Journal* and *The Los Angeles Times*—can afford. The only invitations they accept are those that in the editor's mind have real news value; they only send journalists when it is agreed with the organizers that the paper will pick up the tab. As paying guests, they feel much more at ease to write objectively about what has been shown to them—or to write nothing at all. But, with less affluent publications, even the newsman who is most finicky about interference by advertisers or owners has no qualms about this sort of sport. Not too long ago, the *Denver Post* attempted to abolish this form of "payola," but the editorial staff reacted so strongly that the publisher was forced to reverse himself and publicly acknowledge the practice.

EDITORIAL ADVERTISING

When they cannot get free articles, many advertisers and agencies try to make their paid advertising look as much as possible like articles. Sometimes this is very easy to do, since a number of publications believe that their readers—more often than not their female readers—are mostly interested in practical information about products. Therefore the advertisers are asked to pay for their presence in the editorial pages. This is the usual practice, for example, in a homes and furnishing magazine like *La Maison de Marie-Claire;* it is also routine for *Jours de France* to do an automobile industry advertiser a favor by putting his latest model on the cover.

In April 1972, the noncommercial New York television channel organized a public debate among the editors-in-chief of the major American women's magazines about the relationship between editorial staffs and advertising departments. Some— such as John Mack Carter of *Ladies' Home Journal*— maintained that there was not the slightest bit of influence. Others, like James Brady, who was then editor of *Harper's Bazaar,* admitted that such dealings exist, but he claimed that since he had taken over the magazine he had put a stop to the traditional policy of giving preferential editorial treatment to products of advertisers. Richard Shortway of *Vogue* said that in the magazine business it was a fact of life that those who advertise get editorial space. And he went on to cite the example of the Lacoste dresses which traditionally grace the cover of the January issue of *Vogue*—resulting in sales of 40,000 to 50,000 of the dresses displayed.

What is new here is not that these practices exist, but that they are aired publicly. A newsman writing a "thank you" article does not feel dishonest about doing it; neither does an advertising agency which runs an ad made up to resemble the editorial content of a journal; nor a publisher who has to choose between two items to publish and picks the one most likely to keep his magazine going. At the very most, they might admit that sometimes there are practices they would just as soon not see but which, after all, are a part of their trade. The public is becoming more discriminating and more demanding. When a scandal breaks over particularly flagrant forms of "payola," the people are clued in that such things exist. But they still remain unaware that every newspaper is solicited in the same way and few are capable of resisting one form or another of clandestine advertising. The more that is known about these interactions, the harder it will be for them to take place.

But to be completely independent of advertisers and the powers that be, one must be either very weak or very strong. Absolute independence is enjoyed by the *Canard Enchaîné*, a satirical paper which in all its forty-five years of existence has never run one line of advertising; but it gets by on a frugal budget that would be unacceptable to other journals. At the opposite extreme, publications like *Le Figaro, Le Monde,* or *L'Express* can indulge in the luxury of resisting pressure from an advertiser or an agency because their revenues come from hundreds of clients, not one of whom represents 5 percent of the total. However, one thinks very carefully before falling out with advertisers like Air France or Renault. The trade press, on the other hand, by definition has only a small number of potential advertisers. When one deals with photography or sailing, it does not take very long to see that a handful of companies control the camera and outboard motor markets. To get on the wrong side of them is tantamount to killing the publication. In cases of semi–government-controlled industries, such as oil or aeronautics in France, you present anything but a faithful reflection of the official line at the risk of losing your major advertiser. Looked at this way, the magazine is actually being subsidized, which is why the trade press is hardly anything more than a catalogue, content to stick to the practical side of things. The big publications have more elbow room and can refer more freely to the actual conditions and problems of a given profession or company.

THE MISFORTUNES OF ADVERTISING AGENCIES

Advertising is the most remarkable and visible modern interaction of information, money, and the citizen. Being neither clandestine nor stealthy, real advertising, that which is openly accepted by newspapers, radio, and television from organizations with a "message" to deliver, is itself increasingly on the defensive. The fundamental grievance articulated by J. K. Galbraith in several of his books was summed up by *Le Monde's* Maurice Duverger in June 1972, in connection with the clandestine advertising that was causing such an uproar in France. "Is overt advertising any less disgraceful? Must a state-run institution (French television) become one of the basic elements of the gigantic brainwashing set-up which directs the production of developed capitalist nations toward the plethoric manufacture of objects and household gadgets to the detriment of more useful but less profitable collective facilities?" It is a lengthy sentence, encompassing all the standard terminology: "brainwashing," "capitalist," "gadgets," and "more useful collective facilities." Again the old question rears between revolution and reform. The revolutionary would hold that advertising is evil in itself and should be done away with once and for all; but, because advertising is a necessary evil of the free enterprise system, to abolish it requires doing away with the system itself.[1] Reform—always more complicated and less heady than revolution—means admitting that advertising is a useful economic tool which, in practice, brings on many inconveniences for society and therefore should be modified. It is obviously in the interests of advertising agencies and advertisers to make everyone believe that the only choice is between revolution and the status quo, since they know very well that revolution is far less popular than the status quo. Replying to Duverger, Philippe Charmet, president of an advertising agency, wrote what might have been expected: "In this case, the kind of society in which we live is being questioned; it is a matter of a political choice condemning the economics of free competition." A few years ago, *Reader's Digest* was moved by the same spirit to conduct a slightly simplistic opinion poll: one group of readers received their normal copy of the magazine, the other the same issue with all the advertising removed. Naturally, the second group was less pleased with the issue than the first. How many times have I heard advertising men claim this proves that the reader likes advertising. How does one explain that, in every poll conducted since in the advanced countries, a majority of people tolerate advertising less and less? They are not complaining about the fact that advertising exists, but that it goes too far. Nevertheless, its excesses—its overabundance, lies, unfounded statements, omissions, contempt for the consumer apparent in both content and

---

[1]Nonetheless, one can imagine that some forms of advertising could be done away with short of a revolution. One hundred thousand of the 800,000 highway billboards defacing the American countryside have already been removed following a law passed by Congress in 1965; the remainder are supposed to have disappeared by the Bicentennial in 1976.

language—can be corrected. As the most anarchic element of the economic market, advertising has taken on some thoroughly reproachable and even degrading features. If it is incapable of purging itself, it could be signing its own death warrant. For the moment the problem has not been posed in quite these terms. The new pressure groups such as consumer advocates, government regulatory efforts, the self-initiatives by principled professionals—all of these are now having an effect.

CONSUMER PRESSURE

Increasing numbers of businessmen are coming to view the demands of consumers as part of the normal costs of doing business, like advertising and promotion. To ignore them could lead straight to bankruptcy. This is a modern example of the pragmatic principle that has always benefited businessmen: "If you can't beat them, join them." Nowadays there are few businessmen who dare openly attack the one man who is making them do a slow burn: Ralph Nader. After all, he is increasingly the customer's spokesman, and a good merchant knows perfectly well that the customer (the sucker) is always right. So what is it that these customers want? They want more information. Journalist Max Ways explained this in noble terms in *Fortune,* when he wrote that the way to defend the market economy was to be sure that there was enough of that essential component of a healthy market and a healthy democracy— information. The consumers want to know everything about a product that has not been disclosed thus far. They want labels on canned foods like those on parmaceutical products, giving in detail the amount of protein, chemical additives, coloring matter, and calories. They want the press to carry criticism of products, as it does of the theater and movies, with no hesitation about naming brand names. Why, a reader wrote to his newspaper, is it acceptable for critics to be able to break a work of art or its creator, while no one dares cite a company for making shoddy or mediocre products? It would demand a great deal of courage on the part of the media. When *L'Auto-Journal* decided to increase its readership by conducting no-nonsense tests on cars, it had to give up the manufacturers' ads at the same time. Things are changing in Sweden, which to an even greater extent than the United States is accustomed to high incomes and a high standard of living. The Bonnier press group of Sweden puts out two hugely successful large-circulation magazines which test numerous products and nevertheless receive advertising on a regular basis from even those firms that they criticize severely. Why not? It's an everyday occurrence for the entertainment page of a newspaper to carry an ad for a film printed alongside the review that pans it.

In addition, the Swedes tackled the problems of regulating advertising in a way characteristic of them: they established a consumer ombudsman in 1971. Filling the post is Sven Heurgren, a jurist who has been fighting against dangerous or simply false advertising. By negotiating with the tobacco manufacturers, he obtained their agreement to stop presenting ads showing relaxed couples smoking while walking in the woods, because the image made too close an association between cigarettes and happiness. In one year, more than 2,000 complaints were presented to him by consumers or competitors, and he intervened personally in more than 400 cases, which were mostly settled by discussing the problem with the advertisers. Only sixteen cases had to be brought before a commercial court. Newspapers, radio, and television, which cover and comment on the ombudsman's decisions, are obviously his best lever. In a very short time all advertising in Sweden has become observably more "informative."

CULTURAL REVOLUTION IN ADVERTISING

Recently the Federal Trade Commission rocked the advertising world in the United States to its foundations by subjecting the content of commercials to tougher rules. The new requirements, which many agencies already consider their Calvary, are as follows: 1. substantiation of what is claimed; 2. retraction and correction of false claims; 3. agreeing to citizen and consumer groups' printing counteradvertising to denounce what they consider abusive. And Nader has added his two cents' worth by encouraging firms to attack in their ads the defective products of rivals, a bloody war he hopes will benefit the consumer.

The burden of proof now lies with the media presenting the ads. Consequently, before launching a new campaign, an advertiser must supply the TV channel or newspaper with a convincing demonstration of its claims. In 1970, Gilette had to put on a day-long demonstration for an NBC Television doctor to prove to him its new doubled-edged razor, Trac II, really shaved closer than other models. Two years earlier, this would not have been at all necessary.

Similarly, in 1972, the FCC published for the first time the names of seventeen advertisers who had insufficiently backed up the statements made in their ads. Among them: General Motors, Ford, Volkswagen, Westinghouse, Zenith. No doubt this simple public finger-pointing is more worrisome for the firms concerned than the fines involved, which amount to ridiculously little.

In March 1972, nine Chicago travel agencies were publicly denounced by the city's office of consumer affairs for having tried to cheat the public through their ads. They had omitted to mention, for example, that the advertised hotel prices were for doubles and that single occupancy would be more expensive; that extra hotel costs would be collected even though the price advertised was supposed to be all inclusive, and that some of the advantages mentioned were valid only for part of the trip.

As for correcting errors, the Association of Sugar Manufacturers has had a bitter experience. In August 1972 it was forced to sign an agreement with the Federal Trade Commission requiring it to run full-page ads in seven nationwide magazines contradicting past ads in which it had stated that eating sugar before meals reduces the appetite and makes you lose weight. The FTC-approved correction explained that the way to lose weight is to consume fewer calories than one burns up.

The most recent and least agreeable development as far as advertisers are concerned is the FTC's demand that radio and television offer free time to counteradvertising, which will air the arguments of the public against commercial campaigns. In California one such agency already exists—Stern Concern— which specializes in drawing up the messages of these counteradvertisers. We can thus read in an ad displaying a bottle of pills: "As for plain aspirin there is no persuasive scientific evidence one brand is more effective than another . . . although the major brands cost a lot more. So, next time you buy something for your head, use your head. Buy the least expensive plain aspirin you can find." As one can imagine, such refreshing copy is not run without a fierce struggle with the traditional commercial circles. In the spring of 1972, television channels actually refused to run a spot in which Burt Lancaster explained: "If you have one of these Chevrolets, it could cost you your life. They were built with potentially faulty engine mounts. If one breaks, it could jam the accelerator wide open and knock out your power brakes at the same time. Several thousand accidents have been reported and some deaths have been alleged. Now General Motors has announced they won't give you new engine mounts, but they will install a free safety cable. If you have one of these cars, I urge you—get it to a Chevrolet service man—slowly." The president of the association of radio and television station owners may repeat until he is blue in the face that this is "economic masochism," but once the consumers and their lawyers have access to the same financial means as the producers the entire aspect of marketing will change very fast.

One of the first changes can be seen in a recent spate of commercials on American television, where one advertiser attacks by name a rival product. Up until now such direct comparisons have been taboo in the profession, but early in 1972 the FCC intervened directly with the national networks, encouraging the adoption of this new advertising style. Beech-Nut chewing gum now shows their package of eight sticks of gum next to that of Wrigley's, which holds only seven. Volkswagen insists on the advantages its models have over a Maverick, or Toyota. Lincoln, which up until now has referred in its ads to "the other American luxury car," is getting ready to call a Cadillac a Cadillac. One advertising agency executive has exclaimed: "If this is consumerism, I'm all for it," but the professionals really hope that these fights between kingpins will ward off the threat of counteradvertising from consumer associations, which they find much more dangerous. In the meantime, Ralph Nader is racking up points.

All in all, the cries of alarm from the advertising agencies have died down. They are beginning to realize that they can adapt themselves to this new atmosphere without going under. A report in August 1972 by *Advertising Age* actually predicted—despite all the new sets of rules—that, after five difficult years, advertising should again develop rapidly at least for the following five years.

OFFENSIVE TO WOMEN

Two social groups that have been the favorite targets of advertising will in the future find less acceptable the roles of consuming animals that advertising imposes on them. These are women and children, whose preferences carry great weight in deciding what the family is going to buy; they form the basic public for most advertising. Publications for women and the women's pages of newspapers are for the most part in reality advertising catalogues; TV commercials are almost entirely devoted to selling products for use in the home. Without necessarily being militant feminists, women are declaring themselves to be more and more bothered by the distorted images of themselves that advertising generates. During a convention of journalists representing media devoted to women in Palermo in 1972, the newswomen (there are very few newsmen in this field) pointed out to ad agencies that they were "hanging on to an often stale image . . . one that was more and more flagrantly out of line with the aspirations of their readers." The year before, *Good Housekeeping* concluded after a poll that more than one-third of its readers (mostly housewives over thirty-five years old) had felt like turning off their TV set because of a commerical that offended them. To buttress their case that most advertising directed at women is offensive, the National Organization for Women analyzed 1,200 spot TV commercials. Practically all of them presented women who stayed at home (not taking into account the fact that 45 percent of adult American women work); 42 percent presented women as housewives, 33 percent as being under a man's thumb, 16 percent as "sex objects," and 17 percent as being completely unintelligent. Only .3 percent of these commercials showed women as autonomous human beings leading their own lives. More often than not, these spot films show a woman condemned to domestic hard labor while everyone else in the family—including the dog— leads a good life. Men are constantly giving women advice to which they listen worshipfully. They are never shown buying a plane ticket or traveling alone. Many were depicted as unclean and smelly, repulsive to men until they agreed to spray themselves with a whole gamut of products.

Even if this prejudice is less evident in France, we do nonetheless tell the woman consumer that her husband will love her more if she buys him a six-pack of beer, that she is really lucky if her husband "doesn't get angry when there's a button missing on one of his shirts," or that "now men are going to love women who do the dishes." This is not the language which endears men to their equals—which is obviously how women want to be considered. But here, there is no need for new rules, because the agencies that keep a keen eye out for shifts in the wind will quickly change their tune.

ADVERTISING AND CHILDREN

Parents amazed at how children absorb like a sponge what is presented to them can take no comfort in the estimates of S. I. Hayakawa, former head of San Francisco State University, that before they are eighteen most children will have watched 350,000 commercials on television. Since no one yet knows what the long-range effects of this can be, the natural tendency should be to reduce to the bare minimum this exposure which, even if it is not harmful, cannot in any case be useful. Faced with the growing concern of parental public opinion, the TV networks have agreed to cut back the advertising in children's programs from sixteen minutes an hour to twelve. But, as journalist Joseph Morgenstern has noted, the proper number of commercials per children's hour should be none. Since our society can no longer discuss a problem without taking a poll, the advertisers have counterattacked with the results of an investigation by the Institute of Mental Health which shows that children do not take advertising seriously. School children from five to twelve years old agreed on one point: "Advertising is funny but it's not true"—their attention is attracted more by the story being told than by the product being presented. But, if this is correct, why is more than $100 million a year spent in the United States on advertising aimed at children? Skeptical parents might be interested in Dr. L. Friedman's advice on children and television:

1. Keep television out of the reach of small children. Treat it like drugs, alcohol, and household poisons.

2. Keep TV out of the main living parts of the house—make it an effort to get to the set. Children, unless they are already addicted, will not go to watch TV alone, but will do so automatically if the parents do.

272

3. Never give a child a television set of his own and expect him to control the use of it. He won't, and the responsibility is yours, not his.

4. Spend more time with your growing children; they really do prefer conversation and doing things with parents to watching television.

5. For those who must have artificial sound for company, turn on your television, lie down on the couch, close your eyes, and pretend it is a radio.

Chapter 4

The Urgent Need for a New Ethic

The English historian–philosopher Arnold Toynbee believes that the great crises of our time result from the moral gap between the prodigious progress of science (and the power it has made available to man) and the stagnation of ethical and political concepts. When man unleashes modern weaponry in the name of national and territorial principles of the nineteenth century, the result is the 55 million dead of World War II. This moral gap widens as power grows more rapidly than awareness of its consequences. The scientists of Los Alamos were so pressed by circumstances in 1945 that they devoted all their energies to developing a workable bomb as fast as possible, and none to wondering whether what they were doing was right. Some of those who later considered the moral implications of their work bore the resulting anguish to their graves.

While the media do not have the destructive power of the atom bomb, what power they do have is exercised without restraint. Literacy, material prosperity, and technical innovations have, in only one generation, multiplied the impact of media on society. Yet at the same time intellectual attitudes, professional ethics, notions of propriety, and decision-making processes have scarcely changed. People are only just beginning to realize that they too must evolve, and in any such evolution the media are bound to play a main role. To do this properly, their collective ethic must be revitalized. No one can single-handedly define or even propose such an ethic, but everybody should be conscious of the problems a new ethic will have to confront.

MORE DEMANDING CITIZENS

While journalists crusade to take over some of the power now held by publishers, while politicians fight over the monopoly of the airwaves, the hitherto-silent public is beginning to insist on its own rights. The more far-reaching the consequences of media become, the harder it is to accept the fact that they are subject to no democratic process, that they defend only the interests of whoever owns them, be it a small professional elite or the state. Public demands are going to crystalize around certain set themes which can no longer be ignored.

Access: People now realize that freedom of expression is useless without the means to exercise it. In the United States, emerging minority groups are claiming the right to access. Students, blacks, homosexuals, religious sects all want broadcasting time or their own printed column. In France, in June 1971, Grenoble leftists staged a hunger strike to force the local daily *Le Dauphiné Libéré* to publish the conclusions of their Revolutionary Court. For the time being in both America and France, such demands are made by pressuring people in charge of the media who, for their part, see no reason why they should transform their outlets into a public forum of dubious interest at the risk of dulling their clients' appetites for their products. As long as no law requires the allocation of air time to any and all groups of citizens with a cause to champion, whichever media agree to do it are placing themselves voluntarily in an unfavorable competitive situation. Among the "populist" demands in the United States, at least as expounded by Jack Newfield, is that every organization of 10,000 persons have the right to one hour of television time per week. If Newfield's proposals were implemented literally in a country of more than 200 million inhabitants, television programming could include nothing else.

Nevertheless, the politic of this issue has become so intense that it is leading to violence and blackmail. Revolutionary groups in Brazil take hostages in order to force the military government to read their proclamations over the radio. And at the very moment that Angela Davis was released from jail in June 1972, an extremist skyjacker took over a plane because he wanted television time to speak out in favor of the young black militant. Solutions will be difficult to find, even when cable television permits the existence of free-expression channels, because subsequent demands will be qualitative in nature. An audience of 10,000 will not be enough; the true right to access will mean prime time and major media.

If, as Marshall McLuhan says, television has turned the planet into a global village, is it not logical—thanks also to television—to return to the democratic tradition of the Swiss cantons where decisions were made collectively in the village square? This may not be realistic, but the question will certainly come up repeatedly to the extent that solutions will have to be envisioned.

Equality in information: Even when they are not expressing themselves, the public will decry favoritism in the news—that is, the constant mention of the same names. A taboo against this practice would obviously contradict the requirement that the media—broadcast or printed—report the news. In the words of an American commentator: "The journalist is controlled by this uncontrollable stupidity which is called news!" How to cope with the injustice of this uncontrollable stupidity? To demonstrate this type of inequity in the news, the Junior Chamber of Commerce of Nantes tried to sketch the image of different French cities which emerged from seven publications *(Le Monde, Le Figaro, L'Express, Paris-Match, Le Nouvel Observateur, Elle,* and *Les Informations)* between September 1971 and February 1972. This study showed that, except for Dunkirk, Strasbourg, and Nancy, the cities in the north of France were scarcely mentioned; those most cited were Strasbourg, Tours, Grenoble, Nancy, Nice, Marseilles, and Rennes, in that order; among those, Tours (where Mayor Jean Royer was making news by launching a morality campaign) and Marseilles (drugs, the difficulties of building a proposed industrial complex in nearby Fos-sur-Mer) were depicted mostly unfavorably, whereas Nice, Rennes, and Strasbourg came out well. The Jaycee study brought no judgment to bear on the media, but did ascertain, over a five-month period, that differences in journalistic treatment, which blanketed some towns in obscurity and stigmatized others, are the direct result of the subjective nature of news reporting.

Participation in the media: Since, theoretically, the people are equitably represented in legislatures, why should not this also be the case with regard to the media? This claim parallels that of the right to access. Is it possible that a daily paper might some day have to have half of its editorial staff composed of women, 20 percent of radicals, and 8 percent of farmers? Perhaps, but this would stretch to absurdity the issue involved in the legal employment demands, for example, of the Black minority employees who took *The Washington Post* to court in 1972 because it did not employ a nondiscriminatory percentage of Black reporters. In their words, "American Blacks are painfully conscious of the fact that they are not participating in the writing of American history during this period of change." Not surprisingly, the existence of numerous ethnic minorities in the United States sharpens the problem. When McGraw-Hill bought a group of television stations from Time, Inc., in 1971, Chicano employees, claiming to be maltreated, demanded and were granted participation in management. Among other concessions, McGraw-Hill agreed that a special council composed of one black and one Chicano would meet regularly with station managers to discuss the problems faced by minority groups, that 25 percent of the personnel would be chosen from minority groups, and that a specific number of documentaries dealing with minority group problems would be programmed.

In France, slightly comparable demands are beginning to surface, though they are based on different problems. Although there are no racial minorities outside of Paris, there is a monopoly—or rather a duopoly—on the news: government-owned regional television (which broadcasts only a few minutes per day) and the local daily paper under private control. There are no private TV or radio stations. It means a paltry palette for depicting the nuances of opinion over a whole region. Thus, in March 1972 in Grenoble, an association of readers of the local press was formed to counter "the silences and the commentaries of the *Dauphiné Libéré*, the *Progrès*, and the ORTF which, in concert, define local reality, slant it, manipulate it, emphasize it, or ignore it." The group is attempting to place in the newspapers its own column, to be written by readers and controlled solely by them.

The make-up of an editorial staff should without doubt be based on good qualifications rather than social representation. But once the first criterion is fulfilled, and the employer has a choice between a male and a female editor, he will more and more ask himself: "Do I have enough women on my team to ward off criticism?" The representation of the public in media must be more than merely symbolic.

Knowing the facts: Secrecy is the favorite weapon of those in power; it consolidates their privileges and shelters them from censorship. Nothing seems more unnatural to a government, political party, corporation, or labor union than to reveal what goes on behind closed doors. But thinking members of the public have the gall to insist that they deserve to know everything of general importance which affects them as a group, such as the activities of large institutions. "Freedom of the press" means the right to publish what one wishes, but "freedom of information" means more; it implies the right of the people to know everything that is going on, which was the right at stake in the case of the Pentagon Papers. This behind-closed-doors account of high-level decisions on Vietnam concerned mainly the past, and revealed no strategic information, but it did deal with certain explosive aspects of recent history. One sector of the American press saw no justification in hiding from American citizens how their leaders had involved and maintained them in a drama for which they were still suffering. But other papers, such as Otis Chandler's *Los Angeles Times,* continue to think that this publication was ill-advised.[1]

Sweden and Finland seem to be among the only countries where true freedom of information is written into the constitution. A Swedish law stipulates that "every Swedish citizen in principle has access to all public documents, those of the central government as well as those of regional authorities." Naturally, certain documents are classified, but they are exceptional, and, contrary to the situation in most other countries, publication is the norm. In France, even the limited provisions made for freedom of information are not enforceable. The press itself is a violator, because, by law, publications are supposed to publish annually in their own columns their balance sheets and the names of their shareholders. Only *Le Monde* does this regularly. Another law requires that the taxable income figures for any individual be made available to the public in city halls. This law

---

[1] In France, official archives are theoretically open to the public fifty years after an event. But in practice even after that interval those in charge throw up all sorts of obstacles to their access, even by university professors, to say nothing of journalists.

was never enforced until 1972. Henceforth it will be possible to find out (on a strictly local scale) the amount your fellow citizens pay in taxes, but publishing these figures remains punishable by imprisonment.

Eventually the public is going to demand total disclosure. Heads of industry will have to list the components of their products, businesses their detailed accounts, politicians the source of their campaign funds, governments their policy decisions, and citizens their income tax payments. This means increasing discomfort to those who dislike living in glass houses, but it is the only sure way to stamp out fraudulent practices and the abuse of power.

The right to privacy: It may be contradictory to insist on knowing everything about others and simultaneously seek more protection of one's own private life. But actually public disclosure should be limited to matters with a social impact, and the curtains drawn even tighter around all the rest. The individual himself must organize his resistance to the press and such ominous innovations as data banks. Sweden again is leading the war in fighting the indiscretions of the press by ruling in the code of ethics of the press against the naming not only of those accused of an offense, but those convicted if they are sentenced to a prison term of two years or less. A typical news item would thus read as follows: "A young Göteborg man, aged twenty-one, was arrested yesterday on a narcotics charge." In the small French town of Bruay-en-Artois, a notary public and his female companion were exposed by the media to public vindictiveness with only the lightest circumstantial evidence against them. This never could have happened in Sweden. Which is the more civilized country? France, where the commercial activities and income of a member of Parliament remain cloaked in secrecy but where a citizen can be victimized by the press after a simple police interrogation? Or Sweden, where the situation is reversed?

Data banks can engender outrageous individual injustices. Banks, insurance companies, and public institutions are often requested to conduct an inquiry into the background of an individual. Such an undertaking is routine when the person is being considered for a substantial loan or an important job. Not only is the information gathered without the knowledge of the person himself, it relies heavily on items of gossip furnished by neighbors. Once the information, confirmed or not, is on file, it is there forever and is served up regularly upon the request of various organizations, agencies working hand in glove with one another and the police. Whatever is untrue and defamatory as such cannot be expunged, because the subject himself is not given the chance to refute the misinformation. How many people come up against the stone wall of refusal of a loan or a job year after year because of some dubious or vicious testimony about which they haven't the merest suspicion? This is not a story by Franz Kafka, but the reality of the anonymous world of bureaucratic administration in which individual rights barely count. Safeguarding one's private life is part of the new ethic which must be developed concerning information. The right to refuse publication of your photograph in a tabloid newspaper is only the beginning!

TALKING BUT SAYING NOTHING

An IBM engineer calculated that the average private telephone gathers dust 99 percent of the time; during the remaining 1 percent, it is often used for trivial reasons. At a time when essential social needs such as vital hospital equipment cannot be filled for lack of funds, should society pamper itself with ultrasophisticated and costly means of communication used to transmit poor quality information or inept entertainment? During the first two days of President Nixon's trip to China, every Chinese who appeared on the television screen live and in color was an event. From then on, the reporters began to repeat themselves. By the morning of the third day, they were reduced to relaying their breakfast menus—by satellite, no less. Of the twenty-four journalists present on the trip, only one really knew the language and the country, from his long stay as a correspondent there: Theodore H. White. He was the reporter for public television, which could not afford the $300,000 fee for satellite transmission; therefore he was the only one who had to remain silent until he returned home. The greater the capacity for information, the less there seems to be to say or the more what is said becomes diluted. *Le Monde,* whose initial success led to substantial profits, was able to afford new machines and increase the number of its pages. Articles became more numerous and longer. Unfortunately, this has not meant that *Le Monde's* readers are better informed; the contrary may even be true.

When the paper was only sixteen pages long, one felt duty-bound to read it through. Some people spent sixty to ninety minutes every evening doing so. This is impossible with thirty-two pages. Now the most faithful reader skims over the whole, reading just a few articles in depth. While in some cases "the more, the better" is a desirable social goal, the cases are few and far between. Software—that is, the content of media—lags behind the technical potential of media. Texts published on glossy paper, surrounded by lavishly colored photographs, often are so badly written and have such meager intellectual vafue that they wouldn't even make a ripple on an encephalogram. The greater the number of hours available to television, the more relentless is the verbiage that fills them, because carefully conceived and structured broadcasts require funds that are generally not available to producers. In the United States, the Gannett newspaper chain, which has the largest number of dailies (more than fifty), is a gem from the point of view of management, and its profit ratio is the envy of competitors. But reader letters complain of "rationing of local news, awkward style of writing, haphazard layout, surfeit of special sections composed only of wire service dispatches, outdated articles, and advertisements—all in all, enough to want to make one read the competitor—if there were one!" Wherever territorial monopoly is the rule, there is a notable lack of quality in the product. When, in an American Sunday paper, the reader finds only seventeen pages of news out of a total of 190, isn't the 40 cents he paid for his paper 30 cents too much? The media's right to make large profits from the sale of information should not be contingent on the same quality control as is imposed upon canned goods or automobile manufacturers. Perhaps the day will come when partial control of media by journalists and readers will lead to the investment of at least some of the profits into higher editorial quality.[2]

RENEWED VIGILANCE NEEDED

Are today's media certain to make the best use of their traditional liberty and their newfound power? Are the functions of our Fourth Estate subjected to analysis, discussion, and proposi-

[2]Steps in the direction of correcting editorial errors are now being taken in the United States. Since 1969 the *Louisville Courier Journal,* and, since the summer of 1972, *The New York Times,* publish daily corrections of errors in previous editions. Such honesty has increased the confidence of their readers.

tions elsewhere than in a handful of university studies? Yes, in the United States, where newsmagazines devote a weekly section to the press and other media, where public television has a weekly program on the subject, where journals about journalism are plentiful. But in France one can leaf through dozens of newspapers and magazines, spend hours glued to the radio or television set, and learn nothing about media—except for the politics of the ORTF.

A number of things make it increasingly clear that the media are becoming more and more closely associated with the Establishment in modern society. Young people, workers, and intellectuals have come to consider the media an institution which shields the "system" against any meaningful questioning of the social order. Journalists and publishers hobnob with executives (and advertising men) at lunch, with politicians (of all parties) at dinner, and are much more influenced by these encounters than by the ideas of the social classes with which they have less frequent contacts. Journalists may severely criticize those in power, but rarely to the point of refusing their next invitation. After all, journalists have to keep informed! At the same time, their own intramural conflicts blind them to the image which they project to the outside world. In the eyes of youth almost the world over, journalists stand for the status quo rather than meaningful change.

This image is highly subjective, consequently one sided. Other segments of society blame the media for doing even more than political parties and trade unions to shake up the status quo and promote change. But, if they are active in this respect, it is because the media, by definition, wield a continuing power over the minds of others. Yet as this power increases the legal and intellectual structures of media reveal themselves less and less adapted to handling the social responsibility involved. Paradoxically this instrument of disruption is the one most opposed to changes within itself. The slightest suggestion that certain habits be altered or vested interests bruised provokes shrieks from the press about new threats to its sacrosanct freedom.

This is, in fact, the crux of the matter. Freedom of the press as it now stands cannot perpetuate itself if the profession which benefits from it wants to avoid a clash with the people it serves. Freedom of the press and hence its responsibility will have to be redefined. Since any government interference is intolerable, the press professionals themselves must show that they can rise above their craving for status, power, and/or money. Alas, in most countries, and especially in France, the press is a divided profession.

A simple yet interesting exercise in self-discipline is taking place in Sweden, demonstrating the possibility of finding the means to a minimum common ethic. In a country where freedom of the press and of information really do exist and where, consequently, ample opportunities exist to abuse it, there is also, not surprisingly, a great need for self-disciplinary measures. On another level, a largely liberal press facing a socialist government did not want to risk seeing its rights impinged upon by the latter. The Swedish press therefore opted for a solution widely practiced in Great Britain and other Scandinavian countries—an ombudsman for the press, distinct from the ombudsman for consumers. According to the definition of Leonard Groll, the first person to hold the office in Sweden, "an ombudsman is an intermediary between the public and the authorities. In this case, he stands between the public and the press."

The introduction of a real person to whom one may write or telephone makes it easier for the public to air its grievances and problems. Since assuming his post in the fall of 1969, Mr. Groll has handled about one complaint a day, usually dealing with libelous or erroneous reporting or the refusal of the right to rebuttal. In theory, his power is limited since he cannot force a decision on a newspaper. But in practice, since the press has agreed to act on his recommendations, he is able to correct abuses and redress injustices amicably and without fuss. If he cannot solve a conflict, he refers the case to a higher body, the Council of the Press, whose decisions are binding on recalcitrant newspapers. In one instance, the ombudsman even arbitrated between government ministers and the press organ of their own party, *Aftonbladet,* which, because its editor-in-chief has leftist leanings, had attacked the ministers quite sharply. In its three years of existence, the ombudsman seems to have been a satisfactory institution. First of all, it is surprisingly economical: one man and a secretary in a modest office (total annual budget, less than $40,000), without complicated rules and regulations or other administrative trappings. More important, it was set up jointly by publishers and journalists, and its independence has been solidly established. Even though he is housed by the Press Federation and his salary paid out of member papers' dues, Mr. Groll is actually a judge on leave of absence. He knows that if the press refused to renew his contract, he could easily return to his job as a magistrate. Over the past three years certain newspapers have had to print retractions of mistakes or unproved statements against their wishes, but they all respect a moral contract, and no Swede asks more of the press. It is a system that depends on a consensus and a sense of civic responsibility which is disappearing in the United States and has never even existed in France. This, of course, is another way of saying that the Swedes are more civilized than we are.

Two other experiments deserve consideration: the British Press Council and *The Washington Post*'s own ombudsman. The idea of a Press Council, with the aim of listening to public grievances, first took shape in Great Britain at the end of World War II but, for lack of strong leadership, was not much more than a discussion group until 1963. At that time certain reforms were made which coincided with the appointment of Lord Devlin as its director, a man not involved professionally with the press. The Council's only weapon is being able to publicize the cases which come under its jurisdiction, but this has made it possible for the Council to right a large number of wrongs. As for *The Washington Post,* which covers the nation's capital and has the largest readership of any paper among the people who govern the country from the President on down, it is extremely sensitive to attacks on its objectivity, and has thus appointed its own ombudsman. One of the paper's chief executives, Richard Hardwood, was the first to take on the task of "examining the objectivity and balance of the opinions expressed in the newspaper." The initiative is worthy, but can only work if this paid ombudsman has liberal backers who agree to play along with the idea of self-criticism.

No matter what system is best adapted to the mentalities and habits of a given country, the new ethic adopted by the media should, in addition to coping with the problems raised by advertising, include four essential efforts:

—Allocating more money to checking the accuracy of all information, since many errors are the result of insufficient means to fully cover a story. The education of the general public is making rapid strides; the quality of its daily news intake should improve at the same pace.

—Investigating information disseminated by such institutions as the government, businesses, universities, and public opinion institutes, which are all too often accepted at face value and printed as fact.

—Giving to those in all branches of information—the press, radio, and television—greater participation in decision-making (journalistic and financial) so as to raise their status without endangering efficient management.

—Offering to the general public a direct means of expressing its preoccupations.

This democratic imperative should be a moral obligation on the part of the media, which, no matter what restrictions are imposed on them, still have the overwhelming power to inform. Because they are secure in this privilege, they should bestow its benefits above all upon those to whom they owe their very existence—readers, listeners, viewers, in short, citizens everywhere.

Conclusion

In our time, the predictions made by Joseph Schumpeter and others earlier in the century are being borne out. Capitalism is being threatened by the very success of its own methods. The techniques of rationality devised during the rise of the bourgeoisie served to undermine and delegitimize the structures of the ancient regime—feudal, ecclesiastical, and monarchical—clearing the way for the triumph of free-market social relations and capitalism. Nevertheless, once the foundations of capitalism were secure, the intellectual process, the critique of the status quo, did not cease. Rationality has continued to assert itself, even to the extent of turning on itself and questioning its own legitimacy, as well as that of the social relations and institutions it helped create.

Since the time of Schumpeter, the erosion of established values and the questioning of institutions has been unremitting, with the result, starting in the 1960s, that in industrialized democracies the whole world over the entire "system" has been subjected to a hard scrutiny which, for the first time, is not limited to that of Marxists. When Spiro Agnew accused the media of being the leading instrument of this intellectual dislocation, he was, on that point at least, quite correct.

The media most certainly amplify and accelerate the diffusion of ideas propagated by the critics of a social order which favors the few. Even in the hands of conservatives or controlled by the government, newspapers, radio, and television inevitably play the role of the troublemaker by exposing the absurdities and injustices—in other words, the plain facts—of contemporary reality. This power is, in its very essence, anarchic in that it is beyond the control of any society claiming to be free. It works according to a logic of its own in which exaggeration and one-upmanship combine with integrity and analysis. Trying to check this power on the grounds that it is sometimes faulty or exaggerated amounts to preferring ignorance. But, at the same time, all modern societies, having become as fragile in their daily existence as in their political make-up, must take great care that this razorlike instrument does not fall into incompetent or dishonest hands. The standards governing the quality of information must be constantly raised; those who produce and disseminate it must constantly refine their goals. Only then can they justify their free exercise of the power to inform.

Index

Wolfe, Tom, 135, 148
Woman's Day, 12
Women's Home Companion, 2
Women's Wear Daily, 198
The Wonders of Knitting, 68
Woodward, Robert, 114
World, 134

World Journal Tribune, 24
Wrigley's, 270

Yanne, Jean, 236
Yomiuri, 68, 247

Zenith Corporation, 269